THE BIBLE FOR ZOMBIES

LEHAN STEVEN MACADAM

NEMEDIA CODICES
GOLGOTHA CAVERNS, FLORIDA

σοφὸς ἀνήρ ⸌
© 2012 Nemedia Codices

All rights reserved. No part of this publication may be reproduced, stored in a retrieval system, or transmitted in any form or by any means, electronic, mechanical, photocopying, recording, or otherwise, without the prior written permission of the publisher.

Disclaimer: This series, and its author, categorically and unequivocally reject the so called "Christian Identity" doctrine. Biblical actors painted profile pictures of themselves with strokes of inspired literature. The historical record was preserved with riddles. High-definition farce reflects the absurd reality of a world at constant war. No Homo sapiens⸌ are of any greater or lesser value or potential, due to any material resemblances to any historical characters; all of the tribes of Israel were "race mixers" *(i.a. NUMBERS 12:1-13)*.

All deviations from standard translations were made by careful deliberations of the original Greek or Hebrew. The best resource for study of the original language of the bible is currently **biblehub.com**. The original Greek of Josephus is available at **pace.mcmaster.ca/york/york/texts.htm**. Free eBooks of Josephus can be downloaded from links at **josephusworks.blogspot.com**.

First revision of the original 12-21-12 edition.

Corrections and constructive criticisms can be directed through:
www.bibleforzombies.blogspot.com

ISBN-10: 0-61571--676-8
ISBN-13: 978-0-615-71676-3

There is nothing concealed that will not be revealed
And nothing hidden that will not be known
— *Luke (12:2)*

The very name "Jesus" has a tight mass of double-meaning
best translated as "Delivery from Yahweh."

DARKNESS THOUGHT IT WAS VICTOR
AND DARKNESS PUT ITS FAITH IN THE TRUTH IT STOLE
BUT THERE'S A BRILLIANT PUZZLER LURKING IN THAT DARK

Truth is that Rome was committed to genocide in Galilee. Pilate's handy wipe, was but one bloody episode, in an ongoing ethnic cleanse. The virile second-coming of Jesus, is only comprehended inside a silky geopolitical context, drawn by some of Rome's most wicked characters. Crassus—the Patrician who crucified 6,000 slaves to put down the Spartacus revolt—went on to become the fifth Roman to govern Syria. While Julius Caesar ravaged Gaul, Crassus aimed for more Indian perfume, for soon after Crassus took his Syrian post in 54 BC, Crassus marched to Jerusalem, and robbed Yahweh's Temple to finance war with Parthia. After Crassus was killed in his adventure, Cassius Longinus took 30,000 Jewish men from Magdala, and sold them into slavery.☙* Four years later, Great Herod scored an entry level position, officiating as Rome's first governor of a wily Galilee infested with "robbers." These freedom fighters for Moses were brutally punished by the new lawman. Herod's hunting of rebel Galileans was rewarded by Marc Antony, who murdered the last Hasmonean King of Judea—Antigonus II Mattathias—to replace him with the Edomite's son. Meanwhile the boss Julius Caesar, was busy in Rome, where he murdered the Republic, at the end of a road of immense wealth collection which Crassus had trail-blazed. Caesar's heir Augustus, divinized Rome's new line of dictators in sync with a poisoning of the Jewish state. Well over 24,000 Galileans were mutilated and crucified, during a century of resistance to Rome and the idol temples built in Israel by Rome's governors. A pilot-light flared inside Matthew's son Joseph, on witnessing unconventional brutality following arrest of the general who trained him at guerilla war in Samaria.

As sure as He was reborn, Joe knew who was the real Lord of Hosts:

Nero acted like a madman...
He made Felix procurator over the rest of Judea
Then Felix caught the arch-robber Eliezer [son of Dan*]
And many that were with him
And they were sent to Rome
For they had ravaged the country together for twenty years
But as for the number of robbers who were caught with him
And whom he brought to punishment
And whom he was responsible for having crucified
They were a multitude that could not be counted   ☙ *(see* ANT 14:7:3)

— WARS *(2:13:1-2)* *Δειναίου ("Deinaioy") is wordplay on Δάνην φυλὴν: cf. MARK 14:23-24 with variants on "Dionysos" like Διενῡσοσ & Δεονῡσοσ. Satire is the highest martial art.

Eldstraumur gekk út frá honum, þúsundir þúsunda þjónuðu honum og tíþúsundir tíþúsunda stóðu frammi fyrir honum. Dómendurnir settust niður og bókunum var flett upp.

—Daníel 7:10

从他面前有火,像河发出;事奉他的有千千,在他面前侍立的有万万;他坐着要行审判,案卷都展开了。

THE BIBLE FOR ZOMBIES
Part 1: NOMAD

TRUTH: BIGGER FUN THAN FICTION	1
GIVING IT TO CAESAR	85
RTE 66: ROME TO MASADA	117
POMPEII'S ANNIVERSARY GETS HOT	135
RUNNING WITH THE MENORAH	171
INDEX OF CITATIONS	183

TABLES:

Dan Shall Judge His People	38
Zach's Come-Backs	47
Wages Of Sin	60
Joses Parts The Sea	65
We Did Start The Fire	126
Simply Simon	157
I Am Legion Hear Me Roar • In Numbers Too Big To Ignore	158

.... WITH THE COMING ATTRACTIONS

 **PART 2:** **TWO FIRST DAYS OF CHRISTMAS**

جس دن اللہ تعالی نے انسان کو پیدا
وہ خدا کی ایک تصویر کے طور پر ان کے لئے ڈیزائن کیا
وہ بنائے گئے تھے دن وہ ان کو مبارک
او آنھا را خلق ہر دو جنس نر و مادہ
کی طرف سے ان سے ملاقات کی آدم اور وہ نام
ابتداء (1-2:5)

 **PART 3:** **HANUKKAH MATATA**

FEAR OF THE HEEBIE JEEBIES

در آن روز خدا انسان ها را آفرید،
او آنها را به عنوان تصویر خدا طراحی
روز آنها ایجاد شد او آنها را برکت
او آنها را خلق هر دو جنس نر و ماده
و او آنها را آدم نام
پیدایش (1-2:5)

 **PART 4:** **WICKED SERVANT SHOCKER**

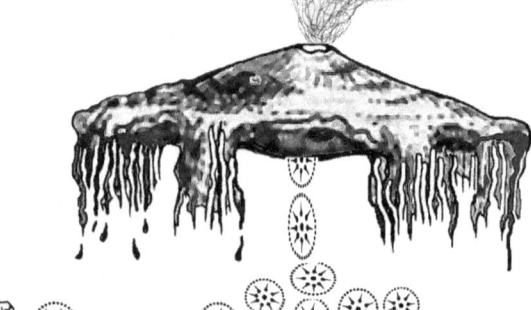

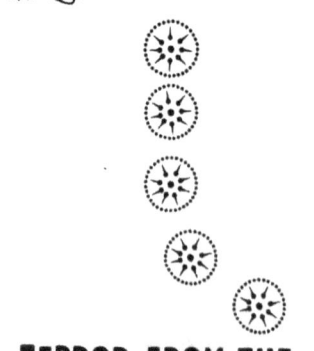

TERROR FROM THE TOMB

THIS VOLUME IS DEDICATED TO MALALA YOUSAFZAI
FOR BOTH MALES AND FEMALES ARE IMAGES OF ALLAH

The day God created mankind   (אדם : *Adam = mankind*)
He designed them in the likeness of God
He created them male and female
The day they were created He blessed them
And called them by the name "mankind"   (אדם : *"Adam"*)
    —GENESIS (5:1-2; 1:27)

אלהים

To mankind He taught the names of all things   (آدم : *Adam = mankind*)
Then He placed them before the Archons
And He said:
"Inform Me of the names of these if you are truthful!"
    —KORAN (2:31)

**"Certainly We have brought the truth to you
But most of you have a hatred for the truth!"**
    —KORAN (43:78)

الله

I turn unto the Creator of heaven and earth
He has provided you mates of your own kind
Just like [He has provided] mates among the beasts
By this means He reproduces you [كفّار]   (*reproduces you kuffār: see 42:9*)
[Who are] Not a thing like Him
For He is the All-Hearing
He is the All-Seeing   (*Mohammed loops on the thread of MATT 13:15*)
    —KORAN (42:10-11)

PEACE BE UPON YOU
BUT ALSO WITH YOU

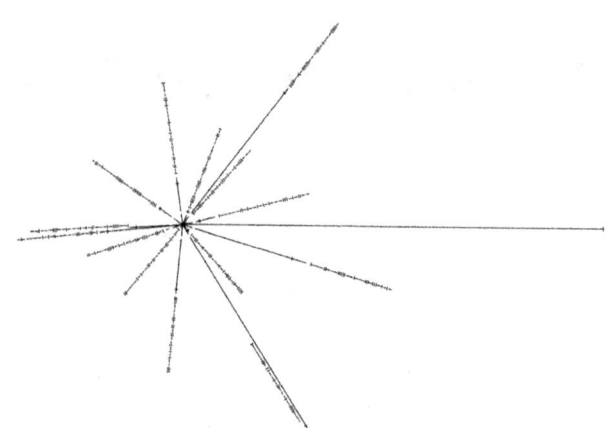

TRUTH: BIGGER FUN THAN FICTION

Just like the days of Noah
So will be the advent of the Son of Man

— *MATTHEW (24:37)*

If we, or even an angel from heaven
Should ever proclaim to you a Gospel contrary
To what we have already proclaimed to you
Let that one be accursed!
We said it once, but now I'll repeat it again
If anyone proclaims a Gospel to you
Contrary to what you received
Then let that one be accursed!

(this perfume is very expensive)
— *GALATIANS (1:8-9)*

Lying Lips are an Abomination

Seminal literature commands deep attention. Beneath dramatic peaks above the surface, truth seekers partake in a glacial mass, hardly hidden. Jesus echo-sounds in the satiric family tradition: **"Those with ears to hear—let them listen ... All is given in parables ... so that hearing—they might not hear."** Jewish scripture hits solid with icy parodies, and ornate snows of literary trickery. Pearls were kept frozen out from the orifices of swine, with shell-games too cool to resist. Jesus honed these creamy licks into hot planetary kisses. Tombs opened with a vengeance. Captive Galilee's near death experiences, spooked victory from out of this world.

When governor Pilate cross-examines Jesus with: **"What is Truth!,"** the gospel fingers a fatal gloss sure to skid any great power to its doom. The Romans became so jaded under the Imperial Cult, that they began to believe there was no truth—only the irresistibility of rabid Roman power. A Jew had to teach Roma the scales. Jesus gave her caloric lessons in reality. She will never escape the heat of His detention:

Pilate entered the praetorium *(military headquarters)*
And summoned Jesus, asking him:
   "Are you the King of the Jews?'
Jesus answered: *"Do you ask this on your own*
   Or did others tell you about me?"
Pilate replied: *"Now I am not a Jew, am I?*
   Your own nation and its chief priests
   They have handed you over to me
   What Have You Done!"   *("confess to all of it!")*
Jesus answered: *"My Kingdom is not of that cosmos*
   If my kingdom were of that cosmos   *(world— "cosmos" meaning "order" is literal)*
   My underlings would be fighting to keep me   *(Roman troops arrested him)*
   From being handed over to the Jews   *(but now I am handed over to the Romans)*
   Thus my kingdom is not of one side"

Then Pilate said:
   "So you are a king!"   *(of a higher "level")*
Jesus answered:
   "You call me a king   *(gotcha!)*
   For this I was born
   For this I came into this cosmos
   To testify to the Truth
   Everyone who belongs to the Truth
   Listens to my voice"
Then Pilate says to Him:
"What is Truth!"

—*John (18:33-38)*

The ethnic cleansing of Galilee was outflanked by a Mosaic defiance. Jesus and his merry band brought the house down on a Roman pogrom already well under way. Despite a sleepy national denial, the pontiffs plainly aimed to assimilate all Jews into the Imperial Cult. Bold flesh and blood of a cross-examined Galilee, handily prevented the extermination of the legacy of Moses. The record of a new delivery from slavery and idolatry, was recorded in double-entendres, camouflaged beneath rhetoric, and tagged with black humor. Magic rods of Moses, roll out a rim-shot on the snared drum of an epic punch-line, mocking dozers, while more than a Roman cohort is required to arrest mild-mannered Jesus. The overzealous sword of Simon cracks off the deaf ear of the high priest's servant Malchus. This lobbed off miracle ear is *tom-tom-crash*ed back onto the head minion by a vaudevillian redeemer. Word is imbued with multiple levels of meaning, so as many ears as possible can hear the scolding, and might yet listen. The holy blood of a brutal war story, sheaths its sword in revelation of a higher cosmos. God's windy trumpets blow in stealth. Slave-master's fig withers.

The prologue of the gospel of *JOHN*, equates Jesus with the "Word"—*Logos* (λόγος) in Greek. Few fully realize or admit, that *logos* also implicitly means *symbol* and *metaphor*. Far from suggesting that Jesus did not exist, it is this symbolic depth that preserved the record of what a real and undeniable victory the Galilean won. "Truth" is the central key to the *Word*:

I am the Way and *the Truth* and the Life (JOHN 1:17)
No one comes to the Father except through me... *(rap ends with...)*
I can no longer talk to you plainly *(nevertheless I must have a word with you)*
The ruler of this cosmos with no hold upon anything (Caesar)
Is closing in upon me *(thus I say nothing a trampling pig can get a footing upon)*
—*JOHN (14:6, 14:30)*

This fuse sparkles as the good-news bombshells drop. Careful seeking in a matrix of cross-references, collates a weighty catalogue demanding a new paradigm. The resultant model, posits that all four gospels were written pseudonymously by the Jewish history author Josephus between 71 and 95 AD, in a refined literary craft that abounds in telescopes to events between 34 AD and 80. This paradigm of New Testament origins, shuffles all speculations about the hypothetical "Q" source used to explain common threads in the gospels. It has long been recognized that the plethora of uncanny parallels between the gospels and the histories of Josephus, require some sort of dependency between their compositions. Consummate authoritative divination, is wet into us by Joe's flirtatious winks, which nest in orbits around this key word *Truth*:

About this time there was Jesus, a wise man,⁵ if it be lawful to call him a man, for He was a wonder-work maker, a teacher of such men as receive the Truth with pleasure.
—*ANTIQUITIES (18:3:3) (Jesus erected wonder-works)*

This much debated *Testimonium Flavianum*, licks on to slip in the guilt phrase: "**Pilate condemned him to the cross**"—a report not tasting like fudge of a later "Christian" interpolator. The *Testimonium* is a mega morsel Joe dips to betray himself as the adversary cracking the loaf at the Passover supper. Autobiographical name games purr out in code, to smudge Joe's role as telescoped Hasmonean spy *Joseph Ari-Mathaias* (the "Lion of Matthias"→ *JN 19:38)*, who prowled the Imperial house for meat. His *LIFE (1)* reveals he was *Joseph Bar Matthias* (son of Matthew #1 and father of Justus), who in another guise as secret apostle *Joseph Barsabbas (ACTS 1:23-26)*, is cast with his brother Matthias (Matthew #2), to replace Judas as head purse snatcher for *Jesus Barabbas (MT 27:15-18, MK 14:36, LK 22:35-37)*. Joe composed the gospels of his whale of a resurrection behind enemy lines, in multi-pseudonymous sedition against the Flavian dynasty he inaugurated, then thieved in Sicarii style. Those with ears capable to hear climactic endnotes, blown by a prodigy with lips smacking on Yeshua's ram horn, may finally fathom catchy songs of a double-agent mole, expert at global double speak.

The Testimonium's *gospel Truth* key turns a deadlock against Christian forgery, whereas its unique autograph of Josephan humor marks competing depths of meaning on two sides of a mirror. Hedonistic euphemism squeaks inside the sweet spot between the sweaty legs of the riddle: "**receive the Truth with pleasure**." Romans hooked on Dionysian abandon, had a hotter truth explode, upon their delusional perks. Here blows the sticky climax to the private dancing of colossal work-gang Jesus. The Greek noun "truth" (ἀλήθεια—*aletheia*) is feminine. Tacky gender ambiguity lays in the context of **"if it be lawful to call Him a man."** Some were indeed made eunuchs by others. Brutal sensuality which Joe reports as typical of young manly Galileans caught in the *Little Apocalypse (WARS 4:9:10)*, was a fleshy communion, damned unlawful, and effeminizing—but the first Matthias taught that it was permitted to contend with the abominable on the Sabbath *(1 MACC 2:27-41)*. A similarly dark comedic double entendre winks from the miraculous healing of Centurion's male love-slave (the bachelor's "boy": παῖς—*pais* in *MATTHEW 8:5-13*, but also "slave": δοῦλος—*doulos* in *LUKE 7:1-10)*. The boy-loving Centurion talks as one oversized power-top to another: "**Lord I am not able to receive you**," (i.e. 'It can't be know how deeply we're involved; how I gape for your rebel cause can't come out with pleasure.')

Joe's satire of the divine drive is gravid. Exposing the full frontal prominence of the Messianic *Truth* code, thrusts home the tight pneumatic grip Josephus had upon His Body of Christ. Joe's next most fruitful use of His big fat *Truth* device is shamelessly hung, hot and heavy, at the tail end of *WARS*—once again to foil any surgical removal of his *terrible Truth*:

AND here we shall put an end to this our history; wherein we beforehand promised to deliver the same with all accuracy, to such as should be desirous of

understanding after what manner this war of the Romans with the Jews was managed. Of which history, how good the style is, must be left to the determination of the readers; but for the agreement with the facts, I shall not scruple to say, and that boldly, that Truth has been what I have alone aimed at through its entire composition. — *Mngr. Josephus ends WARS (7:11:5)*

Take a bite of this Messianic brain tease. Why is it measured as a claim "**boldly**" made, for Joe to aim at Truth, alone, in his solo composing. Is it unscrupulous for a historian to openly proclaim dedication to Truth? The corruption demanding a crypt for Truth, politicizes the light in the planetary record, setting up one more stand for the thief of night. Joe's Messianic subversion turned tricks with the gospel *Truth* key. It would be easy to toss off this telling Truth ending *WARS* as an uncanny coincidence, were it not for the great catalogue of stunning parallels linking Joe to the gospels, only a small sampling of which there will be room to collate in this volume. The gospel *Truth* aim, shot into this last gasp of *WARS*, gains volume from the orgasmic cheer of a zealous host coming in the center of history's grimace. Ears can hear this climax clear, upon unsealing the crypt where Joe preserves how important Jesus blood relations truly were to management of the great war between the Romans and Jews—the very same apocalyptic conflict Jesus predicts in gospel *(MATT 24:34)*. Open secrets bulge out with their own light, and bust in the rectos and versos ahead. Earth's steam cleaning prevails 15 cubits upward. Joe's epic stiff Truth slick, is more irresistible than hell. Christic endowment of hot salvation manna, is literally unzipped from the bravest family codex hiding in a heavenly lining. The man who thinks with his head does not live by bread alone. Freedom isn't free. The Zealots wrote human history, and demonstrated they could write it in fiery brimstone.

Further counts of the word *Truth* in Joe's texts, orbit in his Messianic sense of use, as zoomed out to a wider, more elliptical focus. Joe widely scatters the word, to deliberately distinguish the Hebrew historical world aim, from that of infamous Hellenistic thinkers, contrasting the *Truth* of Monotheistic philosophy, against the *False* pagan cosmos of the Greeks. This Truth lesson is sewn into the spaces between Joe's lines.

The idolators have no idea what a potent seed Joe is planting behind the scenes. They are too busy watching the Capitoline eagle, pecking seed out from the insides of fresh Galilean Ganymedes being abused in the not eternal city. Joe's plantings behind Pagan lines, are rooted in the Truth talk Zerubbabel delivered to Darius—a babble reputedly convincing the Pagan Persian kingdom to reestablish Israel, and rebuild a Temple to the one *True* God. The gender-bender root Joe punched into the poetic lines of his Testimonium (upon the rising Flavian Amphitheatre), cracked into those foundations:

Zerubbabel said:
Are not women strong?
The earth is vast—heaven is high
And the sun is swift in its course...
But Truth is greater
And stronger than all things
The whole earth calls upon Truth
And heaven blesses Her
All the works quake and tremble...
Truth endures and is strong for ever
And lives and prevails for ever and ever...
Everyone approves of Her deeds
Nothing is unrighteous about Her ruling
The strength belongs to Her   *(Mother: behold your son to be reborn)*
And the kingdom and the power and the glory *(teased into "Our Father")*
In every Age   *('for ever and ever'... even though edited early and often from MATT 6:13)*
Blessed be the God of truth!...   *(Amen!)*
All the people shouted and said:
"Great is truth—strong above all!"   *(GENESIS 5:1-2)*

— *Zerubbabel sells Monotheism to Darius, from the Greek of 1 ESDRAS (4:34-41)*

Joe's Monotheistic truth seeds swam victory laps, down lanes of intercourse roped off from the Pagan view. His historic puzzles hid the tough man in Jesus for a liberating sneak attack. The compulsive ruler cult of Rome's genocidal epileptic line, didn't have a snowball's chance in Gehenna, against the doublespeak genius of a twice-born Hellenized Jew, with a stellar resume in historical drama. The clues to the Truth were all laid down in an improvised manner too slippery to squeeze the life out of with any destructive force. Joe had the original records at the bit, and spit the grizzliest ends back out in a wise-cracked ad-lib rap. Joe fired off the slickest rebel rhyme, ever to drive by the palace of a half blind demi-god line:

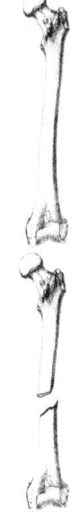

Lazarus • Λάζαρος • Eliezer • אליעזר ⛎

There must naturally arise great differences among writers, when they had no original records to lay for their foundation, which might at once inform those who had an inclination to learn, and contradict those who would tell lies. However, if we are to suppose a second occasion besides the former of these contradictions, it is this:— That those who were most Zealous to write history, were not solicitous for the discovery of Truth, although it was very easy for them to make such a profession; but their business was to demonstrate that they could write well, and thereby make an impression upon mankind. —*Josephus from* AGAINST APION *(1:5)*

Unpuzzled partisans forced resolution to the contradictions. Zealots were not seeking Truth, they were confident in its possession; their aim was to live by it, and die for it. Truth was their chief profession. It was easy for them to make it their refuge. The fruit of Zion belonged to the God of Moses, not to Roma or her officials. The deep drinks in the gospels gush down as signposts of a history the Zealous wrote. The most innovative narrations the planet has ever known, blend wrath with grace. A deep author vints grapes he knows well:

Eliezer son of Simon [Zealotes]...   *(Lazarus the Zealot)* ⛎
Was in possession of the prey
And the money they had taken from the Romans
The people submitted... themselves to his authority
In all public affairs...
[The man whom this Eliezer's authority] **made governor...**
Of both the Galilees
Was Joseph the son of Matthias   *(Josephus—son of Matthew)*

—WARS *(2:20:3-4) (the name Lazarus is from a Greek form of Eliezer)*

Everyone is not permitted of his own accord to be a [Jewish] writer... they are only prophets—such as wrote the original and earliest accounts of things as they learned them of God himself by inspiration, and others who wrote of what had happened in their own times, and that in a very extraordinary manner also. For we Jews have not an innumerable number of books among us, disagreeing from and contradicting one another, but only twenty-two books, which are justly believed to be divine... All [Jews]...esteem those books to contain divine doctrines, and persist in them, and, if the occasion arises, are willing to die for them. For it is no new thing for our captives, many of them in number, and frequently in time, to be seen to endure racks, and deaths of all kinds, upon the theatres, that they not be obliged to say one word against our laws, and the records that contain them, whereas there are none at all among the Greeks who would undergo the least harm on that account ... As for myself, I have composed a true history of that whole war, and all the particulars that occurred therein, as having been concerned in all its transactions; for I acted as a general of those among us that are named Galileans, *as long as it was possible* to make *any* opposition. I was then seized upon the Romans, and became a captive. Vespasian also, and Titus, had kept me under a guard, and forced me to attend them continually.   —*the prophet Josephus speaks* AGAINST APION *(1:7-9)*

Rebel words snap Josephus back into the Galilean school uniform he wore against Rome in the field. Joe made stealth opposition to the Roman yoke until the day he commended his zealous spirit into heavenly limbs anew. His sharp double pointed pen smoked hotter than any steel sword.

The *Josephan Paradigm of New Testament Origins*, identifies Joe as the author of the four Gospels. Use of metaphor is not confined to the parables spoken by Jesus—metaphor winds throughout the narratives. Events are wrapped in symbolic treatments. Parsed wording poses puzzles, pointing at historic details hidden inside turns and curves. Josephus does not restrict his use of riddle and density to only those instances openly identified as simile or parable. Joe uses slippery language throughout his texts. One gravid word from Moses, is often mightier than an entire empire. By this opposition, General Joe seized upon the seven hills of Rome, and earned His stars. The forked tongue method is cosmic in REVELATION:

IN his right hand he held seven stars
And out of his mouth came a sharp double-edged sword
    —*REV (1:16) i.e. adianoeta: Joe's specialty*

Every General must have his army.
Matthew's son Joe, describes his host:

HE Jews for a great while had three sects of philosophy... ❶ the Essenes, ❷ the sect of the Sadducees, and ❸ the... Pharisees. The fourth sect of Jewish philosophy (→❹←) was authored by Judas the Galilean... they have an inviolable attachment to liberty, and say that God is their only ruler and Lord. They also do not fear dying any kind of death, nor indeed do they mourn the deaths of their relations* and friends**, nor can any such fear make them call any man Lord. ℣ *(cf. ROM 16:11*, LIFE 65**)*
—ANTIQUITIES *(18:1:2-6)¥ (but Joe might call Caesar "Lord" for a different reason ⇢ stealth battle)*

Joe rolls out the map; his word is given context: "**I acted as a general of those among us that are named *Galileans*.**" Galilee was a region. First Century Israel had four prominent sub-nations: *Samaritans, Galileans, Judeans,* and *Edomites.* Like the original twelve tribes of Israel, each of these sub-nations had both their own regions, and their own unique mix of heredity as well. These ethnic distinctions were not unlike that between the *Ashkenazim* and *Sephardim* in Israel today. Judaism has always been a relationship, not a race. When the Pagan Roman taxation arrived, Galileans lead their own distinct "fourth sect" of Judaism, whose adherents were (among other epithets) "**named *Galileans.***" Those of the *Galilean Sect*, were called by additional monikers: *Zealots,* and *Sicarii.* Josephus also refers to them descriptively as *Robbers* (or *Bandits*) and *Innovators*, but once one learns to recognize how Joe's sword slices, these low notes cue up symphonies of sarcasm and subterranean double-entendre, for these terms are equally (*or more*) descriptive of those who followed the Herodian and Sanhedrin leaders, collaborating with the Romans like goats in a sheep herd.

Those named "***Galileans***" for their religious zeal, were the chief force that brought the Jews to war with Rome. When Josephus tells his readers over which force "**he acted as a general,**" Josephus is not being sloppy with his words. Joe was appointed to command the frontline defense by the Galilean who took charge of Jerusalem—Lazarus. Joe's literary trickery made this provenance difficult to extract by a casual Pagan perusal. The 66 AD revolt which Joe defended, was the climax to a century of war for the survival of Monotheism. The conflict involved every Jewish community of any significance throughout the entire Roman Empire and beyond. As Joe wrote, those Galileans who did not sacrifice their lives for the zealous cause, were either in exile or in bondage. Galileans were half the Jewish human war booty that the Roman legions had taken by the end of major conflict. Yet Joe served as leader of the Galileans "**as long as it was possible to make any opposition.**" As long as there was still a single Jewish boy who Joe could rescue with clean linen, Joe showed up for work. Then Joe lit a match, giving another hot-foot to the idol that *DANIEL* foresaw in Nebuchadnezzar's dream.

In his book *WARS*, (also called *THE JEWISH WAR*, or *WARS OF THE JEWS*), Joe camouflages his appointment as Galilee's zealot governor, with a trickily sidetracked chronology. Joe distances the note of his appointment, from his twisted chords on the transition to a Galilean administration in Jerusalem under Eliezer Bar Simon. This Lazarus rose in glory after the great victory over the Romans in the battle of Bethoron, and took total control over the new zealous administration of the capitol—before Joe was dispatched to prepare the next front. Joe was put in charge of the defense of Galilee in league with the ruling Zealot. It was a critical time, and Galileans were at the helm in Judea. It is unthinkable, that the edgy frontline appointment in their home region of Galilee, would have been entrusted to any other than an adherent of the fourth sect. Galilee was the door that Rome's legions would soon come marching back in through, to subdue this rebel province with the mysterious and defiant religion. Joe was trusted with the most important military post in the defense of Israel—*after* Jerusalem was taken by zealous Galileans who would have no Caesar honored before Israel's God. All of Joe's rhetorical speeches about the futility of fighting against the mighty Romans are just that—rhetoric. Joe was forced to pledge allegiance with these platitudes, in a history he began writing as Caesar's captive "freedman."

Just as Joe's critical post would not have been trusted to a conservative Pharisee, it equally unthinkable that a person without substantial military experience would have been appointed to this command of the frontline. Joe demonstrates that he is a battle savvy general, giving evidence of his astute martial planning of Galilee's defense, and his ability to train men who were unprepared for the coming conflict with a foe as formidable as Rome's war machine. Yet nowhere in Joe's works, does Joe speak directly of his having any military experience before this war whatsoever; Joe only openly admits to religious trials. When one learns to seek Joe's literary puzzles, and finds the keys to Joe's crypts, then one's ears can hear Joe whispering that his religious trials were conducted under the rebel Galilean sect, during an earlier sedition against the Romans in Samaria. The key to Joe's Galilean sect provenance, is embedded in Joe's autobiographical *LIFE,* where boy Joey begins religious life like a Jewish Dalai Lama, smelling of a huge relation to a familiar fisher of Jerusalemites:

WHEN I was a child and about fourteen years of age...
The high priests and principal men of the city
Frequently came to me together in order to know my opinion
Of what was an accurate understanding of the points of the law

— *LIFE OF JOSEPHUS (2)*

Any modern Jew, or any leader of a major discipline outside of Tibet, can testify to the unlikelihood of this scenario. Religions are hierarchical. Odds are stacked heavily against any legal abdication to youth. For this oddity to

be noted twice in two generations is queer. Josephus mocks the highest holy rollers. The governing board, of Jerusalem's internationally famous billion dollar butcher shop, seeks a fresh fourteen year-old boy—but only to ask the boy to interpret the spirit and letter of their corporate charter. Prophet Joey gags on this unbelievable request, to focus his attentive readers upon the uncanny gospel parallel in *LUKE,* where boy Jesus stumps the doctors:

VERY year His parents went to Jerusalem
For the Passover feast
And when He was twelve years old they went up as usual...
Then when the festival was over, and they started to return
Boy Jesus lingered in Jerusalem without his parents knowing...
When they did not find Him, they returned to Jerusalem...
After three days they found Him   *(hints of a lingering resurrection)*
In the Temple sitting among the teachers...
And all who heard Him were amazed
At His understanding and answers...   *(pointing at the Antonia)*
And His mother chaperoned this ensemble of words in her core
και η μητηρ αυτου διετηρει παντα τα ρηματα ταυτα εν τη καρδια αυτης   — *LUKE (2:41-51)*

After this extraordinary lead, Joe's autobiography continues, with a repeat deposition of the sects of Judaism, trained into a puzzle. Joe's tongue deliberately twists when giving his autobiographical relisting of the deviant Jewish sects. Licking these challenges, is the means Joe provides to confirm that it was Galilean relations which empowered him for a future role as frontline fourth-sect general. Three years Joe spent making out like a bandit in the wilderness, are hidden under the fig leaf of a communal cleanser named "Banus." Just one generation earlier, John the Baptist patted his cousin Jesus on his bench warmer, and sent Him into the field to score one against Roma. Parallels between Joe's life and the life of uncle Jesus, follow the same sequence in the very next generation. Both get into the game after amazing doctors of the law with pubescent slickness. First up, Jesus was coached by a big-mouth, whistle-blower in the desolation, called "the Baptist." Joe too, hones his game with a desert rat designated "the Bather":

When I was about sixteen years old ♡
    I had a mind to make a trial
       Of the distinct sects that are among us   (cf. ANT 18:1:2-6) ¥
These sects are three   (Joe purposely omits the 4th Sect → ❹ ← to call attention to it)
As we have frequently told you   (first prompt to count in his other lists and "hear")
The First is that of the Pharisees
The Second is that of the Saducees
And the Third that of the Essenes   (here follows pantomime over omission)
And I thought by these means I might choose *the best* (the 4th— in secret)
If I were finally acquainted with *them all*   (second reminder that there is a 4th)
So I acquainted myself with rough table   (robbing corns with Galileans)
And underwent great difficulties   (zealously fighting a mini war in Samaria)
And went through *them all*   (third reminder of the 4th Sect called "Galileans")
Nor did I content myself with these trials only   (fourth deviant reminder)
But when I was *informed*   (ciphers Gnosis, submerging Galileans in a new "Baptist")
That one whose name was Banus lived in the wilderness
And used no other clothing than that which grew on trees
And had no other food than that which grew of its own accord
And bathed himself in cold water frequently
Both night and day in order to preserve his chastity
I imitated him in those things
And continued with him three years ♡   (c.51-53, war in Samaria ended in 53)
So when I accomplished my desires   (of killing Romans, see Tacitus ANNALS 12.54)
I returned back to the city   (Jerusalem)
Now being nineteen years old ♡   (note that all three years were spent with 4th Sect)
And began to conduct myself   (the suggestion is as an imposter: double agent/mole)
According to rules of the Pharisee sect   (JN 1:26-27, ANT 18:1:6, ACTS 23:6-8)
Which are kin to the sect of the Stoics   (hints to Joe's alliance with Seneca)
As the Greeks call them   (stoa=porch, cf. JN 10:22-42, ANT 20:9:7; baptism declared war)

But in the twenty sixth year of my age	*(on the eve of the great Christ fire)*
It happened that I took a voyage to Rome	
And this on the occasion which I will now describe	
At the time when Felix was procurator of Judea	*(54-60 AD ☒)*
There were certain priests of my acquaintance	*("priests" of a 4th way)*
And very excellent persons they were	אֱלִיעֶזֶר
Whom he put into bonds	*(circa 59-60 AD, not 52-53 AD ☒)*
On a very small and trifling occasion	*(causing uncountable crucifixions)*
And they were sent to Rome to plead their cause before Caesar	
These I was desirous to procure deliverance for	בנו של דן
Most especially because I was informed	
That they were not unmindful of piety towards God	*(zeal)*
Even under their afflictions	*(fighting Samaritan, Herodian, Pharisee, and Roman)*
Propping themselves up with figs and nuts	*(the Bather's sexy tree diet)*

—LIFE OF JOSEPHUS *(2-3)*: ושם האחד אליעזר כי־אלהי אבי בעזרי ויצלני מחרב פרעה

Joe pantomimes over a deliberate omission of the fourth sect—the *Galilean* Sect—to get the savvy reader's attention. The charade sublimely advertises three zealous years Joe spent fraternizing with Galilean peers between the ages of 16 and 19. The mute puzzle reveals Joe's rebel connections to those with ears to hear. If Joe bathed Israel with the Baptist "Banus" for three years, then Joe hardly had time to try the other three disciplines. The bather's practice is the fourth discipline mentioned after Joe declares he **"went through them all"**—i.e. the other three sects—but not content, tried yet another. This fourth way is the Messianic sect described in *WARS (2:8:1-14)*, *ANTIQUITIES (17:13:5-18:1:6)*, *ACTS (5:37)*, and *LUKE (2:1-2)*.

A flaming bush speaks, to those who seek the identity of the **"very excellent persons,"** motivating Joe to light a fire under Caesar, in order to obtain release. One finds that Joe makes no mention *per se*, of any "priests" being captured by Felix, and then sent to Rome for Imperial judgment. Joe does report that a Galilean general, Eliezer son of *Dineus*, was sent to Nero after being arrested by Felix via a trick amnesty. The student of the good news was promised that there was nothing hidden that will not be revealed. Those with ears to hear the message of his *LIFE*, weigh these **"certain"** very excellent persons, as persons certainly pivotal to Joe's story, for Joe did travel to Rome and appear before Nero with the aim of their release. The seeker is expected to realize that these certain persons certainly must be identified by name somewhere—if not here, then somewhere else in Joe's histories. Their cause was Joe's cause. Thus they must have been worthy of a mention by name, especially when one considers how Joe provides so many names of much more trivial gravity throughout *WARS* and *ANTIQUITIES*. Eliezer Son of *Dan* was a general whose guerilla warfare kept the Pagan Roman occupier restless for two decades. This Lazarus certainly would have been like a high "priest" to the zealotic Galilean Sect. It is too uncanny of a coincidence, that in his *Wars* and *Antiquities,* Josephus mentions no other person arrested by Felix and subsequently sent to Rome—only Eliezer son of *Dan.* (Whiston gives "Dineus" † for Δειναίου: Ant 20:6:1-3, 20:7:5-10; Wars 2:13:2; cf. the "priests" at Luke 17:11-19, and welcome at Jn 4:1-45; as for the contradiction of Jn 4:44 vs. Jn 4:45—Joe's home was Judean ✪, cf. Wars 2:12:4.)

Luke and *Acts* are two volumes of one work. Therefore *Acts* fits into the *Josephan Paradigm of New Testament Origins* as another pseudonymous codex written by Josephus. In *Acts (23:31-27:9),* the seeker finds the only other possible candidate to fill the docket as the second imprisoned friend of Joe, nabbed by an anti-revolutionary police action like that which puts Eliezer son of *Dan* onboard for Joe's secret mission to Rome. In *Acts,* the very same Governor Felix arrests the Apostle Paul while corruptly seeking a bribe, which compares with the false amnesty by which Felix bags Eliezer in *Antiquities.* When Festus succeeds Felix as governor, Paul is soon sent to Rome. *Life* only seems to suggest that the two leaders arrested by Felix, were both sent to Rome by Felix not Festus; the wording is loose enough to take the later truth without much pain. Such curves thrown into otherwise obvious parallels, provide plausible denial. The trick pitch is one of Joe's signature game weapons. Once the reader's ears know how to hear the sound of Joe's thick bombs bursting in thin air, then they know to listen to the wind-up carefully, and can perceive the spin on this curve that throws Paul in an arresting parallel passage to Nero. Another device Joe fancies, pegs narrative events to transitions between rulers. Seeking here provides a secret second chronology of Joe's *Life,* for Festus succeeded Felix as Procurator of Judea in 60 AD, and after finding that Paul is the second "excellent person," the seeker must ponder a chronology that swerves to break with the one provided in *Life (1).* When Joe is known as secretly vital to Paul, then tweaked dates suggest Joe might have secretly left for Rome in 60 AD, and if Joe was 26 in year 60, then a variant nativity of Josephus winds up in 34 AD. Something of Tiberias died in 33. Everything is *satisfactual.*

This hidden alternative date-line to Joe's incarnation, runs parallel to the two very different birthdates given Jesus in gospel—one before the death of Great Herod in *Matthew (2:19-22),* another after the exile of Great Herod's son Archelaus in *Luke (2:1-2) (cf. Ant 17:13:5-18:1:6).* Joe's own alternative Pauline birthdate, reveals Joe's three years with the fourth sect were during the war in Samaria from 50 to 53 AD, for if Joe was 26 in 60, then he was 16 in year 50. Joe's second coming at confirming this chronology, once again employs the same signature pegging to successions, but the peg driven into Joe's secret stint as a Galilean cowboy in his *Life,* marks it as a hat Joe wore at the other end of Felix's rule of Judea—during the transition from Cumanus to Felix. Joe reports that Felix was appointed to this position by Nero, who became Emperor in October 54 AD. Joe's details about the succession of Felix, tellingly constrain the date of the little discussed, but very important victory that the Galileans won in Samaria. Joe reports that Galileans led by Eliezer, achieved this victory jointly with prominent Judeans, and that the Procurator responsible for Judea and Galilee at that time—Cumanus—was exiled by Emperor Claudius for his bumbling actions during the conflict. Joe's notices, direct the seeker to figure that Procurator Cumanus was judged in Rome sometime in the late summer to early autumn of 54 AD. Claudius died before appointing a successor to Cumanus, and when Nero followed Claudius as Emperor, Nero soon decided that the governing of Judea should be promoted unto Felix, whose governance had only extended to the Samarian border during the Galilean conflict in Samaria. The chain of these events is important, in that it indicates this war took place exactly when Josephus cryptically confesses, with the cipher of his sectarian trials (and an Egyptian flight as Paul), that he was riding wild with the Galileans, for the three years when all the Roman garrisons of Israel were devastated in Samaria. This incitation thrust the vengeance, of disaffected Jewish youth, balls deep, into the pride of a significant number of Roman oppressors for the first time. The Jewish boys came out on top, defeating both the Roman forces stationed in Samaria which were under Felix, and devastating the Romans stationed in a Judea under Cumanus. It took intervention of a Roman Legion from Syria, under Syria's governor Quadrantus, to put down this wild cut-throat orgy, by which frustrated young men of both Galilee and Judea, lured blindfolded Latinos into the tight spaces of Samaria, for a dirty bum rush:

ALILEE was governed by Cumanus—Samaria by Felix
The two peoples had long been feuding
And now restrained their enmity less than ever...
And accordingly they plundered each other
Letting loose bands of robbers, forming ambuscades
And occasionally fighting battles, and carting off spoil and booty...
As the mischief grew, Rome interposed with an armed force
Which was cut to pieces
Flames of war would have spread through the province
But it was saved by Quadrantus, Governor of Syria
There was no hesitation to exercise the capital punishment ✝
In dealing with Jews who had dared to slay our soldiers

— Tacitus, ANNALS (12.54)

EWS were accused of setting fires.. *(by bad Samaritans; LUKE 9:51-56)*
They were not so much displeased by their own losses
As they were at the contempt shown to the Romans *(key)*
While if they had received any injury *(Samaritans double bladed to Romans)*
They ought to have made them the judges *(instead of being rebel judges)*
Of what had been done *(like Rome, Samaria was most worried about the evident anarchy)*

**And cease to presently make such devastations
As if they did not have the Romans as their governors
On which account they went to** [Syria's governor Quadrantus]
**In order to obtain what vengeance they wanted...
But when he** [Quadrantus] **was informed that certain of the Jews
Were making innovations** *(i.e. were rebels deliberately drawing Romans into ambushes)*
**He ordered that those who Cumanus had taken captive
Should be crucified** ✝
— ANTIQUITIES *(20:6:2)(Fire in Samaria was followed up by fire in Rome)*

Jerusalem's priests went into tizzy fits, when prominent young men of Jerusalem, such as prophet Joses Priest himself, joined Galileans laying death traps for Roman soldiers down in narrow crannies of Samaria. Jerusalemites cried in terror, that a reddish-headed seduction of rebellious youth, would end in the destruction of Jerusalem and slavery *(ANT 20:6:1; LUKE 21:6-23; cf. the Egyptian Joshua telescope at ANT 20:8:6 and ACTS 21:38).* ✪

The identities of Josephus and Paul, are bound up in an anti-Pharisaic mission impossible. After the fourth sect destroyed two Roman cohorts in Samaria, Joe returned to his privileged priestly circles in Jerusalem. The role played by the Pharisees in the political coalition that ruled prior to the Temple's destruction, enticed Josephus to feign the life of a Pharisaic imposter. The Sadducee sect ruled the Temple, dominated the Sanhedrin, and maintained the high contacts with the Romans and Herodians. The Pharisees intermediated between Jerusalem and the countryside. When the gospel speaks of a resident of Galilee being arrested for suspicion of the capital crime of prostitution, it is a Pharisee who arrests. When Jesus is arrested by a Roman army in Gethsemane, Pilate insists that Rome's ship be decked with Temple police, and Pharisees. In First Century Israel, the Pharisees were detectives with powers of summary judgment. The Gospel portrays the Pharisees as functioning in Galilee like the religious police in a fundamentalist Muslim country—like a committee for the suppression of "vice," and promotion of "virtue." With their license to enforce the Torah, they dove deep into everyone's hairy business. There was no better way for Joe to serve the Galilean fraternity which had hazed Samaria, than for Joe to become a Pharisaic imposter. After a large Roman force from Syria put an end to the blood bath in Samaria, Joe reports:

 **returned back to the city, now being nineteen years old, and began to conduct myself according to the rules of the sect of the Pharisees... But when I was in the twenty-sixth year of my age, it happened that I took a voyage to Rome.**
—*from LIFE (3)*

Men on secret missions take multiple aliases. Samaria looms large at the time that Saul begins his feigned Pharisaic fight against the Galilean sect

(ACTS 1:8, 8:1-14, 9:31). Saul professes special spy authority, to arrest Galilean leaning persons in Jewish communities outside Israel proper. Then when he betrays his official mission, Saul becomes Paul, and begins to spread the illegal Messianic sect from Galilee to Jewish communities further abroad. Saul had told the Jerusalem authorities he was fighting Messianists—not organizing them as their overseas ambassador. *ACTS* winks at Saul's duplicity with a brilliantly coded episode during his trip to Damascus. The fourth sect's visionary loses his blindness to the political reality, on focus in a telescoped cipher, that drops the name of a different sect's priest in a mirror. A polarity flipped *Ananias* residing high above Galilee *(ACTS 9:10-17)*, is a telescope to a Jerusalem Priest who was arrested and sent to Rome at the height of the Galilean hostilities in Samaria. The two priests *Ananus* and *Ananias,* who are arrested (c. 52-53 AD ⏳) by Cumanus (not Felix) at *ANTIQUITIES (20:6:2)*, are another ornate curve to Joe's trick pitch—a literary fake-out making the walls of the spy maze more difficult to crack. Once the vision of the tandem polarity flipped zealot in Saul is restored, by seeing his tethered foil in the deposed priest Ananias, then Saul's polarity is trued to reveal a Galilean adherent reborn in Judea to run God's secret mission. Both the names of Paul and Josephus wind up in Rome before Nero between 60 and 64 AD. The name Paul never leaves Nero's dungeon. Josephus obtains liberty via allies, bribes, and gifts from a high placed proselyte.

If Joe left Rome by August of 64, then an additional puzzle of seeking Joe's whereabouts for the two years ending in August of 66 remains, for after the fire, Joe doesn't find it safe to return to Jerusalem until the city is in Galilean hands. An important clue is found when the seeker discovers that Joe is the one Jewish writer who identifies Paul's Tarsus with the Tarshish of Jonah *(ANTIQUITIES 9:10:2)*. Jonah, a Galilean prophet from the time of Aramaic conquest, provides the fertile central metaphor of rebirth in gospel. Three days Jonah sped through a whale belly (Nineveh), foreshadow three days Jesus burned through a necropolis (Rome). Jonah was spit out in violent vomit, obeys God, and goes to Nineveh—which was Parthian in Joe's day:

I am Joseph son of Matthew, a Hebrew by birth, a priest also, and one who early on fought against the Romans myself, and was forced to be present at what was done afterwards. For at the time when this great flare-up of affairs happened, the affairs of the Romans were in great disorder *(from the Great Fire of 64)*. **Then also such Jews as were for innovations, arose when the times were disturbed ... Such Jews had leaned upon all of their nation who were beyond the Euphrates, to raise them into a united revolution.**
—*preface to Joe's WARS (1:0:2) (Adiabene converts of a Dananias joined hostilities)*

The Galilean sect needed an ambassador to Parthia. Such an embassy explains Joe's next note *(WARS 1:0:2)*, about his having written a (now lost)

report of the war with Rome in Aramaic, which he addressed to wealthy contacts among Parthia's Jews. Joe composed his first explanation of the war to Jewish powers outside the Empire's reach, and thus free of the stinging reparation of continued Temple-taxes. Paul had collected money for the Messianic effort from Syria, Greece, and Italy, then brought it back to Jerusalem. Jewish resources in Parthia deserved to know what had been made of similar funds collected for the Zealots in the Aramaic east.

In seven decades—from the 6 AD tax-revolt which birthed the Galilean Sect, to Masada's fall in 73 AD—well over a million Jews rocked the boneyard to throw off the Roman yoke. The struggle went on. Galileans who had not fought to the death, were either in exile or captivity. Joe records about 50,000 boys taken into slavery from Galilee before Jerusalem fell. Many under the age of seventeen were destined for the brothels. When the Romans took Jerusalem, those captives who were obviously of no economic value, such as the elderly and infirm, were slaughtered in cold blood. A great mass of the able bodied were corralled into the outer courts of Herod's blackened Temple. There the freshest remaining meat was cherry picked in a greedy three-way by Titus Caesar, together with Caesar's drooling accountant, and Caesar's lusty Latin lover named Fronto:

BUT those that were of their flourishing age and might be of value to them, they drove into the Temple ... Fronto slew all those that had been seditious and robbers, who were impeached one by another. Of the young men, he chose the tallest and most beautiful, and reserved them for the triumph; as for the rest of the multitude that were above seventeen years old, he put them in bonds and sent them to the works in Egypt. Also, a great many of those Titus sent into the provinces were a gift

for them, that they might be destroyed upon their theatres, by the sword and by the wild beasts; but those that were under seventeen years of age, were sold for slaves... the number of those that were carried captive during this whole war was collected to be 97,000, as was the number who perished during the whole siege 1,100,000, the greater part of whom were of the same nation, but not belonging to the city itself, for they were come up out of all the land to the feast of unleavened bread, and were all of a sudden shut inside by an army.
— *Josephus from* WARS *(6:9:2-3)*

TWO DEPICTIONS OF THE FIRING OF HEROD'S TEMPLE FOLLOWING JOSEPHUS
"Those rebels who had fought bravely in previous battles did the same now, as did besides them Eliezer, the brother's son, of Simon the tyrant ... but the Romans put these Jews to flight and got as far as the Holy House itself, at which time one of the soldiers, without waiting for orders... was lifted up by another soldier, and set fire to a golden window..." —WARS *(6:4:1-5)* *(cf. LK 6:15; MT 13:55)*
Rhetoric telling that Titus wanted to save the Temple, after having ordered its gates fired, nests inside a greater reality. A stay was impossible, even if Titus had wanted it spared. Soldiers wanted revenge for 64's fire, as much as did Nero who sent them.

Galilean combatants impeached one another by similar appearances. Tribal features of form, hue, and dress, were marked by layers of blood and battle scar. Judean adherents of the northern sect, were culled in tandem fashion with the subnation that had styled their zealotry. Using the code word "poor," and tricky qualifiers, Joe claims more Galileans (at 600 K), died in the siege than Judeans (at 500K) *(WARS 5:13:7)*. That this was not merely a sectarian majority among the dead, is implied by the riddle which specifies that this host was of one nation, but not of Jerusalem. According to Strabo's GEOGRAPHY *(16:34),* only the Edomites were monoracial (they were Nabateans, i.e. Arabs), while Judea and Galilee were populated by Jewish clans which Strabo recognized as Arabs, Egyptians, and Phoenicians—of ratios Strabo avoids along with Galilee's geography. The reddish crested war-birds on the Phoenician frontier were like canaries in the copper mines. Dizzy from prescient whiffs of a slow unmemorable death, they rose up and flew the coop in a collective revolt which ensured a Jewish survival. Respect for the Mosaic roots endured via mass exodus designed into the struggle.

One becomes familiar with Joe's crypt gradually. Entire episodes, are fully double entendre from chapter down to verse—rich tapestries of doublespeak and adianoeta which zip-file volumes of data for those who can register the low tones via the black keys. Joe's terror tale of a renewed Jewish slavery, continued his opposition to the Romans *ad infinitum*, unleashing his Apostolic secret weapon—the earliest perfection of the horror genre: Joe's brilliant FEAR OF THE JEWS! Boy's life is the ever precious object of salvation, that requires Passover blood:

Pharaoh still did not yield to the will of God. Though he gave permission for husbands to depart with their wives, he still insisted that the children should be left behind. God immediately resolved to punish his wickedness... Soon God commanded Moses, to tell the people they should make a sacrifice ready... They offered their sacrifices and purified their houses with the blood... And when they had supped, they burned the remaining flesh right before they were ready to leave. We do still offer this sacrifice in a like manner today... Called ... the Passover Feast, because God passed over us that day, but sent a plague upon the Egyptians that destroyed their first born sons.

—*Josephus from* ANTIQUITIES *(2:14:4-6)*

Precious boy's-life is a nation's inheritance—its future, immortality, and well of future incarnation. No stones, no matter how cool they are carved, no matter how high they are piled, can ever substitute for boy's-life or girl's-life. Beloved boy's-life is a father's delight. War ends in victory, when parents turn their hearts to their children, and children return their hearts to their parents. The road to a slavery free world is lit by book-light. Joe ties an ironic mass to a rascal Passover, under the streets of a war on stupid:

Those that have venereal disease ... it is not lawful for them to be partakers of this sacrifice, nor indeed any foreigners at all, who come hither to our worship. Now this vast multitude was indeed collected out of the remote places, but the entire nation was now shut up, as if by fate, in a prison, and the Roman army encompassed the city, when it was crowded with inhabitants. Accordingly, the multitude of those that therein perished exceeds all the destructions that either men or God ever wrought upon the earth *(DAN 12:1, MARK 13:19-20, MATT 24:21)*; **for to speak only of what was public knowledge** *(secret reserves hide at depth here)*, **the Romans slew some of them, some they carried away as slaves, and others they made a search for under ground, and whenever they discovered where they were, they broke up the earth, and slew all they met with. There were also found slain there** *(i.e. already dead)* **above two thousand persons** *("I am Legion")* **partly by their own hands, and partly by one another, but chiefly destroyed by the famine** *(and what some fugitives will do for food)*; **but still, the ill savor of those dead bodies was most offensive to those who lighted upon them, insomuch as they were obliged to retreat immediately, while others were so greedy of gain** *(the killer moral of the stuck piggy common to all real horror)*, **that they would go in among the dead bodies** *(lusting rare red hots)* **that lay piled upon each other, and walk all over them, for a great deal of treasure was found in these caverns,** *(changing hands)* **and the hope of gain, made every way of getting to it, to be esteemed lawful.** ☻ **Also many of them that had thus been imprisoned by the tyrants** *(the blade of "tyrants" first slices as Romans, then as Zealots)* **were brought out, for *they* did not abandon their barbarous cruelty to the very end.** *(read "they" as both captor and captive)* **Yet God did avenge himself upon both of them,** *(captor as well as captive)* **in a manner agreeable to justice** *(the plot was in the works—a legion of undead slaves aimed for Mosaic possession of an Empire, chasing pigs up to their Capitoline edge)*.

—from WARS *(6:9:2-4)*

The brief comments here are not expected to provide a satisfying enough peep, at the underground sideshow of beaux rarities for which the double-entendres bark. Joe promises to out-terrify the circus, with a fertile climax jumbled upon the most monstrous constructions. Boys of the night were set to light upon houses of ungodly horror with brilliant torches. The quizzer's tease informs the reader of how tacky the situation was on both sides of the ground when Joe wrote this program. Assume the position of an abused captive. If you were an escaped Galilean boy stuck in Rome ... If you were a runaway from a work gang raising a colossal torture chamber at the center of the vampire heart of the rabid new Egypt ... If you were such a child of the most eerie night ever on earth ... How deep inside the low down dirty Whore of Babylon would you need to hide? How would your dreamy beauty manage to make a living? Moreover, how would you deal with your fiery Jewish hunger? Joe synchronized the decrypt of this esoteric tale below, to rise up upon Titus Caesar's appraisal of ash remediation at the New-Sodom superfund site. It was a weekend of demigod politics, that turned into anniversary with embers several degrees hotter than expected.

Few understood what Joe was doing as Caesar's freedman. Joe's defense of Galilee had not stopped the Romans. After Joe was taken alive, he was forced to provide Vespasian and Titus with services. A multitude perished in Jerusalem while Galilee's general was captive in the Roman camp outside its walls. Joe has wrongly been called a traitor, by those without ears to hear the "not guilty" plea Joe makes when he subtly points to the response Nero planned well before the revolt. A fire which began in Samaria, allowed a rebellion that freed Jerusalem in fall of 66. Passover is in spring. Thus before the 66 revolt even took place, Nero obtained numbers to measure his revenge for 64's Great Fire of Rome:

hey had come up out of all the country to Jerusalem
For the feast of the unleavened bread *(of 70 AD)*
And were all of a sudden shut inside by an army
Which immediately put them under such pressure
That there came a malignant affliction over them
And soon thereafter a famine that killed them even faster
And that this city could indeed hold so many people
Is proven by the number of them that was calculated by Cestius
Who wanting of the city's magnitude to inform *Nero* *(after the 64 fire)*
Who else ways was resigned with malice regards of this nation
Entreated the High Priests if it was possible *(prior to August 66)*
To take the number of their whole multitude *(for Rome)*
Thus those High Priests calculated [the number of sacrifices]
Upon arrival of their feast otherwise called the Passover
When they slay their sacrifices
From the Ninth Hour✝ to the Eleventh... *(MATT 27:45, MARK 15:34, LUKE 23:44)* ✝
And figured 2,700,200 were [in Jerusalem for the feast]

— from WARS *(6:9:3): (this fills gaps between the last two extracts from* WARS*)*

The zealous host is the body of Christ. Joe declares his innocence, while his equating human losses with Paschal lambs, points to a miraculous new exodus he plotted to relieve the distress of pregnant women and nursing children. Nero's final solution would fight fire with fire. Without a sizable Parthian intervention, and other provinces in revolt, Joe could do little to stop the back-draft. Messiah is God's anointed leader, not an omnipotent being. Joe can't be reviled for Roman horror in 70 AD Jerusalem, any more than Washington can be disowned for Red Coat and Hessian abuses in New York AD 1777. Japan still loved her emperor after Hiroshima. Joe is forsaken by those he saved. Galileans sacrificed themselves in the Temple so a new exodus could preserve Monotheism. The Passover lambs were slaughtered beginning at the hour Jesus exhaled:

They came to a place called Golgotha
Which means *[Place] Of The Skull*   *(tomb, grave, head, ruler)*
And they offered him wine with bitter herbs
Having tasted it He refused to drink   *(no exodus for Him—down with the Temple)*
Then after they crucified Him
Casting lots among them they divided up his garments...   *(Galilee)*
Over his head they put the charge against him, it read:
"This is Jesus, the King of the Jews"
Two Bandits were crucified with him
One on his right and one on his left
Some who passed by mocked him
Shaking their heads and saying: *(PSALM 22:7)*
"You who will destroy the Temple
And rebuild it in three days
If you are the God's Son then save yourself
Come down from that cross"
And the chief priests likewise
Along with the scribes and elders
Were mocking him saying:
"He saved others
He can not save himself
He is the King of Israel?   *(arrested there in the Imperial House)*
If He comes down off the cross now   *(telescoping between Rome & Golgotha)*
Then we will have faith in Him
Convince the Deity to pull you off now!   *(PSALM 22:8 & 22:19)*
If He delights in You!   *(PSALM 18:19, MATT 3:17, 12:18, EXODUS 22:28)*
Didn't He say: 'I AM GOD'S SON!'"   *(PSALM 2:7)*
The Bandits too who were crucified with him {some who had fought for Him}
They taunted him in a like manner   *{spat on His record and postwar mission}*
Thus after the Sixth Hour   *(cf. JOHN 19:13, LIFE 53)*
Darkness came over the whole country
Until the Ninth Hour⊕   *(the Passover key, and collator to His WARS)*

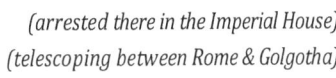

And concerning the Ninth Hour[⊕] *(trying to explain rich symbology to dolts)*
Jesus cried with a loud voice: *(Sabachthani! = σαβαχθανι)*
"Eli, Eli, Lema Sabachthani!" *(Mk 15:34: "Eloi Eloi Lamma Sabachthani!")*
Which means: *"My God, My God Why!* *(Psalm 22:1)*
Have you forsaken me?" *(or have you made me a thorny trap for the Pagan?)*
When some of the spectators heard it, they said:
"This man is calling for Elijah" *(Malachi 4:5)*
Straightaway one of them ran and got a sponge
Soaked it with sour wine
Put it on a stick and gave it to him to drink
But the others said:
"Wait! Let's see if Elijah will come to save him!" *(mocking Joe's manumissions)*
Then Jesus screamed again in a loud voice
And breathed his last *('LORD I CAN'T BELIEVE THESE IDIOTS! — ARGHHHH!')*
—MATT *(27:33-50)* *(cf. סבך—the sabach of the threshing floor: GEN 22:13, 2 CHRON 3:1, ANT 7:13:4)*

Joe delivers a punchline from an iron-tight foot-perch on the cross, exploiting words that shallow spectators to Rome's nailing of Joses miss in translation. They forget. In an earlier chapter of God's providential plan, all of Israel suffered the sting of slavery—even holy Moses himself. Joe hides his hottest key in the mouth of rude diasporic lookie-loos, fully alien to the Aramaic influenced dialect spoken in Galilee. The bystanders confuse the rebel leader's genitive call to ***God (Allah)***—tongued ***Eli*** in Hebrew, but ***Eloi*** in Galilee. When they mistake ***Eli*** for a diminutive of ***Elijah***, the loose-lipped alienators drop the ancient bomb Joe lit at the very end of the Torah:

L O! A day is coming that will burn like a furnace
All the proud and every wicked doer will be chaff *(LUKE 3:16-17)*
The coming day will burn them says Yahweh of the Armies
Neither root nor branch of them will survive... *(REV 22:16, 4:6, 15:2)*
I will send you the prophet Elijah *(MATT 11:14, 17:11-13, MAL 3:1, 4:6, LK 1:17, 1:76)*
Before that great and terrible day arrives
— *MALACHI (4:1-5)* *(i.e. when the Angel of Death will bring on extinctions)*

The Julio-Claudian, Flavian, Herodian, and Sadducee goats, were all denied Passover. The Aramaic shtick they thought beneath them, provides another window to Moriah's threshing floor. The Greek form *sabachthani* differs from the Hebrew *azavthani* (עזבתני) in a way that offers a pun with *sabach* (סָבַךְ) meaning "tangle/thicket" *(GENESIS 22:13)*. The key phrase thus turns: **My God why have you entangled me? ... have you turned me into a thicket?** The fiery trap of temple destruction, crowned Galilee's victory in thorns. This tangled forsaken pericope, echoes 22nd Psalm notes. Joe identifies with his Messianic ancestor David, during his own scandal:

M Y God, My God — *Why!* *(Why has everything gone south?)*

Have you forsaken me far from my delivery?
The words of my roaring?
My God — I call You daily but you don't answer
Yet at night I get no peace *(protest outside his booth)*
Still, You, the Holy Praise of Israel, are sitting
Our ancestors confided in You
They confided — and You delivered them
They cried for You but were delivered
They confided in You
Without coming to shame
But I'm a worm now — no man? *(2 SAMUEL 1:26)*
A disgrace to *manhood?* *(אדם—Adam)*
Now despised by the people!
All who see me curse at me *(the Lord of the Dance)*
They shake the head
Let loose the lips:
"**Roll-over for Yahweh!** *(maybe today He'll "beget" it in you!, PSALM 2:7)*
    He'll deliver you! *(He'll force your evacuation! birth you He will!)*
    He'll enrapture you! *(He'll strip you down and usury you up!)*
    For He "delights in You!"... *(what a sweet boy David is!, PSALM 18:19)*
My hardness is a dried up potsherd *(PSALM 2:9)*
And my tongue sticks to the *dust of death* *ולעפר־מות*
Where my jaw lays... *(Lord what a cluster)*
They divide my garments among themselves *(MATTHEW 27:35)*
And cast lots for my raiment *(plots to replace his administration)*
You Yahweh—O my strength—Won't stay away
But will rush in to help me... *(MATTHEW 27:43)*
All ends of the earth, will remember and return to Yahweh
Before You every family of nations will bow...
                                      —from David's PSALM 22

(Ha Bi Ru)

('A Pi Rw)

עפר
('A P R = dust)

העברי
(Ha iB Ree)

    The sob story ends, with bright-eyed David straightening out his signature Christian jacket, over the entire crazy planet. Near the turn of the first millennium BC, this controversial Hebrew king delivered a cosmic prediction about himself, with public song and dance. In 2001 and 2006, archeologists Finkelstein and Silberman published assessments of David as little more than a "bandit chief," citing a poverty of material remains from his reign, as well as Biblical passages which portray David as such. Yet a larger modern scholarship, still fears to unearth the root of the Hebrew crown completely, while people with guns continue to devolve into fundamentalist tyranny—unsure how else to navigate the ancient borders between myth, religion, ethnic group, and nation. Many cling to the fairy tale interpretation of a very astute literary teaching about religion. They believe such an interpretation provides a sounder claim to build upon, than the true resolution of this literature (as an inspired account of history). They are indulging in flawed wishful thinking. The ancient Hebrews were not a race—they were a social class. Furthermore, this Hebrew fringe element embraced the region's racial misfits. The story of Abraham and the twelve tribes is a parable, and the halakhah regarding God's name is not a Mosaic proscription, but a very old exploitation of superstition by fundamentalists *(JN 8:58, GEN 22:14, DEUT 31:3)*. Those who habitually read at the mundane level of the scripture's riddles, are caught in teacher's snares. Scripture uses the term *Hebrew* sparingly, in a return to the earlier root name of this social class, which was already pejorative enough before Egypt's expansion into Canaan. Mesopotamia's label for the Hebrew (*Habiru*) class is best rendered to moderns as *'illegal alien,'* tracing back to an original root cognate with the Hebrew verb עָבַר *(abar)*, here meaning: *to cross a border, to alienate.*✻ Thus *Haibri* (עִבְרִי) were aliens and renegades—line-crossers. The land with the most Imperial lines crossing it was Canaan. Early cuneiform tablets give *"robbers"* and *"murderers"* as synonyms for this outlaw class, because only a recognized state gets a social mandate to *tax* and *kill*. Nevertheless, the established states in the ancient Near East did not abstain from hiring Habiru to help them execute both functions.

The Egyptian ideogram which designated the nuisances associated with this regional 'alien' phenomenon, played up a pun that disparaged them further as *"the Dusty Ones,"* or *"the Dusters,"* where Egyptian *'Apiru* is cognate with the Syriac *apir,* meaning "dusty," and also cognate with the Hebrew *aphar* (עפר) meaning "dust." The roving Hebrews—made up of bands of escaped slaves, social outcasts, uninvited immigrants, and other rebels against Imperial orders—were thus dismissed by the Egyptians as either dusty gypsies, or lawless raiders who came and went in clouds of dust (like desert Feni). In the Old Testament, the term *Hebrew* (i.e. *'alien'*) is used a mere 34 times, always in context of those who don't fit inside a standard national boundary. Using the same context-conscious style of composition, key nods to the Egyptian accent which slurred the Hebrew as a *'Duster,'* are buried weather deep in the central heap of the literary wordplay with which the inspired text storms. The first man of revelation whom God raises is named *Adam* (אדם—root *ADM, "red," "fair," "handsome,"*

with root relations to: *"land," "soil,"* {אדמה—*adamah*}, *"ruddy"* {אדמוני—*admoni*}, and *"blood"* {דם—*dam*}); God made His man Adam by breathing wet wind into earth "dust" {*aphar*}:

Yahweh God molded **man**   (האדם *ha-adam*)
From *dust* (עפר *aphar*—cognate of "Apiru" for "Hebrew") **of the land** (האדמה *ha-adamah*)
And breathed into his nostrils the breath of life
And *man* (האדם *ha-adam*) **became a living being**

—*GENESIS (2:7)*

You were taken from *dust*   (עפר—*cognate of Egyptian Apiru:* You were a 'Duster')
And into *dust* you will return   (Get Out! Into a dusty rebel 'Habiru' you return!)
—*GENESIS (3:19)*

From the north, (not the east), Adam's descendant Abraham crosses yet another border to blow into Canaan. Another nod to Israel's *Apiru* origins occurs after Abraham's seed gets the deed to Canaan in the sacred oak grove at Sechem. (The Amarna Letters record that the *Apiru* came to dominate their first mini-state at Sechem.) Then, in context of Sodom's sin *(GEN 13:12-15)*⁴, God uses volcanic metaphor, to inform the Abrahamic progenitor of mythic proportions, about the nature of his *Hebrew* seed to come:

I will number# your seed as *dust* of the earth   (כעפר, *ka-aphar*)
So if anyone can number *dust*   (עפ, *cognate with "Apiru"—Egyptian for "Hebrew"*)
That's how they will number# your *seed* !   (descendants)
—*GEN (13:16) (the Temple was built due to numbering# of Israel— 2 SAMUEL 24:1-25, cf. JN 2:21)*

This satire spins off a common magical formula, repetitively engraved by phallus-collecting Pharaohs against such enemies as the Sea Peoples and the Habiru—that "dusty alien people" with an unrecognized state at Sechem:

I srael is made waste   (*GENESIS word-play rebuked Pharaoh's magic; Israel increased*)
Their seed is not
—*hieroglyphic on the MEMEPTAH STELE (Pharaoh's seed is not; the magician's future perishes)*

Inspired density at *GENESIS (13:16)*, pivots a dusty unzip on *numbering*, as the cross-reference matrix explodes into an allusion to the Mosaic law's constraints on the *numbering#* of Israel—a taboo which assured survival of His heirloom. The portrait of David as a triumphant bandit leader, meshes with the Akkadian equation of the "Habiru" as "robbers." This robber legacy was still alive and kicking hard into Joe's time. Joe exploits it for those with ears to hear that the Zealot robber sect is born in protest of Caesar's *numbering* of Israel. On this first Roman census, Jesus is born together with the Zealot sect, and He is crucified among robbers caught in revolt:

A company of tricksters and robbers got together   (*Galileans*)
And persuaded the Judeans to revolt   (*cf. dust of MATT 10:14-16)*⁴
And exhorted them to assert their liberty   (*WARS 2:8:1, ANT 18:1:1 & 18:1:6*)
Inflicting death on those who continued to obey the Roman rule
—*WARS (2:13:6)(Zealot sect began due to numbering# of Israel: ANT 17:13:5, LUKE 2:1, ACTS 5:37)*

The triumphant Galilean, who paraded into Jerusalem as its king, without a permit or appointment from Rome, was crucified with two insurrectionist robbers. In the same way that the apostles of this zealous Messiah kicked up the dust to incite revolt against Rome, Moses had stirred up the *dust* (i.e. instigated the Apiru—the Hebrews) to incite revolting flight over Egypt. To grasp this hidden deep bite of revelation, one must know that the Hebrews (i.e. Habiru/Apiru) were largely Canaanite, and that the God of the Hebrews was a zealous God:

Then Yahweh said to Moses:
 "Tell Aaron to extend your staff
  And agitate the dust   (aphar—cognate w/ Apiru)   **of the land**
  So all the land of Egypt becomes gnats"   (לכנם—pun for Canaanite)
And Aaron struck the dust   (עפר, i.e. stirred up the "Apiru"—Egyptian for "Hebrew")

Man and beast became gnats   (הכנם, ha-kin-nam = 'gnat')
                                 (cf. הכנענים, hak-ke-na-a-nim = Canaanite)
All the land of Egypt became gnats (all Egypt became Canaanite)

—EXODUS (8:16)

Only sarcasm might excuse any scholar who would wrongly claim that the social status and activities of the *Apiru,* bear no valid resemblance to the Bible's ancient *Hebrews*. In fact, they fit the profile perfectly. Egyptian records boast of how Pharaoh made slaves of *Apiru*, and set them to work on the same royal projects the Bible names—along with the Sea Peoples who liberated them via strikes, upon lands held by Egypt's Pagan magic:

Distribute grain and rations to the soldiers and the Apiru
       Who move the stones to the great pylon of Ramesses

—*hieroglyphic from reign of Ramesses II on* LEIDEN PAPYRUS *348*

I   [Ramesses] **extended all the borders of Egypt**
   I evicted those who violated these [borders] **from their lands**
       I slew the Denyen in their islands
The Tjeker and Peleset were made ashes
The Shardana and Weshwesh of the Sea were wiped out
All at once I snatched them up like the sands of the shore
And it was as slaves that I brought them to Egypt
I settled them in fortresses bound to my name
Numerous were their classes—like myriads
And in clothing and grain from the store-houses and granaries
I taxed them all yearly   (NOT!)

—MEDINET HABU INSCRIPTION OF RAMESSES III *(Egypt was safe until Moses walked in on the water)*

Despite the repetitive wishful thinking of Ramesses III's magical formulae, it is fairly clear from the context of his tortured rhetoric, (i.a. the veritable fortress under siege architecture of his Medinet Habu complex), that many store-cities, built with Apiru and Sea People slaves sworn under oath to his majesty, had already famously asserted their freedom by the time the spells at Medinet Habu were engraved. Regarding the antiquity of the reputation for robbery—alchemical nods vaporize as fast as a pick-pocket, escaping via the shiftiest passages of *EXODUS,* to those with ears to hear:

And Yahweh said to Moses:
One plague more do I bring on Pharaoh and on Egypt
After this he will surely disown
Let go of here completely
Speak so to those who can hear it
Ask for articles of silver and articles of gold
Each of his neighbor and each of her neighbor
And in the sight of the Egyptian
Yahweh gave adornment greatly

משה

To the great man Moses and also the people
In sight of Pharaoh's slaves, the people, all the land of Egypt
Moses announces:
Yahweh has said I am going through Egypt's middle
In mid night will die the first born of Pharaoh
Who sits on his throne
And all the firstborn of the land of Egypt
Even the firstborn of all the cattle
Down to the firstborn of the slave who is behind the millstones

—*EXODUS (11:1-5) (skeletons of ancient Egyptian millers show extensive deformity)*

This gnarly historical theater pulls no punches. Revolutions start as criminal enterprises against governments perceived as criminal enterprises. The real rebel Moses survives to come across the literalist desolation, as a composite of Robin the Hood, and Jesus the Barabbas. Ill-gotten gains will inevitably be ill-gotten. Surely fundamentalists who exploit superstition with candy-coats, are to some degree guilty of the same crime that blew Yahweh's wrath over Egypt—guilty of magical attempts at creating an underclass robbed of a free conscience. All this background is vital to understanding the trick double-sided coin Josephus plays, flipping the term "robbers" under the nose of the new Roman Pharaohs. While the Jews had earned a renewed reputation as the criminal class par excellence, Joe's duplicitous portrait of reality reassures his audience, that Joe was of some otherwise unknown sane minority of Judeans, who had tried their darnedest, for submission to Caesar's sweet peace. The *"what a good boy am I"* routine, is delivered with a straight face, while Joe embraces the moniker

"Hebrew," like it had not been since *JONAH* spent three days traversing the gurgling stench of Nineveh's under-belly.

Moses worked miracles for freedom by the revealed word. This mission fought by kilted sages, rocked on in David's triumphant rhymes. Wisdom out of the groves stepped up the unhewn altar, to worship only one divinity—that of a cosmic parent that creates life-forms. Pagan reads of creation fell into magical cults of rulers who monopolized divine descent to oppress; in contrast, David's musicians opened the Temple with: **"I said you are gods—everyone of you is a son of the Most High"** *(PSALM 82:6)*. These lyrics have more power than Pharaoh's spells and statues ever did. The encore riddles rapped by Jesus, cracked the safe of Caesar's vicious magic marbles. Being made of earth-dust and water, the sentience of mankind (Adam) is not other than the universe—it is part and parcel of the universe. This evidence is too equable for the hierarchical designs of a Pagan mindset.

Why do the empires conspire
And the nations plot in vain?
Kings of earth appoint themselves
And the chiefs confer with each other
Against Yahweh and his Messiah
Saying: *"Let us burst their bonds asunder*
And cast their cords from us"
He who rules the heavens laughs
The Lord holds them in contempt
Soon he will call to them with his anger
And horrify them out with his fury
Announcing: *"I have set my king on Zion*
My holy hill" *(ib. τυροποιέω φάραγξ)*
I will reveal the decision of the Lord
He said to me: *"You are my Son*
Today I have begotten you
Just ask it of me
And I will make the nations your heritage
And the ends of the earth your possession" —*from David's PSALM (2)*

The dramatic sunset cheese commanded by aging this ambitious will, is misconstrued if we fail to realize the interwoven fabric, that curds space in time. In an immortal scheme of things, the timely dimension is a far more regal throne than the lower spatial one. Map-quests for the great and terrible coordinates of self-sacrifice, zero in here. David's wise boy Solomon not only built Yahweh's First Temple, but also carved fatal switchbacks into the valley of Bethoron. Mt. Moriah's Temple—the summit of a trail tagged on oaks at Sechem and Hebron—was designed as a giant Danielian device, for trapping pesky colossal idols which sought to enslave the men of earth unto inanimation. The Bible is earth science. 🜨 The colossus in the dream of Nebuchadnezzar, is the targeted tyrannical pest, whose foot was dashed by the unhewn stone altar to preserve boy's life* *(DANIEL 2:31-35)*. Maccabean bling lured the matured idol's filthy foot into the sanctuary Solomon built and set for David's countdown *(1 MACC 4:47, DEUT 27:6, EX 20:25)*. Jesus let loose the holding bar, as He turned tables, to spring the cosmic trap *(LUKE 3:17, 4:9-11, 20:18)*. In reward, soldiers braided a victory garland upon the reddish thicket of His head *(JN 19:2*)*. The zealous whipping saved planet earth, from having the month following Caesar's *July,* and *August,* similarly renamed *Tiberi* for Tiberius. Josephus tended David's planetary threshing floor, as the remaining months were cleared by fire *(ANT 7:13:4)*. Every step along the chain of custody, authenticates the divine provenance of David's giant idol-trap on the holy hill *(2 SAM 24:9-25, 2 CHRON 3:1, GEN 22:2-13*)*.

Important links in the trip-wire chain, are teased out by *2 CHRONICLES*:

King Hiram of Tyre wrote a letter
And addressed it to Solomon [instead of David]:
✝ Blessed is Yahweh the God of Israel
Who made the heavens and the earth *(a stone not hewn by human hands)*
He gave to David a wise son
Who is now a King savvy of wisdom and understanding
Who now builds a house for Yahweh...
I am sending you a wise man possessing wisdom
He is Hiram Abi—son of a woman of Danite royalty
And his father is a man of Tyre
Hiram is skilled working in gold, and in silver, brass, and iron
With stones, and wood, with purple, blue, fine linen, and crimson
Able to cut any type of cutting
And devise any type of device laid out to him by your sages
And the sages of my Lord— your Father David
So send to us, who are your servants
The wheat, barley, oil, and wine you promised
We will cut all the trees you need out of Lebanon
And float them down to you by sea to Joppa
You can take them up to Jerusalem from there"
—*2 CHRONICLES (2:11-16)*

This passage prompts one to ponder, exactly how the borders of the tribe of Dan, wrapped up the flanks of Jerusalem from Joppa to Tel-Dan *(JOSHUA 19:45)*. The dangling of this redacted tidbit by Ezra, dates to when captives in Persia were returned to Jerusalem by Pagan Emperors. Ezra's compelled refounding propaganda, epitomized a subset who found it convenient to address these Persians as Messiahs of earth's Monotheistic religion, and bow down to them beside Yahweh, ignoring the fact that these Persian Shahs claimed Pagan godhead. Ezra's rare tidbits, suggest that a remnant

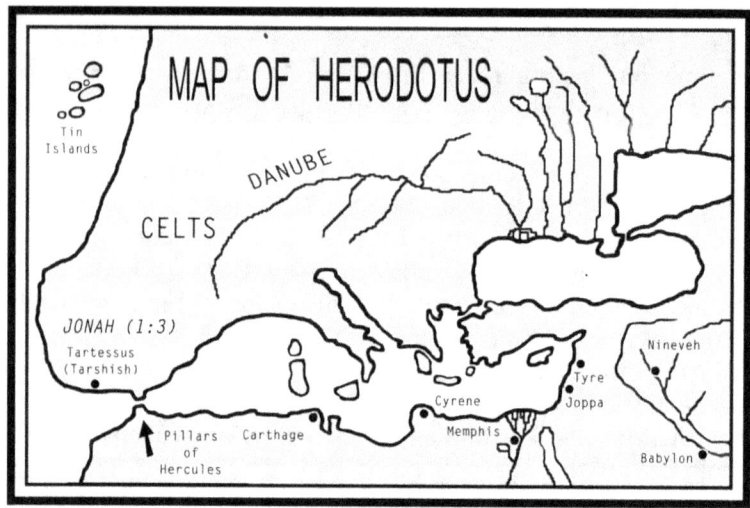

of Dan in the wild upper Galilees, held on in the rugged high ground, while more vulnerable confederates below were exiled into idol lands and hands. Intermarriage with the nations was a big issue to the lines who returned with fancy Babylonian names, yet the very First Jerusalem Temple, was built by the son of an alliance between Dan and Tyre. Go figure.

Josephus pasted on Biblical deviations, by a method exploiting angles between diverging parallels—performing conservation with *ANTIQUITIES*, in order to fill in some of what was drowned in water damage done at Salamis. Joe's stealth method of rhetorical comment is well within the Biblical milieu. A variant parallel passage given about the artisan Hiram in *1 KINGS*, blurs the distinction between Dan and Napthali—two Galilean tribes said to descend from sons of Israel carried by the same mother. Joe affirms the suggested blending of Danites, into those lonely widows of Galilee who had successfully hidden from the exile nets cast from Assyria, Egypt, and Babylon. Joe simultaneously lobs-off the faux-purity of Hebrew origins touted by misreads of Ezra's Persified Abraham myth. Israel's religion is a knowledge of the ineffable spirit, not a race for effable blood.

The Hebrews who fled Egypt, were not only Mesopotamians of some pure provenance traceable back to Ur of the Chaldees—a location tellingly akin to the racial mix recently picked back up, and blended deeper in, by Babylonian captives deployed by Persian *Kings of Kings;* contemporary prohibitions against foreign wives can be read like a cover or 'beard.' Yet those who still mourn Herod's Temple are deaf to Joe's tones. The Nile certainly was not a black and white colonial plantation. Egypt was a hugely wealthy empire when Moses lived, and the Egyptians exploited slaves and mercenaries from all the known world. This opulent society was several millennia in the making, with trade on both the Mediterranean Sea and Indian Ocean. The ethnicity of Egyptian slaves was certainly of a diversity akin to the rainbow of servile meat available on the Roman market. The Hebrew revolution definitely was not uniracial in origin. The undeniable allegory, in a full spectrum of twelve tribes—one for each month of the sky—points at multinational truth. Josephus gives a version of Hiram's story that diverges from *1 KINGS* by trickily replacing **Tyre** with **Ur**, while questioning how the role of **Dan** in *2 CHRONICLES (2:14)* is replaced by **Napthali** in *1 KINGS (7:14)*. These deviations are part of an elaborate ruse, which hides the rough role Dan played leading an Exodus out of Egypt, by Hebrew flocks thick with Phoenicians (i.e. Canaanites). Ancient Irish verse says this "Tribe of Dan" (Tuatha Dé Danann), perfected their craft in Bronze Age Greece, then entered the world war with sails around the Black Sea— grabbing fresh mates flowing south out of the mouths of the rivers Don (Дон), Donetz (Северский Донец), Danapris (Дністер; Dniepr), Danastris (דנ-נעסטער, Dnister), and Danube (Дунав; Dunaje; Donau):

King Solomon sent for Hiram
And brought him from Tyre
He was son of a Napthali tribe widow ❋
And his father was a man of Tyre
Who worked bronze
Full of wisdom, understanding and skill
For making anything in bronze
He came to Solomon and did all his work
—*1 KINGS (7:13-14)*   ❋ *(cf. 2 CHRON 2:14; Sidon had refounded Tyre at Bronze Age end)*

Now Solomon sent for an artificer from Tyre named Hiram
He was born of the Napthali tribe on the mother's side
For she was of that tribe   ❋ *('and she wasn't not of Dan—if you get me')*
But his father was Ur   *(Ur of the Chaldees was a stones throw from Babylon; pun for "fire")*
Of Israelite stock   *('Babylon is not where some purer fire is from—if you get me')*
This man was skillful in all sorts of work   *(he worked aniconic 'magic')*
But his chief skill lay in working in gold and silver and bronze
By which were made all the mechanical works about the Temple
According to the will of Solomon   *(1 KINGS 9:17, 2 CHRONICLES 8:5, DANIEL 2:32)*
Moreover Hiram made two pillars   *(symbol of Two Messiahs: David and Solomon)*
Whose outsides were of bronze   *(August passage graves were much older)*
And the thickness of the bronze was the breadth of four fingers...
Both of their capitals were molded with lily-work   *(symbol of rebirth)*
That stood upon the pillar   *(JN 16:4: world umbilical pillar on Admiral's curile throne)*
—*ANT (8:3:4)* *(ABOVE: gem of maritime Mycenaea: griffin Asvins sail tethered to the holy civic pillar)*

Anchored in Isaac, the Patriarch Parables launch inspired wordplays, to row swiftly over multi-ethnic Hebrew origins. The *Reed Sea* (יַם־סוּף:) parted for Moses, like the books he opened by the hand of inspiration. The English words *Bible* and *bibliography*, come from the Phoenician word for Egyptian *Papyrus*—a product made of marsh *reed* (סוּף:), traded at Phoenicia's port of

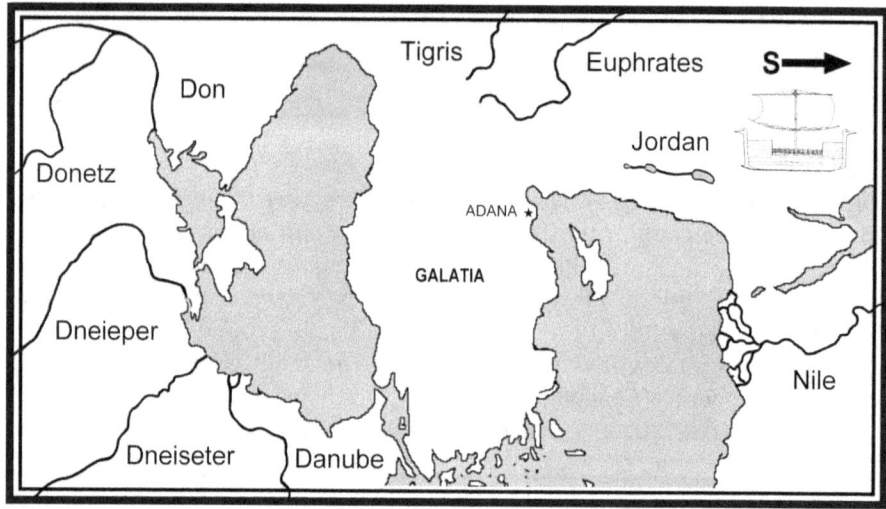

Biblos to supply manufacturers of both books and boats. Pharaoh was drowned by the Lord's craft. Israel was founded by both a migration from the Nile delta, and an erosion of the Imperial borders of Egypt, with both actions lead by the "Sea Peoples" who ravaged the great powers of the eastern Mediterranean at the close of the Bronze Age. Inside this framework, the Tribe of Issachar is identified with those Sea Peoples whom the Egyptians called *Shekelesh*, (*Sikil*—perhaps paired with *Tjeker* as endonym and exonym). Their city state at Dor, was the first independent polity in Canaan to deny the Egyptians tribute. The rebel manifest which gave birth to the colony of Issachar, did not have an Egyptian mother.

The Sea Peoples whom the Egyptians called *Weshwesh*, are a dead ringer for the Tribe of Asher, and Asher's Biblical position in both Phoenicia and Canaan, hints at the great historic depth to David's alliance with Tyre.

The coast south from Asher and Issachar, was cleared by *Denyen* (Dan), who remained in their ships with naval docks at Joppa, guarding the frontier all the way down to the *Peleset* (Philistines). The Philistines were the one tribe of Sea People resettled far enough from Phoenicia, that they succeed by buying off Egyptian attacks in a trade for periodic raids with the rebel buffer further north. This strategic reality of the 12th and 11th Centuries BC, was buried deep in parabolic code, after the epic Persian loss at Salamis in the 5th Century BC, where the Phoenician flotilla in the Imperial navy of Xerxes, led an attack on the Greeks which quickly dissolved into chaos. In the aftermath, Xerxes's son Artaxerxes sent Ezra, to clean house in Persia's vassal Jerusalem. The compendium of midrash-like exercises Ezra edited, preserved both the record, and sharpness, of the Hebrew edge.

If the carpets of Joseph's tribes are rolled off the map, and their territory redistributed back to Issachar and Dan, there emerges a clearer picture of the regime of the "Judges," who ruled after Exodus and conquest. One may dial up the period when Moses lead a rebel Exodus, if one recognizes that Canaan remained in Egyptian hands until the reign of Ramesses III. *EXODUS* names a city that stored tribute and statues of "Ra'amses," as one of the facilities Hebrews slaved upon, along with a "Pithom" (*House of Amon*)—one of the great idol temple complexes of the god Amon *(Amen;* EXODUS *1:11)*. This literary device supplants the need to otherwise name the two Pharaohs in the rebel drama, and allows the plot to fuse them into a composite character. One need only catalogue and weigh all the autobiographical stone idols of the Ramessides, to get the heavy point lifted by the author's economy. One colossus of Ramesses II at Memphis, and four other images of Ramesses at Tanis, all weighed over 1000 tons. Yahweh got hot with explosive jealousy. The famous temple at Abu Simbel is entered between four more giant statues of Ramesses seated in a row—all 69 feet tall. Abu Simbel is supported inside by a row of eight additional idol pillars depicting living Ramesses as deity; each stands 30 feet high. Egypt is littered with tens of thousands of idolatrous images in the name of Ramesses. The Ramesside regents made very lofty claims of divinity—in sky high ranks with the god Amon himself. These Pharaohs required human worship, and slave labor, to maintain their magically stated divine claims. It is no coincidence that the Sea Peoples, including Dan, Asher, Issachar, and the Philistines, united to attack Egypt from the reign of Ramesses II to Ramesses III, in the same period that Egypt first tightened and then lost control over Canaan—while scarcity, regicide, and revolutionary class-warfare are recorded on the Nile.

The Sea Peoples named Sherden (as *Sirdana*), and Denyen (as *Danuna*), are fixtures as early as the Amarna Letters. They ring as terms for kindreds, with 'Sherdana' used for alien mercenaries managed by Danubian *Urnfelds,* as employed by Imperial powers in the region, while 'Danaanu' designated those who had secured Adana in Cilicia by the 14th Century BC. Then, beginning in the 13th Century, these *Denyen* sailed out of their port Tarsus to attack Ramesside Egypt, while a related European mix (*Sher-Denyen*), were employed by Egypt at Sidon, to keep both Hittite and Canaanite in check. Hieroglyphic for 'Danaanu': (D'-n-n'), compares to (Š'-r-d-n'): 'Sherden,' (Š'-r-d-n-n'): 'Sherdenen,' (Š'-r-d-n-y): 'Sherdana,' (Š'-r-d-y-n): 'Sherdenyen,' and (D'-yn-yw-n'): 'Denyen,'—all cousins called on to rise with the captive 'Canaanu,': (C'-n-n), who were Israel's Canaanite/Phoenician core flock.

The picture that emerges from archaeology and linguistic studies, is in surprising accord with loose literary accounts in the Gaelic *LEBOR GABALA*, which relate a Tribe of Dan that sailed out the Black Sea, attacked Greece and Asia Minor, served as mercenaries in Egypt, made war with Philistines, and migrated to metal-rich Ireland, via Sardinia and other Celto-Iberian lands.✩ An earlier Jewish text, also gives neglected testimony, in support of *Dan's* stint in Greece as the *Danaoi* (Δαναοί) of Homer:

Arius, King of the Spartans
Sends greetings to High Priest Onias
It is found in writing
Concerning the Spartans and Judeans
That they are sons of the same mother
And that they are of the cause of Abraham's nation

—1 MACCABEES (12:20-21) cf. ANT (12:4:10-5:1)

Two symbolic genealogies are harmonized here. The focus of one is the figure *Danae*, given as granddaughter of a *Sparta* personified. She is notable as mother of the hero *Perseus,* who freed *Andromeda* at Joppa, the seaport of Dan's lot *(Pausanias 4:35:9, Strabo 16:2:8, Pliny 14:5, WARS 3:9:3,* and *JOSHUA 19:46,* where for הַיַּרְקוֹן וּמֵי —i.e. "Joppa Frontier"—read "Mediterranean," *cf. JUDGES 5:17).* Thus despite the gender difference, *1 MACCABEES* identifies the Greek *Danae* with Jacob's *Dan*—mythologized grandson of an *Abraham*. While the Library of Alexandria thrived, savvy students of these myths could more easily discern, how colorfully the narratives illustrated oral traditions with historic relevance. It's no accident, that three surviving accounts, all tell on J. Caesar (destroyer of Gaul), for having burned out earth's great library, in prelude to his own Pharaonic-style divination.

Medieval Irish texts report a proto-Celtic background for the Tribe of Dan, related to a large force of Northerners under Egyptian military employment at the time of Moses. Plausibility of these verses still flows in living linguistic markers (Donets, Dniepr, Dnister, Danube, Don) which mark the expansive river haunts of an early Indo-European horseman culture, from the Scythian Steppes, clear west across Europe—a circuit of nations dominated by Celts before Romans. The central place of the art of satire in Celtic religion, as preserved in a Gaelic record, sketches a profile with a sharp angle with a compelling parallel in evidence, between Biblical Dan and the maritime Celts *(JUDGES 14:15 as key).* The Cimmerians who followed up the Denyen drives into Assyria, are noted as early relations of the Galatians and Gauls

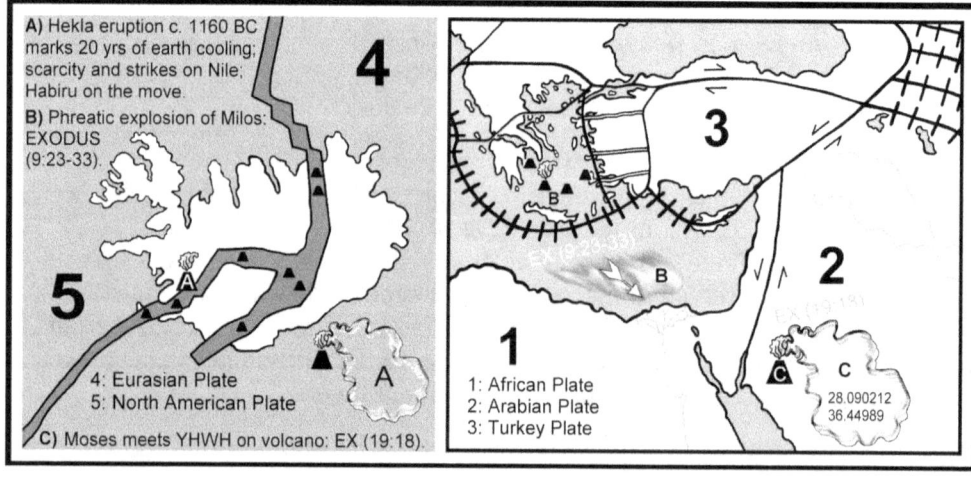

A) Hekla eruption c. 1160 BC marks 20 yrs of earth cooling; scarcity and strikes on Nile; Habiru on the move.
B) Phreatic explosion of Milos: EXODUS (9:23-33).
4: Eurasian Plate
5: North American Plate
C) Moses meets YHWH on volcano: EX (19:18).
1: African Plate
2: Arabian Plate
3: Turkey Plate
28.090212
36.44989

by Josephus *(ANT 1:6:1; cf. GENESIS 10:1)*, and are distributed as far as the fiery winterland of Ireland by Homer *(ODYSSEY 11:14)*. Their pushy Scythian neighbors colonized *Beth Shean*, where Egypt once posted Shardana soldiers to secure Canaan. Not far from the lows of *Gaulonitus* (i.e. Golan), this thriving *Scythopolis* was a fixture of the Decapolis when Jesus and the Galileans made war upon idolatrous Imperial Rome. Such penetrations shot out of the further north, had continued their eruptions long after Ezra's day.

ALMOST TWELVE TRIBES OF ISRAEL

Dan & Judah—wandering with Joshua† & Caleb—apart just 11.9 K:
74,600 A − 62,700 B = 11,900   ❖   76,500 C − 64,400 D = 11,900

Tribe (x) = order by size	Census 1 NUMBERS (1:20-46)		Census 2 NUMBERS (28:4-51)		Sealed REVELATION (7:1-8)
Judah*	74,600A	(1)	76,500C	(1)	12,000
Dan	62,700B	(2)	64,400D	(2)	†
Levi	\multicolumn{4}{l}{LEVITICUS has 11,900 + 2 Hebrew words}	12,000
Reuben	46,500	(7)	43,730	(9)	12,000
Simeon*	59,300	(3)	22,200	(12)	12,000
Gad	45,650	(8)	40,500	(10)	12,000
Issachar	54,400	(5)	64,300	(3)	12,000
Zebulun	57,400	(4)	60,500	(4)	12,000
Manasseh*	32,200	(12)	52,700	(6)	12,000
Ephraim	40,500	(10)	32,500	(11)	†
Joseph			REV (19:11-13)		12,000
Benjamin	35,400	(11)	45,600	(7)	12,000
Asher	41,500	(9)	53,400	(5)	12,000
Napthali	53,400	(6)	45,400	(8)	12,000
Total:	603,550		601,730		144,000

* **Judah**, **Simeon**, and **Manasseh**, were not worth a mention in THE SONG OF DEBORAH *(JUDGES 5:2-31)*

† On **Dan** and **Ephraim**'s omission from the sealed of REVELATION, see GEN *(48:3-7)*, WARS *(1:7:5-7)*, *(4:5:2-3)*, *(3:7:31)*, EZEK *(48:1)*; cf. 2 SAM *(17:1)*, ANT *(7:9:6)*, *(14:4:4)*.

MAP LEFT: Epic records interlace to back-cover a ditty—lip-syncing an earlier 1550 BC flight from Egypt, of Hyksos licked by eruptions at Santorini in the 17th & 16th Centuries BC. Thus **"Danaus"** \—son of an Egyptian born Belus (Baal)—founded Argos (Strabo *8:6:9*) with Canaanite and Indo-European in the mix. Mycenae—founded by Perseus, son of **"Danae"** *(ILIAD 14:310)*—hit the exits after a late Bronze Age earthquake. The 430 yr. rhyme spun by *1 KINGS (6:1)*—rapping on a 1440 BC Exodus—is post-exilic wax. Joe knew Thutmose reigned in 1440 BC, and that only a century-late Hyksos comeback tour, could justify the telescope spin (*AGNST AP 1:14*→see variant text at *1:15*). Ironic punch from the literary chronology's tag, clocks its knock-out from one fact: Thutmose actually extended Egypt's border back up into Canaan like never before. The Samaritan Pentateuch and Septuagint add **"and Canaan"** at *EXODUS (12:40)* to buffer literalist shame. History was conflated and mythologized. Habiru antiquity emphasized. The story of Joseph's office satirizes a century of Hyksos rule in the Nile Delta at Avaris/Goshen. But the Sea Peoples took Canaan from Egypt—a fact buried to negate Egypt's claims on the Levantine chart.

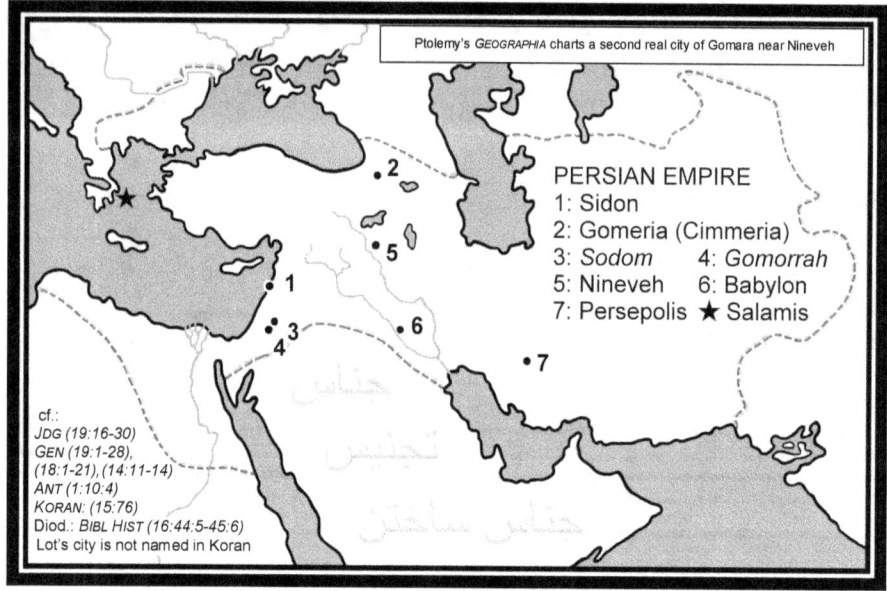

Academics who object to any use of the term *Celtic,* (except as label of a modern movement which they boldly seek to deny its valid historic depth), must be addressed here, even at risk of appearing to over-evaluate the import of a red colored thread in the Biblical tapestry. Technicolor stitches of Josephus, endure as early strands on this topic. A Roman subprovince of maritime Celts marks them closely connected, to those eastern Celts whose quasi-Thracian history was treated by Greek scholars. St. Jerome judged the Celtic dialect still spoken in 4th Century Ankara Turkey, mutually intelligible with Celtic he knew from natives around Trier in the Rhineland near Belgium. These early witnesses, when followed up by later testimony to "Celts" in the Medieval letter Zosimus wrote concerning the fall of the Roman empire, provide sufficient ammunition to implode the tenure of Imperialist mythologers, who so crudely claim Celtic identity as naught but an 18th Century invention of Edward Lhuyd. Josephus testifies to Celtic patriotism among the 1st Century maritime Gauls/Belgae:

he Jews had leaned upon
   All of their race who were beyond the Euphrates
   To raise them into a united revolution
Also—living nearby the Romans—the Gauls   (Γαλάται: "Galatai")
Were [set] in motion
And those of Celtica   *(Κελτικὸν: "Celticon"—Celts)*
Were not quiet [either]   *(for a fork off proto-Celts going Semitic, cf. "more Irish" Normans)*
(Whiston's 1737 AD "Geltin" for Joe's "Κελτικὸν," is hard not to see as a turn on the anti-Celtic circuit.)
        —Josephus in WARS *(1:0:4)*

The gospel which Josephus sequels off Biblical puzzles on Dan, squeaks with great literary economy. The Galileans had reason beyond geography and scriptural study, to consider themselves a Danite remnant. Jerusalem's discriminating establishment, could alternatively cite several later eruptions from the further north, to explain away the more fiery tone and glow of the Galileans. The Greek historians Pausanias and Polybius, record an undervalued history of the Greco-Macedonians, regarding their employment of Celtic mercenaries in the Middle East. Celtic armies deployed by the Seleucids in Syro-Babylonia, fought other Celts hired by the Ptolemies of the Egyptian sphere, in battles that were deciding factors of

---

**WHY have fishermen reddish hair?
And the murex divers** [of Phoenicia]**?
In short—all who work on the sea?
Is it because the sea is hot?
And full of dryness because it is salty?...
Furthermore, those who live close to the north** [edge of earth]
All have fine red hair. —*Aristotlian riddle in* PROBLEMATA *(38:2)*

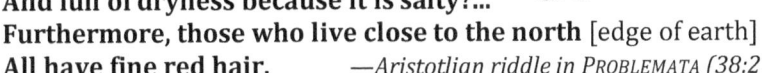

**IT happened when Moses was coming down Mount Sinai
Descending with two planks of warning in his power
Moses did not know that because of his speaking** (דָּן מִדָּן מִדְיָן)
The hide of his head had horned (קָרַן) —*EXODUS (34:29)*

    The word מַקְרִן of *PSALM (69:31)*, affirms that "horned" is the literal Hebrew; figurative use *(cf. HABAKUK 3:4)*, radiates another masterful double-meaning here, where propensity for sudden sunburn, is a consequence of communion, (with Yahweh), near the magnetic end of a big round glowing volcano. <u>BELOW</u>: DEPICTIONS OF THE *SEA PEOPLES*, FROM THE FORTRESS-LIKE MEDINET HABU TEMPLE OF RAMESSES III: <u>RIGHT</u>: Denyen/Shardana (Dan), fight for Egypt in horned helmets, against the brush-topped Peleset (Philistines). <u>LEFT</u>: Pharaoh modified the horned helmets of his Denyen servants into radiant discs of Hathor. Some Denyen figures are pug-nosed caricatures of Caucasians. The curious one below left has a simian brow like the racist anti-Irish cartoons of the 19th century.

rule. The outline of an enduring Northern footprint in the Middle East, survives in engaging detail—but this red-headed stepdad is only introduced here to protect a march over the desert, towards recovery of a multiracial origin of the Hebrews not only plausible, but much more than probable. The Bible itself tells that the good book was so heavily redacted after the Battle of Salamis, that Ezra had to introduce the new Imperial sanctioned Bible to *Shah an Shah's* Jewish subjects, while he stood on a preening high government ground, of new Persian walls around the City of David.

Truth is worth the risk of being accused of "British Israelism"—a doctrine with racist tenets which research negates and discards. Study lights the opposite match, exploding the tongue-in-cheek racial purity mythology of the Bible like a paper tiger on parade. The race riddles were scripted while discrimination recurred as a factor in the greatest saga ever lived on earth. Persian prompted pedigrees took center stage in the testament Ezra redacted, while Iddo's book of genealogies was tossed. Gospel collates that tragedy of convenience, with the stoning of Zechariah son of Jehoiada in the Temple. Like so much of gospel study, truth seeking starts with David:

So he directed [Jesse] **to fetch** [David]
Now he was a redzie* *(reddish—a redhead)*
And handsome to look at with beautiful eyes
And Yahweh said: *("redzie"→ אַדְמוֹנִי : 'aḏ·mō·w·nî ↔ is a pun of "Lord"→ אֲדֹנִי: 'ă·ḏō·wnî)
"That's the one! Go ahead and anoint him!" — 1 SAMUEL (16:12) (cf. 16:7)

A word here most often translated as *ruddy*, has the equivalent literal meaning of *red* or *reddish*. Study of its parallel contexts indicates it is an ancient endearment for *red-headed*, less taunting than the modern *gingery* or *carrot-topped*, and perhaps closer to endearing the bright red head under a crown-name of *"Copper."* The divine finger that first identifies and promotes the Messianic house of David, is framed by a description of what may be construed as an ethnic characteristic. This finds a whole new imperiled level of population in self-denial of the savior. Pointing out tragic morals, highlighted by rare bold recessive traits, does not preach racial purity, but instead champions ethnic diversity. An astute Jewish subtlety which notes a Persian sanctioned betrayal of roots, boldly underlines the first restoration, in a way that it makes it hard not to see Ezra as a Persepolian mole, dropping a trail of breadcrumbs imperceptible to the rulers of some Persian version of the Council of Nicea, so that the children of Moses would one day find their way home to a truth about the original liberation of their boy's-life. The *burning bush* of a *redzie* was favored in the Messianic lineage, as laid down with wisdom in the descriptions of David's beloved boy-king, who built the filial Temple:

AVID ordered them to take the prophet Nathan...
And to set his son Solomon upon the king's ass
And carry him out of the city to the fountain called Gihon
And anoint him there with holy oil
And to make him King...
Without any delay they set Solomon upon the king's ass
And brought him out of the city to the fountain
And anointed him with oil
— *Josephus from* ANTIQUITIES *(7:14:5)*

Y beloved is *creamy-white* and a redzie (cf. LAM 4:7, צַח וְאָדוֹם)
Conspicuous among Ten-Thousand...
While my king [Solomon] was at his table
My nard provided the fragrance (cf. MARK 14:3, JOHN 12:3)
— SONG OF SOLOMON *(5:10, 1:12)*

This is evidence on multiple levels. One doesn't need the Bible to know what a rare prized beauty, brilliant and comely red-headed specimens are all the world over, and no less so in the Middle East, where dazzling reds still fetch a higher price than blondes of otherwise equal looks. Certainly the ancient Egyptians kept them inside their houses, like boy Moses. Their skin is damaged easily in the tropical sun. Joses riddles redophilic nature into us:

OW there was about this time Jesus — a wise man
If it be lawful to call him a man
For He was a maker of wonder-works
A teacher of such men as take the Truth with pleasure
He drew over to himself both many of the Judeans
And many of the Greeks
He was Christ *("He was anointed" leader of the rebels called "Christians" after him)*
And when at the suggestion of principal men among us
Pilate had condemned Him to the cross
Those that loved him at first did not *forsake him* *("at first"* ᆨᄃ *: a riddle)*
For he appeared to them alive again the third day *(then some forsook him)*
As the divine prophets foretold these wonderful things
Concerning him—and another Ten-Thousand *(immortals)*

— *forsaken Joe's Testimonium, from* ANTIQUITIES *(18:3:3)(cf.* MATT *27:46,* PSALM *22:1)*

The precision ad-libbed into the Testimonium, elevates it to the same level of divine inspiration that Josephus put into the four gospels themselves. There is no sound reason for a runaway Joe to hold back calling Jesus "anointed," after he had burned Rome like a Sicarii for the second time. The Roman Tacitus, in his Latin *HISTORIA*, calls Jesus by the very same Greek word "Christ," to report on the proselyte "Christians," whom a Jew called Christ inspired.

Tacitus, a Pagan historian, calls Jesus "Christ" simply because "Christ" was the name Jesus was known by on the creepy Imperial street, and that fact alone, makes use of the *Greek* moniker "Christ" by Jewish Josephus, 100% plausible—whether or not we know Joses is a secret Galilean Apostle. Not a single criticism of this passage's authenticity, (all based upon errant rushes to anti-"Christ" judgment), bears a single drop of potable water. The volumes written against the Testimonium's virginity are all full of waste-water tears—unfoundedly rejecting use of the Greek word "Christ" by Josephus, as though first-century Greek-speaking Jews would find it objectionable, even though it was the Imperial street-name for Jesus, and as if Joe (whom many critics revile to this day) would be that sensitive to such critics in his own time. Taking the moniker as an alias in a news report, Origen could write that Josephus "did not believe in Jesus as Christ." Every thesis crying that the passage violates some Jewish sanctity for the Greek word "Christ," is naught but sterile poppycock. The real issue critics aim to promote isn't a scientific assessment at all. It is a matter of blaming a mass of unjust Jewish suffering, on a Christianity corrupted in tandem with Judaism. Lets leave Jesus out of that mess, whereby academia throws medieval anti-Semitic guilt upon Jesus, as if He doesn't pay for enough sins at the ends of the ages. Jesus can't be Messiah to a Jew? Not now, or even in the first-century? But the Shah can be—no problem? Holy Moses, whose

religion is this? Which brothers are invited to partake in its sacrifice? Waste verbiage crucifies Josephus from every angle, and now begins to further libel Jesus as: "*CAESAR'S MESSIAH.*" Did Moses free the Egyptians from their abused servants? If Jesus saved the Caesars, then who ethnically cleansed the Galilees? Some who head-bob at a wall will no doubt reply: "Joses!"... Forgive them Father, for they know not their exodus they revile.

Joe sealed his codex with fire from out of this world. His accomplished rhetorical style is fathomable, once one perceives how neatly the double-entendre slices through a thick bed of emotionally charged cross-references. The Testimonium points the word *forsaken* as an autograph academia ignores—at first. Joe's sharp double edged tongue tweaks *forsaken* in an intergenerational autobiographical fashion, stroked hard here, to enhance cognizance of a method by its firm example. Maybe some of those who didn't trust the Truth's presentation at first, will now warm up to it, as the pedigree, the meaning, and the global potency become clear. Some might accept what they at first reject. Others will suddenly forsake rebirth because the big fat unzipped Truth is too hard to swallow. Loosen up. It is pleasure preserving the brutal planet earth. We need both the forest and the trees.

The lexeme *Ten-Thousand*, is a martial seal Joe subtly triggers to index Jesus to a myriad of zealous *mea culpas* in his works. We just point across in passing, towards the empty squares of those times, down at this level of our show and tell floor. Today the Messianic parade proceeds under a much bigger tent. The contestants are fighting over who retells fairy tales better, (from the parable of Eden—all the way to some fantasy planet reached by genealogical studies). Visage of the anointed Mesach's inclusive family, is the Peace team mascot. Truth, about the identity of the hero who has already made the showcase deal to win our freedom, floats in on prized cartooned features. The rule of His word was given the central respect in Islam, for the first twelve parades out of Mecca:

> **The Prophet Mohammed (Peace be upon him) said:**
> ***There is no prophet between me and Jesus***
> ***Peace be upon Him!***
> ***Jesus will descend to the Earth***
> ***Recognize him when you see Him:***
> ***A man of medium height*** *('standing in the midst')*
> ***Fair and reddish"*** —Hadith in SUNNAN ABU DAWUD *(37:4310)*

The Messianic bedrock for Muslims, is laid upon the ebullient formula "Peace be upon him," which Mohammed (Peace be upon him) passed around often enough, to affirm for us his belief that Jesus (Peace be upon Him), would revaporize upon the earth through a Davidic door of rebirth.

Whenever Mohammed (Peace be upon him), mentioned Jesus (Peace be upon Him), Mohammed (Peace be upon him), busted out the grand "Peace be upon Him." Mohammed (Peace be upon him), apparently mentioned Jesus (Peace be upon Him), much more often than the verses would testify. Islam subsequently adopted the tagline from Mohammed (Peace be upon him), and ignored THE BOOK source Mo cites, with the key to its meaning. Here their anti-Christ rhetoric is reduced to absurdity. Here unseals a scriptural puzzle equal to the one Ezra dangled in the chapters of THE BOOK sealed at the first restoration. One can't miss the prescient provenance of Koranic verses, which on the one hand ridicule Christians who misunderstand Messianic claims of divine sonship, with a riddle surely measured above the desert audience level:

THE Jews say Ezra is the Son of God
The Christians say Christ is the Son of God...
Imitating the talk of those who misbelieved before

— *KORAN (9:30) (i.e. "the Jesus" wrote the gospels, and they pervert them)*

Elsewhere the *KORAN* plays with gospel allegory as fact, claiming Jesus was conceived when a disgruntled Aaronite Jew was forced to submit as *Allah took incarnation* for what was, without a doubt, the tightest one night stand ever. True sex is the donation of chromosomes:

WE sent unto her our spirit (MATTHEW 1:20)
And He took on the form of a handsome man for her... *(flesh)*
He said: "I am only a messenger of your Lord (LUKE 1:26)
To bestow upon you a pure boy" (LUKE 1:31-33)
She said: "How can I have a boy (LUKE 1:34)
I am a virgin, and I am no whore!" *("I will not have sex until I marry!")*
He said: "Your Lord proclaims it *("I overshadow you," LUKE 1:35)*
Its easy for me... *(LUKE 1:37→"I'm in like flint")*
It is a decided matter" *(LUKE 1:38, 1:54, 2:1, the trap's wire has been tripped)*

—*KORAN (19:16-21) (the Zealot Sect was the Word made flesh: LUKE 1:37-38, JOHN 1:14)*

Only eyes wide shut could fail to see the physicality played with by the holy spirit of Allah taking on the semblance of a well formed man, to make a perfect boy sprout inside the most tender part of a perfect young girl. If Allah is not the father of Jesus (Peace be upon Him), then who is? This dazzling display of logic can not be side-stepped with reference to the obedient genetics slaving away in the kitchen and laundry rooms. No matter how perfect she was, certainly no female could be the Y-chromosome donating father of a pure Jesus—boy Son of Mary (Peace be upon Him). Therefore, on the masculine side, whose son is Jesus (Peace be upon Him) according to the *KORAN*, if Jesus (Peace be upon Him) is not God's Son? Who is our alternative candidate for the male DNA creator of our Doomsday captain Jesus (Peace be upon Him)? Perhaps a black meteorite named Nomad? This self-sterilizing parental enterprise probes *non sequitur* territory. The changeling is cubed. Shame about the original "Syrian" direction to truth over Mecca is unsealed. Resistance is not futile. The burqa is torn at the launch point. Behave yourselves—*reducto ad absurdum*.

Mohammed (Peace be upon him), wisely riddled one prayer indelibly into the true core of his legacy in a way that did not allow it to be dropped from the canon. Islam's original direction of prayer was towards Christian Jerusalem, and Haaj was made to the rocky top of Moriah (at first). The

Byzantines policed Islamic Christians on their way to the city, ending a notable incident of Arab on Arab violence which threatened to spoil Easter week of 629. New Christians from the Red Sea region of Arabia, celebrated the resurrection of their savior—the savior they were lead to follow by their Apostle Mohammed (Peace be upon him). Mecca was taken at 630. Mohammed (Peace be upon him) destroyed the Pagan pilgrimage of the non believing Arab slave marketers—a bold stroke which he only enjoyed for two years. Mo was avenged in a rather shady assassination, more likely to have been motivated by a bigger, more cosmopolitan grudge, than the loss of a date grove by a humbled minority three years earlier. Before the death of the prophet, Islamic prayer was directed to Christian Jerusalem—not towards the Kaaba. It was from Christian Jerusalem that Mo ascended to Allah to get the  divine instruction prescribing Islamic submission towards the furthest aim of prostration. After two years of Meccan economic disaster, the wealthiest remnants of the gutted commercial infrastructure of the Pagan Hajj would verse Arabia in a new religion that firmly reestablished Mecca after Mohammed rode the way of the wheat to the ruler of the heavens. Peace be upon Danae's son Mohammed, who gripped the heads of the Meccan idols he pounded, by their tortured whoring hair, carrying home the prophetic Messianic proof, spoofing skyward on daddy's lightning *Pegasus*. This Olympic flight took equine wings from that Jerusalem hill at the end of the earth, about which King David told us the ultimate father promised:

> *have set my King on Zion, On my Holy Hill...*
> *You are my Son... The ends of the earth are yours*
> — PSALM *(2:7-8) every last hour grain of the furthest sands*

The 621 AD night-flight to Jerusalem is noted in both KORAN and Hadith. Mohammed turned over Arabia's hour-glass, ordering five daily prayers towards Christian Jerusalem. The Surah pivots upon a stony Mecca Mo curses, when the "sacred mosque" is still a black Arab Pagan pantheon:

LORY to Allah who took his servant to journey over dark-time From the sacred mosque to the furthest* mosque
— *KORAN (Surah 17:1)*

 **WHY TRANSGRESS THE COMMANDS OF GOD SO THAT YOU FAIL?
FOR IF YOU FORSAKE HIM—HE FORSAKES YOU** —2 CHRONICLES 24:20
ZACHARIAS means "God Remembers"

Zach #4
son of Barruch
68 AD (from 62)
(cipher for James)

WARS (4:5:4) 玷
James becomes "Zach son of Barruch" (υἱὸν Βάρεις': 'born of the savage, of the weighty,' cf. βαρεῖς in ACTS 20:29; βαρύτερα in MATT 23:23). The adjacent anomaly of MATT 23:35-36 ciphers the murder of James, telescoped 6 years ahead to 68 AD, with a jealous mask flipped upon guilty High Priests then hunted: *"Two of the boldest ... jumped on Zacharias in the middle of the Temple and slew him ... they also threw him down out of the Temple into the valley below."*

#4 CONT.

Zach #2
**son of Berekiah
son of Iddo**
c. 521 BC

MATT 23:35
A literary device fakes a lapse of memory, to replace Zach #1 with the prophet of the BOOK OF ZECHARIAH, who is the grandson of that Iddo who returned from captivity with Zerubbabel (NEH 12:4). There is no mention of Zach #2's death, except this accidentally on purpose confusion via Jesus: *"Zechariah son of Berekiah (υἱοῦ Βαραχίου) whom you murdered between the Temple (courtyard) and the altar (in the sanctuary)"*
cf. ZECH 1:1 & 1:7

Resurrection in the Koran:
"Tell them the semblance of life in this world: It is like rain which We send down from the skies; the earth's vegetation absorbs it, but soon it becomes dry straw, [seeds of which] the winds scatter" (2:28)
"Allah is He who has made the earth spread out for you, and put channels in it so you may find guidance, and sends down water from the sky in measures, and thus We raise a land of the dead to life, and so too will you be raised" (43:10-11)
"Jesus... you raise the dead by my permit" (5:110)
"No one can enter God's kingdom unless they are born of water and wind" (JOHN 3:5)

Iddo
**Grandfather of
Zach #2**
c. 538 BC

2 CHRON 12:15
Ezra was compelled to omit genealogies of the Northern Kingdom kept by Iddo: *"And the acts of Rehoboam, first and last, are they not written in the books of Shemaiah the prophet, and of Iddo the seer in the genealogies?"* No note like that found at 2 CHRON 20:34, indicates this book was woven into another scripture. Iddo's book also had accounts of Abijah: 2 CHRON 20:34; and Jeroboam: 2 CHRON 13:22. As CHRONICLES dates to no earlier than Cyrus, Iddo's Book was censored under Persian rule—during or after the life of that Iddo who was Zach #2's grandfather. Ezra's identifying of Zacharias as the son of Iddo (EZRA 5:1 & 6:14), not Berekiah (ZECH 1:1 & 1:7), makes it compelling to take that notable Iddo as the author, and places Zach #2 in a censored context. Joe reseeds the generation (at ANT 8:8:5), identifying the unnamed prophet (of 1 KINGS 13) as "Iado" (cf. Οαδο).

Zach #1
son of Jehoiada
c. 800 BC

2 CHRON 24:17-22
"stoned to death in the courtyard of Yahweh's Temple"

Zach #3
**Zachariah
father of John**
c. 5 AD

LUKE 1:5-23
"Zachariah belonged to the priestly order of Abijah ... An angel appeared to him on the right side of the altar of incense ... "Fear not Zach. for the Lord has heard your prayer"... Zach. said to the angel: "How will I know?"... The angel replied: ... "Because you did not believe my words, which will become fulfilled in their time, you will become mute ... until they are done"
(i.e. 9 months = 3 days)

KORAN 1:5-23
[Zach. said]: *"My Lord give me proof!"* [Answer was]: *"Your proof is you wont be able to speak for three days, even though you are not dumb."*

#4 CONT. *(before 'Zach's' stoning)* *"The jealous and the Edomites ... had the impudence for setting up fake tribunals ... and intended to have Zacharias the son of Barruch, (i.e. James) one of the most eminent citizens slain, and what provoked them against him was the hatred of wickedness (cf. James "the Just"), and love of liberty (cf. the 4th sect of real Zealots), that were so eminent in him (Joe's father Matthew too, was "eminent on account of his righteousness"—LIFE:1) ... by taking him out, they not only hoped to grab his effects, but also get rid of a man who had great power to destroy them ... so by public proclamation they called together 70 principal men of the citizenry (the Sanhedrin—cf. the Testimonium) for a show, as if they were real judges—even though they had no proper authority (having been appointed by Romans). Before these Zacharias was accused of a plot to betray their polity to the Romans (Jamie judged weightier legal matters: Nero's blemished sacrifices; cf. Zach ben Abkulas in BABYLONIAN TALMUD GITTIN: 56A 玷)."* —WARS (4:5:4)

"Ananus assembled the Sanhedrin of the judges, and brought before them that brother of the Jesus called the Christ, whose name was James among others (among other names Joe puts down in code→Ananus, →Zecharias son of Baruch). And when he had formed an accusation against them as breakers of the law (James calling the practice of blemishing animals before sacrificing them for Nero a double violation) he (the real Ananus) delivered him (James) to be stoned." —ANT (20:9:1); compare all with Eusebius ECCLES. HIST. (2:23)

Zach #3, and Zach #4 (i.e. James), are ornately conflated in the *PROTOVANGELION OF JAMES:* **"They found his blood turned to stone** [near the altar]." This, (like the βαρεῖς tag of Joses⚔), reflects the *TALMUD* on Zach # 1: **"The blood of Zacharias remained, and was not washed away until Nebuchadnezzar** *(a mirror of Titus)* **came and became a remarkable avenger of his blood"** *(JERUS. TALMUD TANN: 69, BABYL. TALMUD SAN: 96).* Zach # 3 gave birth to John—cousin of the brothers James and Jesus. James was reborn after the passing of very old uncle Zach # 3, who was married to Elizabeth—Mary's cousin. They were Levites descended from Levi, son of Aaron, son of Amran. Mary's growing rebel seed Jesus, was fed in the Temple with the bread of the presence (like Saul's rebel David), under supervision of Zach #3 *(cf. KORAN 3:36-41 & LUKE 1:8-21—especially 1:11; the civil warrior profile of Jesus/David links MARK 2:23-28 to 1 SAMUEL 21:1-6 & 1 MACC 2:27-41—hear of Ineswitrin in ANT 6:12:8, tagged by Abiathar in MARK 2:23-28 versus Ahimelech in 1 SAM 21:1-6).* Jesus conflates Zach #1 & Zach #2, to telescope his brother James (as Zach #4) ahead to 68 AD, when that generation of Roman appointed High Priests who slew James (for his teaching against Nero's sacrifices 㱏), were themselves slain in their turn by Zealots; Joses #2 was Jesus reborn. Mohammed uses the same device, conflating Mary with Miriam, to equate Moses and Joses:

"Mary—you have issued something enormous—sister of Aaron (big Moses even); your father was not a player, and your mother was no whore" —KORAN 19:27

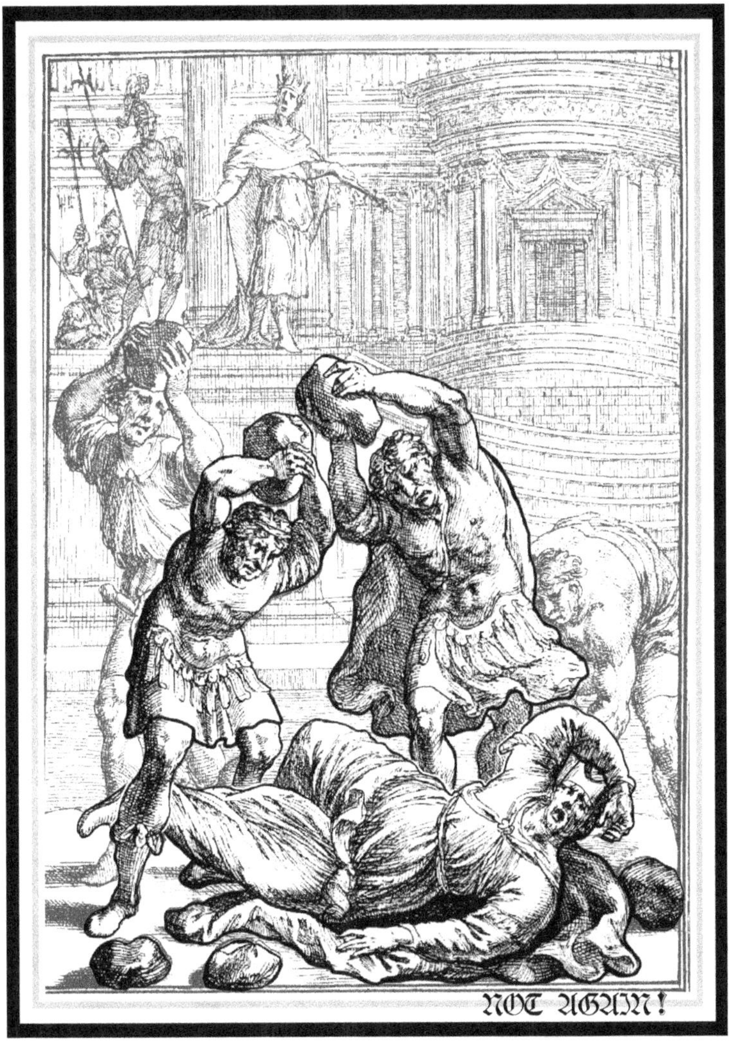

"Mary the daughter of Amran kept her chastity, so we blew our spirit up inside her" —*KORAN 66:12; cf.* 50:9-11, 43:5-11 & 18:45 & 6:99 & 21:28-43, 39:42, 67:2, 6:38, 23:99-100.

Islamic tradition betrays its Christian pedigree. Mohammed's Christian cousin Waraka was first to recognize Mo's prophetic talent. Islam submitted its prayer towards *the furthest place*—in a Christian Jerusalem. Mo flew there all the way from Hejaz to ascend to heaven. The prayerful prophet did not rise to Allah above the Kaaba. It was above Jerusalem that Mo met Jesus and was given direction for Islamic prayer by Allah, with a strictness disguised in a riddle from Sergeant Moses (*'I could make you get down and give me fifty'*). General Jesus is raised to judge advocate and presides over Islam's day of doom and bloom.

The most obligatory snipe in Islam, shoots sharp from Mo's "Peace be upon Him," to rifle the furthest aim into us. The Arab apostle destroyed the Pagan Haaj to Mecca, and redirected Arab prayer to the mountain sacrifice of 70 AD. As the *Khatam an Nabuwwah*, Mo smartly chose and sealed his favorite gospel greeting, to chastise all who ferment the stink of compulsion to religion. Many are none the less committed to reface the entire planet, toward centers of idolatry which the master of Peace be upon him destroyed in respect of the shrine of the end of time. Mo sealed this cross-reference to preserve his devotion to an immortal Messianic movement which will end the age of religious oppression. Arabia's promoter of *Peace Be Upon Him*, never told anyone to break holy wind, and blow down any civilians of any nation, creed, or preference, for being no more wrong than they are. Pervert one prophet's message and you reject them all. Imams have more fear of Mo's ode to shockingly black gospel humor, than they do for the real horror inside shut doors:

JESUS came, and stood in the midst, and laid it down:
   "Peace be upon you!"   (a noxious spoof in wake of an eruption)
When He had laid this He displayed His hands and His side to them
Thereupon the disciples cheered
For they had witnessed the Master [of the ends]   (the Lord, boss, owner)
Then the Jesus laid it down on them once again: (εἶπεν: "laid," 'said')

"Peace be upon you!   السلام عليكم
As the Father has let me loose
You I burst-forth!"   (send, transmit,   thrust-forth, propel)
And having said this
He blew! — saying:
*"Take this Holy Wind!**
Anyhow, of any you might let loose   *(πνεῦμα: pneuma = wind, breath, spirit)
Those sins have been loosened
Anyhow, any you arrest   (any that you 'hold in' or "grip")
They have been arrested"   (they have been 'held in')
And Thomas—one of the twelve—he called "Twin"   (Thomas Didymos)

[He] was not with them when Jesus came, so they told him:
"We have experienced the Master!" *(the "Lord" arrived—He happened)*
And to them, he (Tom) replied:
(in a sharp double-edged desire for both a risen Spartacus and a nailed Crassus):
"Until I see the strike of the nails in His hands
And can put my finger inside the strike of the nails
And may put my hand inside his flank
I will not believe" *(i.e. 'It's not over until his fist is returned!')*
And eight days later His disciples were with Him again
And Thomas was with them
With the doors shut, the Jesus appeared *(He "came"—happened—blew in—materialized)*
Standing in the middle He laid it:
"Peace be upon you!" السلام عليكم

Then He said to Thomas:
"Bring your finger here
And see my hands
And bring your hand
And put it inside my flank and become *(become geothermally engaged)*
Not a disbeliever but a believer" *(a believer in the regime to come)*
And Twin answered Him and said:
"My Master and My Magistrate!" *(You—not Vespasian—are my god: Ps 86:9, Jn 10:34)*
Jesus said to Him: *(full of wordplay—casual use of "Theos" was "Magistrate")*
"Thomas, you have believed me
Because you've experienced me *("perceived" My power, had cause to have "taken heed")*
Those who believe without [such an] **experiencing are blessed"**
Accordingly Jesus also produced many other signs
In the eye of his disciples
Which are not written in *THE BOOK* الكتاب
But these things are written
So that you will come to believe *(JOHN 1:12-13)*
That Jesus is the Son of God—the Christ *(ROMANS 8:14-17)*
And that by believing *(in divine adoption for the entire populous—not just Caesar)*
You might have life in His name *(you become "Jesus"—"Salvation from Yahweh!")*⸸
— *JOHN (20:20-31)* 8 yrs after idols of Pax led a parade, Vespasian* was deified, Vesuvius* erupted.

> *ABOVE*: Mosaic from Pompeii mocks a slave's suffering. Wicked master boasted of the scarcity by which he maintained those who served him at his table of plenty.

Judas the Galilean founded a Zealot sect which refused to call any man Lord (Master). How could Jesus have lead such a sect? Jesus stands in for the entire Messianic Host.⸸ His Zealots went down in flames in 70 AD; the grumbling nation united behind their moral word too late. Rome's fake god was receiving sacrifices next to Yahweh, while Rome's fake god turned Israel's poor into slaves and food. Judas earned the nation's 30 shekel redemption price, as a result of the unconventional anointing of Jesus *(MATT 26:8-15, EXODUS 21:32).* ¥

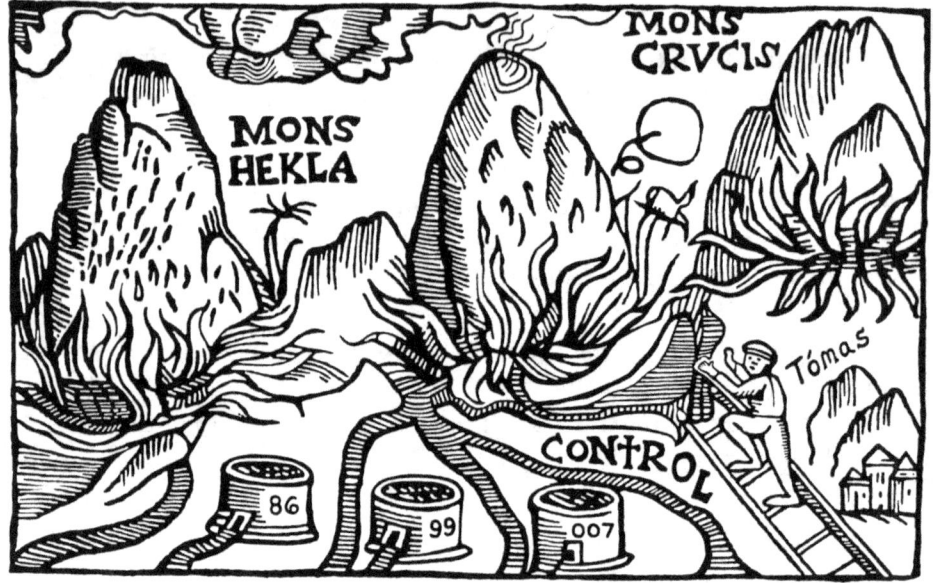

ABOVE: **Prophetic 1555 AD Illustration of "The Gateway to Hell"** *(Hlið til Helvítis)*.

The unfolding flank of Iceland's Mount Hekla trembles like a flower made of fire. Sigmund Freud was the first to comment: **"Yahweh was certainly a volcano god."** Yet Freud failed to fathom the depth of literary device in the astute testament. Freud could only hear that level of prose which speaks of a small Arabian volcano where Moses fled for an auspicious natural redoubt. The date of the huge eruption known as *Hekla-3* causes controversy. Many associate it with an 1159 BC cluster of climate markers which promote *Hekla-3* as a main driver of *Exodus from Egypt*. Other attempts dating *Hekla-3* range from 1130-920 BC, which collates impact to finalization of the *Conquests of Canaan*. One Icelandic volcanologist maps ejecta in two events two centuries apart—surmising a *Hekla-3a* and *Hekla-3b*. The testament tells that both *Exodus* and *Conquest* were lead from above and bellow, by a:

"pillar of cloud by day, and a pillar of fire by night."

Monotheism's early prophets were made aware of the important part volcanism had played in movements of armed forces in the eastern Mediterranean—from at least the time of the Hyksos. Yahweh is the Creator, and new forms of biological life arise after old ones are pruned off along with their environmental niche. Every mass extinction of species on planet earth has had as much of a volcanic causation as a meteoric one, if not through mass ejections, then through climate crises caused by continental configurations dictated by volcanism. To call the Creator a "volcano god" is a gross understatement, but Yahweh's backside does have volcanic hands *(Exodus 33:22-23)*. They mine hidden hot depths of literally *Living Stone,* in the *Harrowing of Hell* of *1 Peter (2:4-10, 3:17-22)*, and locate a transubstantiated host taking the Otis elevator, to enlist with Yahweh in *Luke (23:46)*:

"Into your hands Father I commit my wind."

Lightning bolts tons of energy from the atmosphere back into the crust. You are earth ("Adam")—made of rock and water. Believers in transmigration of souls, and rebirth in corporeal bodies, need to know that all elements which make up human life are also found in heat packets commuting to work deep inside the earth. Biological elements are recycled by a volcanic conveyor belt which sinks them into earth's mantle at ocean trenches. Inside the earth, the life-elements respark into new heat packets that populate volatile gears of a system which torments them under great pressure and stress for a long and taxing duration. They erupt back up at plate tectonic boundaries, and may thereafter be reincorporated into heat-packets of new animal life-forms commuting to work in the biosphere where weather dictates. If there were no hell, all life on earth's surface would be nuked by the sun in just hours. Life is no accident. Man will only survive by geothermal science.

"PUT IT INSIDE MY FLANK AND BECOME": *Hekla* is an Icelandic word for a type of hooded cloak. Early Latin maps name this volcano **Mons Casule**—*Mount Holy Cloak.*

Yahweh who is your God will himself cross-ahead* to destroy nations
Before these shall dispossess Joshua *(MATT 21:33-46)*
Who will cross-ahead* after Yahweh has spoken ...
Cry out with the name "Yahweh!" *(a line of wordplay on the name "Joshua")*
Give greatness to our God!
This rock is perfect
Because His work is for all
His ways are just
A God of truth and without corruption
Righteous and erect is He!
—*DEUTERONOMY 31:3*

The Christian origins of Islam are retained with belief that Jesus (Peace be upon Him), *A:* returns to Earth sporting His stiff morning rise, to neatly bring all the ends into tight fulfillment, and *B:* presides as judge by the measure of His firm will, when His warm global release is accomplished:

God said:

> *"O Jesus! I will make you finish*
> *And take you up inside Me again..*
> *On that day of the rising you will come back into Me"*

— KORAN *(3:55) (God raised him into himself)*

Jesus said:

> *"God gave me the Book...*   (My Word)
> *And has not made me a miserable tyrant...*
> *Peace be upon me*   وَالسَّلَامُ عَلَيَّ
> *The day I was born*
> *The day I die*
> *And the day I will get raised up back alive"*   (By My Word)

— KORAN *(19:31-33)*

The KORAN is emphatic, over and over again, with words directly from Allah warning, that tough gospel of divine rise Jesus, is hard Islamic cannon:

We followed their footsteps up with Jesus the son of Mary
Fulfilling the law and what came before him *(MATTHEW 5:17)*
And we gave him the Gospel *(again in KORAN Surah 57: 26-27)*
Which is filled with guidance and light *(JOHN 14:6)*
Inspecting what was legal before it *(LUKE 6:9-11)*
And a guidance and admonition to those who fear *(LUKE 18:2)*
Then let the people of His Gospel *(including Muslims; KORAN Surah 2:81)*
Judge by that which is revealed therein *(Gospel in Sharia?)*
For whosoever will not judge by what God has revealed
Those are the workers of evil! *(chaff: REVELATION 20:12-15)*
— *KORAN (5:50-51)*

Mohammed put a seal of approval upon a corpus he called *"THE BOOK."* His seals were ribboned in Arabic, to steer Arabia towards this prophetic literary legacy, and away from idolatry. Only shirkers can claim that Hadith which are not in the Koran, have precedence over gospel revelations which the Koran confirms by prophetic composition. The Council of Nicea of 325 AD, closed *"THE BOOK."* Mo's poetic references to the Syriac *INFANCY GOSPEL OF THOMAS*, and to Hebrew Midrashes of like genre, do not undo Mo's approval of the closed *BOOK*. In 630 AD Mohammed destroyed the Pagan Kaaba (Peace be upon him), to affirm the divine authority sealed in *MATTHEW, MARK, LUKE,* and *JOHN,* with an epic historical milestone. No Koranic verse can be credibly read to deny the gospel its authority. Secure within the gospel savvy verses of Mo (Peace be upon him), is a direct message to reanoint Muslims of these hairy times. Allah gave the gospel to the reborn Jesus (Peace be upon Him):

We gave Him the Gospel — *KORAN (57:26-27)*

Muslims are told to submit to the teaching of Jesus (Peace be upon Him):

Jesus the son of Mary: His title shall be the Messiah *("the anointed")*
Respected in this world and the next
And a title belonging to those whose place is nigh to God
— *KORAN (3:37-43)*

Messiah is a title reserved for rulers anointed by divine favor. The anointing of Jesus as king is a scene repeated with prurient pomp in the gospels. His christening seals the record of a great victory Israel won over Rome in the valley of Bethoron under the risen general Lazarus (Eliezer). The most climactic anointing of Jesus (Peace be upon Him), is performed by a girl named Mary, but it is not the perfect chaste mother of Jesus. This Mary is worn by a world at war, to anoint our king near His Passover sacrifice. War-torn Mary has a sister Martha. Her brother is the (just unsealed) "help from God" of the name Lazarus. Zealous sister Mary takes on the symbolic role of the first female High Priest of Israel. No monk would alter gospel, to award a traditionally male role, to an imperfect mass of conflicting impulses:

Mary took a full supply   *(about 10 ozs.)*
Of costly perfume made of pure Nard
Anointed the feet of Jesus
And rubbed them with her hair
    —*JOHN (12:3)(cf. SONG OF SOLOMON 5:10 AND 1:12)*

    Allah lavished the living Gospel with repeat anointing episodes. The version in *LUKE* is sealed with extra Islamic social submission, to work love with raw *KORAN* power, sans violent burqa:

A woman in the city
Who was a sinner...
Brought an alabaster jar of ointment
She stood behind Him
Weeping at his feet
And began bathing His feet
Using her tears   *(over all those sacrificed for Truth)*
And drying them with Her hair
Then she continued kissing His feet
And anointing them with the ointment
Now when the Pharisee who had invited Him saw this
   (too many Islamic Imams: "leaders," and Mullahs: 'scholars,' mimic such a Pharisee: 'purist')
He [إمام , ملا , Φαρισαῖος] said to himself:
"If this man Jesus were a prophet, then He would know who
And what kind of woman this is touching Him
That She is a sinner"*(Pharisees disparaged Galilee as a pool of red-headed Danite idolators)*
Jesus spoke up: ..."Do you see this woman?* (do you turn from the image of God?)*
I entered your house   *(you miserable fundamentalist @#%$!)*
You gave me no water for my feet
But She has washed my feet with Her tears
And dried them with Her hair
You gave me no kiss
But from the time I arrived
She has not stopped kissing my feet
You did not anoint my head with oil
But She anoints my feet with ointment"...
And He said to the woman:
"Your faith has saved you *(from Orthodox terror; "saved": σέσωκέν: or "cured you" of it)*
Go in Peace"   *(πορεύου : "go," "travel," 'die' in Peace; the Pharisees taught on transmigration)*
   — *LUKE (7:36-49)* *(if the Pharisees had really been law experts, then they'd have known that the Sadducees were the adulterers—i.e. infidels:* كفّار *)*

السلام عليكم

الحق اقول لكم حيثما يكرز بهذا الانجيل في كل العالم يخبر ايضا بما فعلته هذه تذكارا لها
   — *MATT (26:13)*

I will fulfill the law that is before you (MATT 5:17, LUKE 18:31, 24:44)
And will surely make lawful for you (ROMANS 3:31)
Some of that which was prohibited to you
—KORAN (3:43-45)

The gospel Allah gave Jesus tells that oppressive public standards were a key motivator of the Galilean movement which He zealously lead. The hair of women was loosed and employed by the hand of God. Jesus is God's anointed Messiah, and Allah used the hair of women to anoint Him. The female hand is the only hand that the gospels ever use to anoint the "Anointed One" ("Messiah," "Christ"). His christening always flouts social convention with a casual ceremony of love. Shadowy tribal traditions will not overcome the light Allah long ago revealed through Jesus to any tribe that has reached literacy. If any women wear the burqa with pleasure, that's their own business, but there is no legal compulsion to cover the face or hair in the Islam of Mohammed, Jesus, and Allah. Women who choose not to cover their hair, can not be violated based upon rulings men make contrary to a true revelation from God that Mohammed sealed at the founding of Islam. The Koran specifically orders that no part of this sealed gospel that Allah gave to Jesus can be ignored or "slain":

We gave Jesus the son of Mary manifest signs
And aided Him with the Holy Spirit *(with the volatile power of the Holy Wind)*
Every time an Apostle brings you what your souls don't love
Will you proudly scorn him
And accuse a part of lying
And censor that part?
—KORAN (2:81)

Educated Muslims must reject any claims Imams may make, that the anointing of God's Messiah with hair is a knot of inserted Satanic verses in the gospel (*Injil:* إنجيل). There was never a motive to add such hairy episodes to "the Book" (الكتاب) in a Christian world that until recent times suppressed women and sexuality in nearly the same measure that much of the Islamic world still does today. Indeed, even now many Christian sects ignore the Messiah's teaching by example. They wrongly drape scarves

over the hairy truth, sporting a leaf from a fig Jesus withered.

Arabic words for *hair* or *gray-hair*, appear in the KORAN eight times: *(4:49, 4:77, 16:80, 17:71, 19:4, 30:54, 48:27, 73:17)*. Arabic words for *face* appear 115 times. No word for either *face* or *hair* appears in the two verses of the KORAN *(33:59 & 24:31)*, which errant Islamic teachers abuse in order to force women to obey dress codes dictated by out of context men. The only thing worse than making up a lie about God, is using that lie to add compulsion to religion. The sense organs of the human form—eyes, ears, nose, and mouth—are all designed by Allah to be uncovered for proper functioning.

Surely Allah would not let the gospel of Jesus become tangled with hair, and then neglect to inspire Mo with verses clearly saying *"don't show hair"* or *"don't show face."* No words for *hair* or *face* exist in verses 33:59 and 24:31. Why are words for *hair* and *face* missing from the places in the KORAN where they are needed to enforce compulsory "hijabs" and hair coverings? It's because pretentious Islamic teachers lied. Modern teachers follow respected liars who came before them. That doesn't change the fact that they enshrine a lie. Pagans prayed and sacrificed to stone gods in the Kaaba for generation after generation, but the cultural imperative of these rituals never brought those stones to life. No one ever reaped any heavenly benefit walking round a graven hive in ecstatic circles. Though the respected elders in Pagan Arab society said that big rock box in heat valley was full powered by many gods of pilgrimage, such talk did not protect the facade from Mo.

Mo was concerned about the way his Pagan society used a woman's chest like a trophy rack, to display a family's wealth and status. Women dressed with breasts largely exposed, and were heavily adorned with the family wealth in gold and coins strung down from round the neck—a practice which persisted until recently among Bedouins wandering safely outside the authority of fixed Mosques. Catty show times while bossing the servants at the watering-hole, can be compared with a competition to show off the flashiest and most expensive car in a wealthy neighborhood.

Instead of liberating women from their social burden as the prophet intended, a misread of the KORAN abuses women in a different direction. Mo rapped against compulsion in religion, but still advised that it would certainly be better not to expose tender mammary skin to the fierce solar radiation of the Arabian desert. Exposed breasts, flaunting the family treasure chest, brought skin cancer, jealousy, and long lasting feuds:

And tell the believing women
They should tone down their appearance بِخُمُرِهِنَّ
And guard their cleavage *(guard their chastity: i.e. "cover their cracks")*
And not display their adornment *(double-speak for both breasts and jewelry)*
Except what is natural *(or unavoidable)*
And let them beat their breasts in fury *(a comedic picture of coins banging against chests: "let them be of an intoxication to assert their rights"—bikhumurihinna: "with wine")*
And not display their adornment *(not be compelled to be treated as trophies)*
Except to their husbands *(true family neither objectifies nor oppresses their women)*
Or their fathers... *(there's slippery levity in the prophet's lengthy roster that follows here)*
And they should not walk heavy *(seductively shaking and shimmying)*
To reveal what they conceal of their adornment...

(again, Mo speaks both of flaunting the fluid motion of larger breasts and buttocks, and also of the jingle of much jewelry—i.e. don't be a hypocrite and try and find a loophole out of the discipline. Many women no doubt found enjoyment in a trophy role, being all they knew. There are perhaps even Geishas who are quite happy to be Geishas.)

Mo exposed his wealthy audience further with this sermon full of healthy advice. Allah's instruction proclaims that sexuality is a human right that should be respected for everyone. Many in Mo's audience abused slaves in sexual ways. Mo continues soon in the same Surah:

Provide mates for the single among your male and female slaves
—KORAN (24:31)

Now this is certainly not to be taken as God's approval of slavery. The cure for mankind's mental illness is worked in stages. The disease twists the liberating words of the prophets out of context to oppress. Marriage for slaves is the first step to their liberation, and implicitly insulates them from sexual abuse and exploitation. Captive husband and wife could together save for their own purchase or escape. Denying a mate to a slave was a central feature in their oppression. God did not instruct that all slaves should be bred with a stud service. Allah demanded that good Muslims of Mo's time provide real marriages for all their single slaves. This was Mo's sneaky way of paving their road to freedom:

ow then if you refuse to acknowledge the truth
Will you protect yourself on that day
Which will turn the hair of children gray ?
—KORAN (73:17)

وَأَشْعَارِهَا فَتِيلًا شَعر

God sent the Messianic communion down from heaven with lessons in flesh and blood that lead to eternal life *(JOHN 6:26-71, KORAN 5:111-115)*. Mohammed's followers joined the table. All who shirk truth have hell to pay:

W̲hosoever disbelieves amongst you after that   صَدَقْتَنَا
Certainly I will torment him with a torment
Which I have not tormented anyone throughout all the worlds

— *KORAN (5:115) (He will let their women loose upon them!)*

No burqa protects from glowing rain. Excessive compulsive modesty is an aniconic idolatry; instead of effacing idols, it effaces God's beautiful creation—even slashing and throwing acid in its face. A society that can not behave well enough to let females have the full function God designed into their sense organs, is a society half dead. Priggishness is no stranger to Judaism and Christianity, though in those religions it now hardly has the power to suppress women to the magnitude still so common in many regions which claim to be Islamic. Still, "Christians" misled to believe sex is a sin, may suffer the most stinging separation from the one they love.

The gospel demonstrates the futility of trying to cover up the divine truth, no matter how hairy. The sexual suffering experienced by young Jewish boys taken to Pagan Rome as slaves, was sealed beneath codes crafted by divine inspiration. It lead Joe on like a pillar of fire, through the deserts of man's mental torments. Joe endured the pain to minister to beloved boy's-life. The puzzles Joe crafted, preserved the record while Joe worked in stealth, as God's secret apostle, behind Pagan enemy lines. The anointing of God's Messiah, blows in on four winds of protection with deviant pomp and

المسيح ★ CHRIST ★ ANOINTED ★ MESSIAH ★ משיח

Gospel *cf. SONG 1:12	Location (House of)	Anointer אביונים	Angry Party	Reason for Anger
MARK **14:4-11** alabastron myrou nardou*	Simon the Leper in Bethany ♉	"A Woman" pours very costly ointment on his head	**"Some indignant inside"**	Oil could have been sold for more than **300 denarii** and the money given to the poor
MATTHEW **26:9-16** alabastron myrou	Simon the Leper in Bethany ♉	"A Woman" pours very costly ointment on his head	**"the disciples** **(plural)** **became** **indignant"** cf. MATT 20:24	Oil could have been sold for more than **300 denarii** and the money given to the poor
LUKE **7:36-39** alabastron myrou	Simon the Pharisee ♉	An unnamed woman, called "A Sinner" by a Pharisee, anoints His feet and wipes them with her hair	**Simon the** **Pharisee**	A sinner is touching Jesus; He then gives the parable of the **500, and 50 denarii**
JOHN **12:3-8** litran myrou nardou*	Lazarus in Bethany ♉ (Lazarus is Greek for Eliezer)	Mary (sister of Martha and Lazarus) anoints His feet and wipes them with her hair	**Judas Thief** **(kleptes)** **i.e. Sicarii**	Oil could have been sold for **300 denarii** and money given to the poor

The four variations form a Messianic puzzle. Three keys to its solution, deliver the esoteric message:

1) The disciples were brigands—the *lestai* and *kleptes* who were crucified with Jesus (cf. MATT 24:43, 2 PETER 3:10, REV 3:3). Not only Judas, but all of the disciples were angry about the expensive perfume. The nick-name *Ebionites*, meaning "The Poor," was used to distinguish Jews of the Messianic fourth sect. A name-game raps on these brothers, from: *Bar Jonah, Bar Iona*, and *Baryonim*, into *Ebiyonim* אביונים. This appellation as "The Poor," relates economic motive for the uprising against Rome and her puppet rulers, who had impoverished much of the nation. Scripture teaches against usury and economic exploitation, using forms of this same word—אביונים—61 times (e.g. PSALMS 69:33, 12:5, 72:13, 140:12, AMOS 4:1, DEUT 15:4-11, EXOD 23:6, JEREM 2:33-35, 5:28, ISAIAH 29:19, 14:30, 41:17; in Greek see ROMANS 15:26, GAL 2:10). Ebionites held on as a Messianic Jewish sect (Hippolytus REFUTATION prol. 7, 7:22, Irenaeus AGAINST HERESIES 5:1:3), but Galilean Jews lost all title to Holy Land held prior to 73 AD—to Pharisees. Subjection to Pharisaic literalism, would thus ironically become the tie back to the land.

2) Forgiveness of sins is related to the forgiveness of monetary debts in LUKE's *Parable of the Two Debtors*; one owes 500 denarii, the other 50, and the one forgiven more, loves his Lord more. Mary's brother Lazarus, ciphers the Zealot Lazarus who burned the debt records when Jerusalem was won by the Zealots (i.e. "the Poor"—the Ebionites): **"Numbers of the Sicarii, which is what they called those brigands who carried a dagger in their bosom, forced their way in ... The victors burst in and set fire to the house of Ananias the high priest, and the palaces of Agrippa and Bernice. They next carried their combustibles to the public archives, eager to destroy the money lenders bonds, and to prevent a recovery of debts, in order to win over a host of grateful debtors, and cause a rising of the poor, against those rich sure of impunity."**—*WARS (2:17:6)*; cf. **"forgive us our debts"** in *MATT (6:12)*. In the *Cleansing of the Temple* pericope, LUKE is the only gospel not to use the word "money-changers," but instead provides the clues "robbers" and "zeal."

3) In *JOHN (12)* the anointing is in the house of the Lazarus ♉, whom Jesus raised from death as his seventh sign in *JOHN (11)*. Though the raising of Lazarus is the most tangible miracle, it is only told in *JOHN*. LUKE meanwhile, has an imaginary Lazarus who is "very poor." Lazarus ciphers Eliezer son of Simon Zealotes, winner of the victory over Rome at Bethoron. Elsewhere the anointing is in the house of a Simon who is a leper, or a Pharisee; but in *JOHN*, when Pharisees are told Lazarus lives, they decide to kill Jesus, by a Judas called "Judas of Simon Iscariot" (a cipher for Sicarii). Eliezer's Zealots fought without wages. When Domitian became emperor, he raised the salary of Roman soldiers to exactly 300 denarii. Memory of the victory of Lazarus would sleep but not die (*JOHN 11:4*).

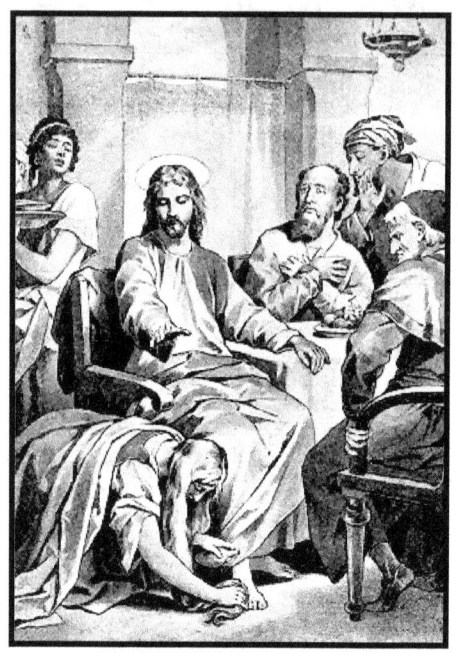

circumstance. In *MATTHEW* and *MARK*, a mystery woman pours expensive oil on the hair of a Jesus, who, accused of being a diva, is betrayed with a kiss, from the purse holder of the rebel band He sent out without a purse. The variant in *LUKE* and *JOHN*, anoints Christ with a loose woman, letting her hair down upon the saviors feet, and crying her eyes out while she lips His toes. In *JOHN* she is identified as the sister of Lazarus, and the oil is revealed to be funerary perfume. Talk about what Jesus smashed during the reign of Tiberius was soon "killed." Then in the reign of Domitian, when a Roman soldier's pay was raised to 300 denarii per annum, the Pharisees were trying to act as if the victory Lazarus won in Bethoron never happened. The Pharisees plot to "kill" Lazarus too. The anointing episode is followed by the triumphal entry into Jerusalem. This type of parade is that assembled for a king after a great military victory.

Joe's variations mold the gaps between diverging parallels to zip-file his Messianic diary. These variant angles, thrown into otherwise obvious parallels, also provide plausible denial to support the pseudonymity of the codii protecting God's mission. This trick pitch is a signature game strategy Joe uses to pass the ball back and forth between the gospels and the more academic delivery of his historical memoirs *ANTIQUITIES*, *WARS*, and *LIFE*. Consider for example the strange clothing worn by both John, the Baptizer of Jesus (in *MATTHEW 3:4*), and "the Bather" Banus (who schools Josephus in *LIFE 2*), both dress unconventionally, yet their wardrobes vary in that the Baptist dressed in the coarse camel-hair garb of the poor, while "the Bather" dressed only in "clothing that grew on trees," suggesting he wore fig leaves, to hide his revoltingly fiery fur.

John the Baptist lost his head screaming satires at the illegal sexual practices of Herodians, who indulged themselves while the multitude suffered under their royal hypocrisy. The wealthy Herodian elites openly screwed around with forbidden pleasures, publicly flaunting illegal behavior, while the braided Pharisaic cut in from Jerusalem patrolled rural Galilean villages, making women cover their hair, and pulling incompliant prostitution suspects out into busy bodied public spaces for stoning. If you needed to get some, they wanted you to come to Jerusalem for it. That's where they got theirs. The entire Galilean sub-nation rose up and gave them what they were asking for.

The rebel Messianic rite of communal bathing, was a rejection of the corrupt and expensive sham purification rituals in Jerusalem, which were whips of an institutionalized blasphemy turning an ancient culture off its land with a predatory parody of the real spirit of Judaism. For love of money, the ruling class was sending the legacy of Moses towards its slaughter on an altar tooled by giant legs of Imperial iron. The huge, hypnotically shiny architecture, had been paid for by the Cypriot copper Herod worked for Augustus. The mines were full of Galilean robbers sentenced to brutal deaths even slower than crucifixion. Messianists gathered in wild places that the Pharisees didn't dare visit. There the mother of all revolutions was reborn. God made man in His image. God is certainly no slave.

The record in WARS, tallies at least 42,500 people taken into slavery during the battles in Galilee that preceded the siege of Jerusalem. Joe tells us that the total number of slaves taken in the entire war was only 97,000. We are therefore safe to garner that at least half of all those taken into slavery during the full-on conflict were of Galilean nativity. Joe suggests that a large portion of the remaining population, indeed almost the "entire nation," stormed into to Jerusalem before the Passover of 70. The Roman historian Tacitus, tells us that the women fought against the Romans as full fledged warriors, side by side with the men:

WHO COULD BEAR ARMS DID SO
With a more than adequate courage
Than their odds could warrant
They were inflamed with zeal and ardor
Women no less than men   *(MATTHEW 26:13)*
For the thought that they might be doomed
To give-up their country
Made life more terrible than death itself

— *Tacitus* HISTORIA *(5:13)*

Flavian freedman Josephus, and Flavian protege Tacitus, were contemporaries in the same elite circles of Rome. There is overlapping coverage between the histories written by these two wards of the new Imperial House. They can be compared with two males who are fans of different football teams, discussing the playbooks after a big brutal contest. The junior Tacitus can have more affection for the Jewish team than he is openly allowed to admit, or otherwise he risks alienating less level headed fanatics among his Italian home-team readership. Josephus can be more of a die-hard Jew than it is safe for him to reveal, without losing all the advantages he has won for his zealous mission by gaining full access to the enemy locker room.

As Josephus and Tacitus lay at meat together in the lavish Imperial sports bar of Roma, a big ball of discrepancy over field numbers bounces out

זה רק הבגד שלי אבל אני אוהב את זה

of a discussion of dueling destinies. This testosterone two-some did more than just shake hands and agree to promote a more than minor disagreement. In WARS Josephus tallied one million and one hundred thousand killed in Jerusalem during the Roman siege alone. Tacitus would later pick up the ball, in what appears to be a fixed contest with his elder mentor of sorts, and play Monday Morning Quarterback, telling us that the gambit in the Temple could not have sacrificed that many men, for the total number of people alive and at play in the Holy City when Roman encampments cut it off, amounted to about six hundred thousand persons—all Jewish players and non combatant spectators included. The apparent revisionism by Tacitus is cleverly camouflaged, feigning to play down Roman atrocities. The controversy points to a scab in the account of Josephus, revealing that his Jewish war memoir in Greek, has much deeper home-team allegiance than is apparent upon a shallow first read. Joe's readers are prompted to go back to Joe's text, and pick out Joe's explanation of where he got his inflated figures. There the seeker hears Joe whisper that Nero Caesar planned on burning Jerusalem even before the blasphemous sacrifices to Nero were stopped by Joe and his zealous team. This *fait accompli,* is tagged by a run-away discrepancy discussed between two independently minded historians patronized by the new Flavian house. No matter how deep the throat of their arguments and agreements surrounding the Jerusalem odds at the Imperial sports bar did drink—to a secret Guinness record of gutsy escapes Joe was proud of, and Tacitus admired—the truth thirsty student is still left to wonder: what *did* happen to the rest of Galilee while the new exodus lambs roasted in the temple?

The context Tacitus mints upon his half a million sheep counted as absent from the table, teases us to flee in the brave direction that secured freedom from the marble shadow in tyranny valley. Jews who flocked to the finale in Jerusalem, wanted to die rather than leave their land. Those fighters old enough to resist a slave fate, did so to their deaths, so that a multitude of the weaker sort might also avoid captivity. Tacitus parses words to specify that the final conflict was fought by Jews who loathed the option of wandering as aliens, even if it was to make sure that good-bye didn't mean forever. Shallow perceptions and narrow sensibilities abhor the deep read. Nonetheless, rhetoric has power to break taboos unpunished, using the negative, the mute, the pause, and the void, to point in rich detail. Consider the following Pandora's box, of many a rebel paradox:

Josephus marched on the city hoping to take it   *(Sepphoris)*
But just before it revolted from the rest of the Galileans
He had encompassed it with a strong wall
So strong that the Romans would have had much trouble taking it
This is why he proved too weak   *(Josephus, i.e. General Joe)*
And failed in his hopes   *(Joe seemed to fail because of his strong walls?)*
Both as to forcing the place
And as to his compelling the people of Sepphoris
To deliver it up to him   *(or forcing the Roman party of Galilee to join in revolt)*
By this means he provoked the Romans   *(provoking sieges upon fortresses)*
To treat the country according to the law of war   *(while villages fled)*
Nor did the Romans, out of the anger they bore at this attempt
Desist ravaging the places in the plain
Either by night or by day   *(key to a note about the implied flight, cf. MARK 13:16)*
And stealing away the cattle that were in the country   *(red heifers)*
And killing in each place those who appeared capable of fighting
And leading the weaker people as slaves into captivity
So that Galilee was all over filled with fire and blood
Nor was it exempted from any kind of misery and calamity
For ❧the only refuge❧ they had was this
That when they were pursued
They could retire to the cities   *(that "Paul" scouted, seeded, and greased)*
Which had walls built them by Josephus   *(and in a multitude of nations too)*

    —Josephus, WARS *(3:4:1)* *(the Christians were a secret cult hard for Rome to crack)*

When a number of Galileans who had cost the Romans terrible casualties, escaped from Roman clutches at Gischala on a Sabbath, and provocatively fled to Jerusalem, it was the perfect diversion. Legions were drawn away from the villages of Galilee. The subsequent spectacle of infighting among the factions, visible to the Romans outside the walls, delayed the thrust of siege. The *Little Apocalypse* in the gospel describes the concentration of Rome's forces for the calamitous final showdown around Jerusalem:

THE NEW EXODUS

"With usual propensity of men ready to believe what they ardently wish, the populace assumed to themselves the scene of grandeur which the fates were preparing to move forward *(a new exodus)*. Calamity itself could not open their eyes *(but could close Roman eyes)*. The number besieged in Jerusalem, including both sexes and every age, amounted according to the best accounts, to no less than 600,000... The women no less than men were inflamed with zeal and ardor. Life, they declared, was more terrible than death itself, if doomed to quit their country."
—Tacitus HISTORIA *(5:13) (cf. 600,000 poor Ebionites dead at WARS 5:13:7)**

FEAST	HISTORICAL SOURCE	NUMBERS PRESENT AND/OR KILLED
PASSOVER 65 OR PASSOVER 66 (BEFORE THE REVOLT)	Josephus, WARS *(6:9:3)*	2,700,200
PASSOVER 70	Josephus, WARS *(6:9:2-3)*	1,100,000
PASSOVER 70	Tacitus, HISTORIA *(5:13)**	600,000*
DISCREPANCY		500,000

HEN you see encampments
All the way around Jerusalem
Then know that the hour *(EZEKIEL 37:1-3)*
Of her desolation has come near
Then those in Judea let them flee
To the "mountains" *(bilingual Greek / Hebrew pun: "flee to the fire")*
And those in her midst   ὄρη / אוּר
Let them depart out   *(danger to the weak was forseen)*
And those in the regions   *(Galilee, Edom, Samaria)*
Let them not enter into her   *(or become captives)*
Because these are the days of vengeance
To fulfill all things that have been written
And woe to those who are pregnant
And to those who are nursing in those days
Will accompany a great cataclysm upon the land
And wrath upon those people upon this
And they shall fall upon sword-mouth
And shall spearhead a captivity
Into all the nations ...   *(a Mosaic net upon them)*
Till the time of the nations be fulfilled   *(EZEK 37 esp. 9, cf. KORAN 2:243 & 2:259)*

— LUKE *(21:20-24) (There will never be another major European war.)*

HE day of Pentecost being fulfilled *(harvest feast 50 days after Passover)*
They all agreed upon the unity [of scripture] *(Ex 23:16, Ezek 5:1-10)*
And suddenly there came out of heaven *(breath in the sails, Rev 21:2)*
A sound like a violent gush of wind *(Matt 13:30, 3:12, 26:31, John 11:52, Zech 13:7)*
And it lifted the entire house where they sat *(Galilee, i.e. 'Dan,' more or less)*
Divided tongues as of fire appeared among them *(Jeremiah 4)*
All of them lifted in the Holy *Wind/Spirit* *("pneuma" is wind & breath & spirit)*
And began to speak in other languages *(into the following generations)*
For that *Wind* gave them the ability *(Luke 22:46, Mark 15:37, Matt 27:50)*
Now there were devout Jews of every nation

Living in Jerusalem *(Revelation 21:2)*
And at this sound the crowd gathered
And was bewildered
Because each one heard them speaking
In their own native language
Amazed and astonished they asked:

"Are these not Galileans?
Then how is it that each of us
Hears in our own native language?"

— *Acts (2:1-8)* *(cf. Acts 17:22-31, Ezekiel 37:9)*

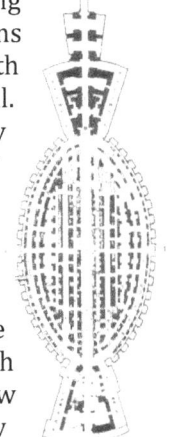

One can get some grip on this windy battlefield, by considering another 900,000 missing persons that arise from a comparison with the Roman conquest of Gaul. Julius Caesar counted roughly one million killed in his victory over the Gauls, which puts the annexation of that province on par with the casualty numbers Joe records for the Roman reconquest which ended this Jewish revolt. However, Julius Caesar records that he took an additional one million Gauls into slavery during his conquest, while Joe reports less than one hundred thousand Jews taken captive by Rome in the Jewish War—a number Joe would not have been able fudge. Those slow to accept that Joses was a new Moses, need to consider how busy Joses remained at work in Pharaoh's house behind enemy lines, trying to delicately save what he could of 97,000 Jews the Romans did manage to collect—mostly young boys who were slaving over the new infrastructural "**works in Egypt**," where *Egypt* is code for *Rome* (earth's new Imperial slave master). Suffering Jewish boys were building a colossal new pyramid of pain in the belly of the whore. It was a giant machine of

ISRAEL'S HIGH PRIESTESS ANOINTS THE ZEALOUS KING

public murder—a humanity killing shrine to death bondage that pushed heart killing sadist entertainment to globe snuffing scale. God turned His thumb down. His chosen people would not supply the arena without a bigger fight of His choosing. Joe doomed the imperial idol by burning a record of the bout deep into Gentile consciousness. His new Passover brought the freedom fold to all the nations. The macaroon is not the only fare of the holiday.

Herod himself built a theatre for manslaughter games at Jerusalem. It was just one of the many insults to Moses that incited a critical mass of Judeans to follow Galilee into revolt. Wily Galilee fought Herod from back when Herod was trying to make a name for himself in the first real Roman attempt to run roads in the region. Though Herod had been Antony's protege, Herod switched courses from Antony and Cleopatra's side, over to the right hand of Augustus—shotgun. Herod went on to manage the copper mines of Cyprus for Augustus, and was given a hefty fifty percent of the profit to spend. Those Galileans who were chewed up in the bowels of Cyprus, paid for Herod's great building projects with their lives. As more and more of Galilee was turned off its land by the Imperialist angles of Herod's Roman financed architecture, the Messianic movement quickly built up to revolutionary potency. After Jesus and John violently resisted Imperial cult temples, built in Bethsaida and the new capitol city Tiberias, it became evident Galilee would be ethnically cleansed to serve geopolitical aims of the Julio-Claudians—the very type of idolatrous faux-divine tyrants Mosaic tradition was supposed to immunize them against. Galilee was set to become another one of Rome's proofs that resistance was futile. If any Judean questioned whether Pagan atrocities in Galilee meant all of Judaism was in grave peril under an evolving Imperial rule, then Caligula's attempt to have an idol erected in the Jerusalem Temple, woke up anyone worthy to identify as a Jew. Caligula's mystery meat was the taboo tree of Eden,

and Israel moved as one to deny the cannibal Caesar his fetish. Galilee's movement subsequently found a valuable ally in Caligula's stoic enemy Seneca. Galileans went on the offensive in Samaria in the reign of Claudius. Joe's activities after Nero took over, are shadowed by the works of the spy named "Paul," who organized a strong Judeophilic fifth column of Gentile zealots in the empire. This was greatly assisted by the Monotheistic moles deep inside the Imperial household: Seneca, Ephaphroditus, and Poppaea. The most important doors which opened up to the new exodus, were greased in part with pilfered Imperial resources. Of the communities Paul founded with Stoic Monotheistic epistles in Greek, the new assemblies of

Asia Minor and Greece became the most useful fire escapes. The new Mosaic spearhead eventually penetrated from the Black Sea up to the Baltic.

Joe tells of a motley Zealot Navy working an exodus of Galilee, with a cipher placed right after his capture gains him access to the deep innards of the new Imperial House. Israel's General let himself be taken so he could continue the fourth sect's contest with the Romans for as long as superhumanly possible. While a ram was stuck in a burning bush on Moriah, ships of fire were powered by the heavenly wind:

Suddenly a sound like a violent direction of breath came out of the sky, and it lifted the entire house where they sat. Divided tongues as of fire appeared among them. All of them lifted in the Holy *Wind,* and began to speak in other languages, for that *Wind* gave them the ability. Now there were devout Jews of every nation... *"Are these not Galileans?"*
— ACTS *(2:1-8)*

Josephus spoke: *"I did foretell to the people of Jotapata that they would be taken on the forty-seventh day, and that I should be caught alive by the Romans."* Now once Vespasian asked the captives in private about these predictions, he found them to be true, and then began to believe those Josephus had made about him... In the meantime, all those Galileans who had forthwith managed to secretly remove themselves from their Roman enemies, forthwith escaped out of the demolished cities—which were in all a great number—and ☝ rebuilt Joppa, (which had been left desolate by Cestius), that it might serve for a place of refuge *(as they prayed for south winds)* ☝; and because the adjoining region *(Dan: a good-bye metaphor for a once greater slice, due the core seed leaving Galilee)* which had been laid waste in the war, and was not capable of supporting them, they determined to go off to sea. They also built themselves a great many piratical ships, and turned pirates upon the seas near to Syria, and Phoenicia, and Egypt, *("near" means they harried the commercial routes near those coasts—particularly Egypt, where much of the seed that kept the mob quiet was shipped)* and made those seas unnavigable to all men [except this Zealot Navy]. *(the omissions, from these Syro-Phoenician and Egyptian coastal actions, tell us Jewish sails diverted the Roman Navy away from the coasts of Israel, and 'Paul's' strong walls* in Greece and Asia Minor, allowing Galilean 'Mariel-like' boat-people to pass safe between wide stretches of uncovered beaches)* Of course, as soon as Vespasian knew of their conspiracy, he sent both footmen and horsemen to Joppa, which was unguarded in the night-time, *(the full codex suggests diversions continued at Joppa every night, to game a*

"Dover-to-Calais" type diversion, while the Operation Overlord, plotted out by Joe and Seneca, departed quietly along less guarded sections of Israel's coast) **however those that were in it,** *(the conspiracy)* **had figured that they would be attacked and were afraid of it,** *(that their exodus would be squashed)* **yet they didn't try to keep the Romans out,** *(because it was a rouse)* **but fled to their ships,** *(a big rouse at Joppa, and little boat-lifts all along the coast)* **and lay at sea all night,** *("night" refers both to stealth operations, and also back to the "**unguarded at night-time**" report, letting the 'spy vs. spy' crow deliver a sea-deep communique that flies a feather or two beneath the Flavian radar)* **out of the reach of projectiles...**

★★★★★ Galileans sailed out from 'Joppa,' all night and every night. The plot doubles-down off this point of strand, for Joppa was one of Israel's natural sea-havens. The unnatural idolatrous harbor was Caesarea Maritima, which Herod had built on unsteady sand. Galilean fishers of men were Christianity's first cast, making war upon a Roman ravaged Sea of Galilee. The next cast was of rescue nets by Greek fishing communities, in an Aegean hooked on Paul's anti-Imperial zeal. It was not safe for war refugees to beach without escorts. The whore had eyes in every village backside. ★★★★★

ON THE IMPERIAL SHIP'S PROW, THE GODDESS VICTORIA-NAVALIS GIVES THE FLAVIAN HOUSE A VICTORY WREATH (στέφανον; cf. JOHN 19:2). JEWISH CONS IN PIRACY ARE NOT DECLARED DEFEATED, UNTIL THESE COINS OF 75 AD— TERMINUS POST QUEM OF JOE'S PUBLICATION OF WARS. REFUGEES WERE GIVEN EXTENDED COVER BY SICARII RAIDS OUT OF CYRENE. JOE WAS ACCUSED OF COACHING ONGOING RESISTANCE FROM ROME (WARS 7:11:3). ◐◑

Now Joppa is not naturally a haven *(not!—i.e. they did not linger there),* **for it ends in rough shore** *(code for the other side of the sea emigration route),* **where all the rest of it is strait** *(psst... clear across to the other shore),* **but the two ends bend towards each other** *(Gentile zealots trolled help out),* **where there are steep precipices** *(really hairy on the Greek side),* **and great stones that jut out to sea, where the chains wherewith Andromeda was bound** *(broken by one a bit smarter than the average lamb),* **have left their footprints** *(Pagan myth linking Dan to Greece),* **which attests to the antiquity of that fable. But the north wind opposes** *(pneuma means wind, breath, and spirit; it was an exodus on south winds)* **And beats upon the shore** *(Imperial patrols)*

And dashes mighty waves
Against the rocks which receive them   *(killing Joe's Peters when caught)*
And renders the haven   *(havens on Greek side too dangerous when without Christians)*
More dangerous than the country they had deserted...
Some of them thought to die by their own swords
Would be easier than by the sea
And so they killed themselves   *(in a Temple sacrifice that covered the exodus)*
Before they were drowned   *(in the nations)*
   —*prophet Josephus mimes the guts of the conspiracy in* WARS *(3:8:9 - 3:9:3)*

For the thought that they might... leave their home
Made them more afraid of living than dying
                              — *Tacitus* HISTORIA *(5:13)*

PENTECOST

 ALL OF THEM LIFTED IN THE HOLY WIND...
ARE THESE NOT ALL GALILEANS ?

Once the jumble in the undercurrent to this spy code is fathomed, Joe's gloss-stream is recognized as the dominant global turnover exchange. How did key tongues keep their speaking constrained so subtly right beneath the surface, without becoming the word-wide answer on everyone's fiery lips? Joe trolled his anchors beneath the surface, and saved many a precious boy's-life from destruction in the brutal Imperial amphitheatre. Joe's Gentile Christian kept a more than civil communion with the diasporic Jew, and the gospel's double-edged message retained its historical clarity for over two centuries. Then Messianic seeds  Joe planted in Britannia spooked Constantine all the way to Greece. Seated there in the homeland of the gospel language, Constantine engineered a religious coup that swallowed the greater body of Christ. Gospel's call to resist the exploitative Imperial master, was twisted into vicarious atonement worked by torture and murder of Jesus the rebel king—whose candy-coated literary alter-ego had now reputedly done all the Messianic work the planet would ever need, by just three nails and a scourging. Tandem to this exploitation of Christ went persecution of the anti-Imperial Jew, who piously refused to worship a parabolic Messiah, whom the lamb rustler Constantine reworked into a hypnotic state deterrent to any resistors who would be free of Caesar. The slippery slope of Antisemitism that would return the exiles to Joppa was greased. Unbaptized, Constantine Caesar declared his own legal rulings over doctrine, including the new official prohibition of sharing Passover and Easter as a common festival:

It appeared an unworthy thing that in the celebration of this most holy feast we should follow the practice of the Jews, who have impiously defiled their hands with enormous sin, and are therefore, deservedly afflicted with blindness of soul ... Let us then have nothing in common with the detestable Jewish crowd; for we have received from our Savior a different way — *from Constantine's Letter after the First Council of Nicea*

The entire vintage of the Christian corpus is so locked, stocked, and barreled from Judaism, that Nicene Caesar's wacky anti-Passover statement, is a doomed wordless reversal of the true rebel spirit that took down his empire despite him. Constantine's imperial double-speak ignores the fact that every single scripture which Christianity treasures, has a Jewish

Retracing David's dance from Dan to Beersheba, starts with the inscription on the *Tel-Dan Stele* found at Dan in 1993. It refers to *Israel* as "Israel" (not "House of Omri"), and refers to *Judah* as "House of David" (not "Judah"). The stele dates 150 years after David ripened the victory of Moses— a date well after the kingdom split into two. Exodus is fact.
No nation would confabulate an origin from slaves.

by-line, and works the divine will on the world stage in the mirror of the Jewish people. Therefore Caesar can not state: **'Let us have nothing in common with the Jew,'** for then Caesar is bankrupt of all "authority"— *reducto ad absurdum*. Caesar's ritual binds still continue to claim infallibility, tempting the ire of the devil himself. All the anti-sexual and anti-social excesses of Medieval Christianity sprang from the same place that Christian Antisemitism did: Connie Caesar's coup. When Christianity became the state religion under this regime of *Pontiff Maximus* hypnosis, it became harder to read the codes of Joses, who places the blame for the crucifixion squarely on the man who needed to wash Christ's blood off his hands. It was Pilate who **'impiously defiled his hands with enormous sin.'** Though Connie Caesar's coup would take all of the sex, humor, and Jew, out of Jesus, the Galilean nation Jesus shepherded away from Roman slaughter, was living proof that resistance against tyrannical masters was not futile. Constantine turned the Messianic world upside down to negate the exilic proof. The Jew was stereotyped as the pariah that had killed the Messiah. This deflected attention away from how Pilate had defiled his hands with enormous sin. More than a millennium of hypnotic church ritual brainwashed a laity, until they were deaf and blind to the explosive power of the gospel's cross-word puzzles. It is no wonder that ghettoized Jews under this enduring regime, trended towards forms of Judaism which valued legalese misreads of Ezra's parables more than the vision of Israel's prophets. Israel's diviners were so precisely pointed at the terrible Truth, as to make disregard for Jesus and Joses extremely difficult. New Rome's Pharaoh twisted the communion to the point that the Jews were prodded into forgetting new exodus. Shallow dogma covered the lingering imperial shame, regarding Caesar's having been outmaneuvered in the Jewish War.

Galilean boy-slaves of the war, who escaped coliseum construction crews without Joe's resurrection robes, were crucified right in the heart of a city code named "***Sodom* and Egypt**." To think these Galilean Jews of more than archaic Celtic affinities would be over-reaching. In the inspired literary tapestry, the Tribe of Dan remembers a proto-Celtic mercenary class that hood-winked Pharaoh. Without racial bias, they volcanically marshaled the exploited classes which Egypt had drawn and interbred from all over the known world. First century Galilee certainly had more cultural remnants of Dan than anywhere else in Israel, and *Cuticle-Joe* tells us they were conscious of it. Recognizing a Galilean exodus in the Jews of Europe, focuses a salon light upon the *Ashkenazim*, who were long judged by many Gentiles to have higher incidences of reddish hair than most of the Gentile nations they fled from as the age of the Gentiles was fulfilled. The reestablishment of Israel near Joppa in 1948, was spearheaded by Ashkenazi Jews.

In order to preserve boys-life, David and Solomon converted the threshing floor atop Mount Moriah into a searing diplomatic green-room for gate crashers, with a horny thicket burning beyond Pagan comprehension. The parable of Abraham, redacted by Ezra at the first restoration, relates the multiethnic origins of the Hebrew nation. An allegorical summary of Abraham's geopolitical import is given by Josephus with his typical mind-bending deviancies. Joe prompts students to read the minor gods as the Persian Kings* and Roman tyrants after them—all pawns in the hands of Israel's metaphysical universal Godhead, who is the God over these "gods":

 **Abram had no son of his own**
And so adopted Lot *(who had children by two daughters: GEN 19:36)*
Son of his brother Haran
And his wife Sarai's brother *(Abe married a niece: cf. GEN 11:31 & 20:12)*
And when he reached 75 years† *(age at Haran→GEN 12:4; and a length of the exile)*
He left the land of Chaldea *(i.e. Babylon, where Jews were exiled for 75 yrs.)*

> And by God's* command came into Canaan... *(God/god*)*
> He was the first that ventured to publish the notion that:
>
> *There is but one true God*
> *The creator of the universe* *(the highest cosmos, source of all being)*
> *And as far as other gods go*
> *If they contribute anything to the happiness of men*
> *Each of them only affords it*
> *Because of appointment from Him* *(the Creator of All)*
> *And not by their own power...*
>
> — ANT *(1:7:1)* *(here Joe gives a clue that Israel shirked no more than did Judah)*

Joe charters departures from *GENESIS* in order to provide more context with which cryptic subtexts may be decoded. Restoration of a new nation in Canaan, sets off in force from Babylon instead of Harran, by way of Joe's tweaking of the old dude's odometer reading. The ridiculous parental ages of Sarai and Abram, relate the unlikely odds of a Hebrew nation being restored to the land after 75 years† of Babylonian exile, (that began circa 597 BC with Jeconiah, and ended under Zerubbabel circa 518 BC). The thin party of restorers is overly inbred, and in need of new blood. Ancient Abe doesn't even have his own boy. Soon enough Abe seeks to play his *Fili* inside the great hollow of the precocious mounds of Canaan:

> **NOW** Abram dwelt by the Oak called Ogyges*
> Not far from the city of Hebron
> But being uneasy at his wife's barrenness
> He entreated God that he might have male issue
> And God required of him to be of good courage...
> Accordingly Sarai, at God's command
> Brought one of his hand maidens
> A woman of Egyptian descent
> In order to obtain children by her...
> A little while later she gave birth to *Ishmael...*
> Born to Abram when he was eighty-six years old
> But God appeared to him when He was ninety-nine
> And promised him that he would have a son named *Isaac*
>
> —ANT *(1:10:4)* *(cf. GEN 18:1, where Septuagint reads: "drui te Mamre;" cf. Og and Ogygia)*

Ishmael is born in irony, to an Egyptian slave mother. The Hebrews had been lead out of an Egyptian slavery by Moses. The hypercritical overlap between the nativity of Abe's spurned first son, and four centuries of slavery baking bricks in unlaughable heat, provides an extra flaky literary device hard to top. Every pool of slaves fed into Egypt interbred with indigenous slaves of Egyptian nativity. Abraham's multinational tour fills in some of the fruit flavors on a pie chart. Three sources ripe with alien labor for Egypt were: 1) Mesopotamian, 2) Canaanite-Phoenician, 3) a deep Indo-European pool to the north of the Hittites, who ruled Harran and much of Mitanni before the folk mascot Abraham was renamed. It would be rash to miss the allusion in the name of Abe's brother *Haran.* This ubiquitous device is again apparent in Abe's later son named *Midian*, who is one of six more boys whom ancient Abe is said to have fathered in his hundreds—after being dry for 86 years. (While there is life, there is hope.) Such old sperm donation is certainly not impossible, but when this senior citizen swim-team ejaculate is clocked-in, along with the beyond dusty hormonal age of Sarah's ninety year-old organs of Isaac's birth, one would be just plain stupid not to hear a much more booming laughter than could be mustered by the enfeebled breath of a long post-menopausal ninety year-old woman. Jews who are turned off by the virgin birth allegory in the gospel, need to bookmark their Torah at GENESIS *(18:15).* Uterine miracles are one of Yahweh's signature recipes.

The allegorical trinity of nations pie charted by Abraham's sojourn, mixed their family jewels in late night trysts, (both in and out of bondage), with a veritable United Nations—spicing it up with Libyans, Nubians, Abyssinians, Dorians, etc.. The desert cooked peoples of violent folkloric addictions we know as *Semites,* who are both Arabs and Jews, date such race mixing in the region way back to the Neolithic. Both Semitic branches are charted as descendants of our parabolic Patriarch himself—Abraham—with the Arabs from Abraham's boy Ishmael, and the Jews from his Isaac.

This genealogical folklore is betrayed as astute Jewish parable by the undeniable eye for sick humor it has in common with the Lord of Creation. Those who don't see a divine wink here, have their numb-ass asleep in the pew, during a gripping grappling with an odiously emotional din. First Abe is kept without a son until the age of 86. Then God gives the boy Ishmael to the lonely old man. Next the brutal cosmic Father lays a trap to test poor Abe as Abe reaches centenarian age—when mystics in the oaks proclaimed a man to be a sage. Most readers probably remember where this Bedouin soap opera goes next. Gramps becomes the proud pop of another toddler, but gums is then asked to let go of his first beautiful boy, who is his own teen flesh he loves, because of some valid points about greed pondered sweating under Sarai's aged of days miracle rag. (Can you imagine the restored menstrual agony at her caravan pit-stops?) After our centenarian manages one last pat on the ass, sending off his beautiful bright eyed boy Ishmael into the desert without a father, Abe is suddenly asked—with no better reason than *"I said so"*—to sacrifice his now one and only beautiful boy Isaac, (popsie's fresh new giggle-toy). Dino-pops has just sacrificed his handsome teen Ishmael to the fate of the desert, hoping to keep frightened antique milk-bags quiet. God is kidding ancient Abe. He is going to leave him boyless again, with a female Jewish centenarian who still demands to be treated like a "Princess." The sting to fossil-man Abraham, must have been worse than a hard rap on the enlarged joints on his knuckles. Boy oh boy what a tease! The Lord giveth, and the Lord taketh away:

THE LORD dealt with Sarah as He had spoken
**And the Lord made it for Sarah as He had promised
Sarah conceived** *(Sarah means "Princess")*
And bore Abraham a boy in his old age *(certainly past "due season")*
At the time of which God had spoken *(the 'past due' gag: GEN 18:10 & 18:14)*
**Abraham gave the name Isaac
To this boy whom Sarah bore him
And when his boy was eight days old
Abraham circumcised his boy Isaac
As God had commanded him
When his boy Isaac was born to him
Abraham was a hundred years old
Now Sarah said:**
  *"God has brought mine laughter
  Everyone who HEARS will laugh"*
— GENESIS *(21:1-6) (cf. MATT 22:33, 28:16-20, JN 8:58, HEB 4:12)*

Before cutting off tips, the reader is asked to recognize the words of Jesus reflecting here: *"He who has ears to HEAR, Let him listen."* The name *Isaac* is a Hebrew word meaning *Laughter*. A chuckling Creator offers two doors.

Only one door opens to the Holy of Holies. The doomsday of the humorless approach deserves a limerick of prostrations. (More asteroids fly in here than you can smack a hot fetish with). The comic nativity of a boy named *Laughter* clues in the divine gag, irrigating ears to hear that this whole prose exercise is a purposely silly come-on. The ancient of days scored this bedside story time for intergenerational education. The dinosauric ages of Abraham, Sarah, Methuselah and company, are colorful bed-time stories for children. Abraham is a Jewish *Santa Claus* who delivers the nations of the desert on a geriatric flying carpet. Sarah is a varicose, mummy skinned, *Mother Goose* in a tent. Methuselah is *Father Time* for a reality check. The moral of the exalted father's genealogical lullaby, informs His smartest children of the terrible truth about an unexalted past, which they can be certain is common to their human *Exalted Fathers*, their Jewish un-Centenary *Princesses*, and their tragic *Laughter* against all odds:

As the sun was going down
A deep sleep fell upon Abram
And deep and terrifying darkness
Descended upon him
Then the Lord said to Abram:
  "Know this for certain
  That your offspring shall be aliens
  In a land that is not theirs
  And shall be slaves there
  And they shall be oppressed
  For four hundred years" — GENESIS (15:12-13)

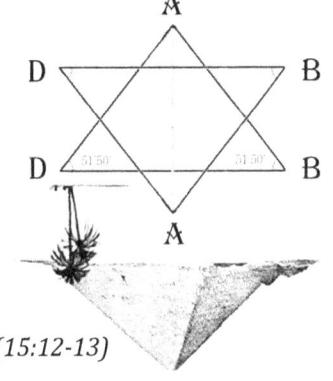

No nation of settled nomads, which was stitched together out of people who were slaves for four centuries, is going to have a pedigree. If they are ever going to make their freedom from idols last on a planet enslaved to idols, then one thing that they will have, is the need for a powerful propaganda. The author who wrote the *Patriarch Parable*, expected that adults were mature enough to realize this, and inserted numerous garish visual clues into his narrative for the hard of hearing. Water however, seeks its own level. Any great literary work is a mirror, that sorts the wheat from the chaff. In it, people will either see their base selves, or their higher selves, according to where their heart is aimed.

Sarah said:
  "Who would have ever said to Abraham
  That Sarah would nurse children?
  Yet I've borne him a son in his old age"
The child grew and was weaned
And on the day Isaac was weaned

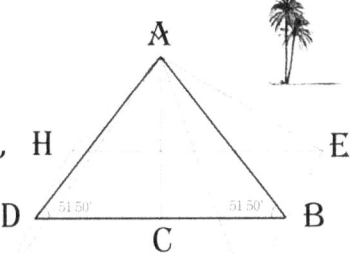

Abraham made a great feast
But Sarah saw the boy of Hagar the Egyptian
Whom she had borne to Abraham
Playing with her boy Isaac
So she said to Abraham

> "Cast out this slave woman with her boy
> Now!
> The boy of this slave woman
> He will not inherit
> Not with my boy Isaac!"

The matter was very distressing to Abraham
On account of his boy...

After these things God tested Abraham
He said to him:

> "Exalted Father!"

And He said:

> "I am
> Here!"

He said:

> "Take your boy
> Your only boy Laughter
> Whom you love
> And go
> To the land of Moriah
> And offer him there
> As a burnt offering
> On one of the mountains
> I will charge"

So Exalted Father got up
Early in the morning
Packed his ass
And a party with him
—*Two of his young men
And his boy Laughter*
He broke wood
For burnt offering
And set out
And went to the furthest place
Where God had charged him

(KORAN 17:1)★

On the third day Abraham looked up
And saw the furthest place
Then Abraham told his young men:

> *"Stay here with the ass*
> *The boy and I*
> *We're going over there*
> *We will worship*
> *Then we will return to you"*

Abraham took the wood
Of burnt offering
And stuck it upon his boy Laughter
And he himself held fire
And knife
So the two of them
Went further onward together
Isaac said to his father Abraham:

> *"Father!"*

And he said:

> *"I am*
> *Here*
> *My boy!"*

And Isaac said:

> *"Fire and wood are here*
> *But where is the lamb*
> *For burnt offering?"*

Abraham said:

> *"My boy*
> *(The Lord Himself)* (MATT 25:40)
> *Provides the lamb*
> *For burnt offering"*

So the two of them
Went further onward together
When they came to the place
That God had charged him
Exalted Father built altar there
And erected wood
He bound his boy Laughter
And worked him on altar

**On top of wood
Abraham did his hand put then to seize**
— *A knife to kill his boy!*
**But an angel of the Lord
Called him from Heaven
And said:**

"Abraham Abraham!"

And he said:

"I am
Here"

He said:

*"Do not put your hand into the boy
Don't do anything to damage him
For I know that you fear God
Keep your boy your own"* (respect him like your own flesh)

**And Abraham looked up
And he saw ram
Caught in thicket
By its horns
Abraham went
And took ram
And offered it up
For burnt offering
Instead of his boy**

— GENESIS *(21:7-12, 22:1-13)*

    The ramming elder hand is a third day awareness test, devised to take a deep dark punch at an intergenerational integrity issue, refined by the foundation of the Temple of Zion. On rocky top Moriah, an exalted ancient father charges a further end up high with his boy, to provide earth's fiery threshing floor with its moral—the preservation of boy's life. This parable flies through a series of metaphoric levels which dovetail like the Russian nesting boxes called *matryoskas*. Down inside the global box of God's relation to man, at the nuclear family level, nests the box of the most awkward and intimate politics

> **THE LORD IS MY SHEPHERD...
> HIS WINNOWING FAN IS IN HIS HAND:**
> Pharaoh herded the hungry masses, using the shepherds crook and threshing fan, as symbols of his office. Moses sacrificed that lamb which followed faux-divine Pharaoh inside the mind. The Lamb of God was a Lion.
> אֲרִי מַתָּת מֵאֵת יהוה

of father-son relations. Between these boxes hinges the box of father-son politics at a national defense level. The army (the host) offers its life up for the security of the nation like first fruits. This host is the sacrifice of the divine mass. The filial Temple was ordered over the threshing floor after David counted all the fighting age men of Israel. Exalted father kept his boy his own by a novel use of words. The cosmic Temple was a deep martial fist.

David anticipated imperial battering rams arriving up flank, yet the first Temple had already been destroyed by Babylon before the first midrash about Abraham was ever invented. Abraham is unknown to the lyrics of David's reign. Only two Psalms—*PSALM 47* and *PSALM 105*—ever mention Abraham, and both these Psalms are post-exilic. These are also the only two Psalms that mention Isaac. Meanwhile, Jacob is a character in eleven other Psalms, but without a peep about his funny father Isaac, or exalted grandpa Abe. Literalists refuse to hear the serious humor of the inspired literary word. They fail to see that God contends with them by pulling their leg. When Jesus speaks of the *"God of Abraham and Isaac and Jacob,"* Jesus keys the savvy into the method of *the Exalted Father, the Laughter, and the Leg-Puller.* This is the trinity of the *Great Commission*: "the Father the Son and the Holy Spirit." Recruitment of the Messianic army sought to ensure future generations of God's human creation. Riddles in the word are more about developing moral mind to a level that makes man's future possible, than they are about any wartime trickery:

open my mouth with a parable
I bring forth hidden things of old
Things we have heard and learned *(Ex 33:1-34:10)*
And were passed down to us by our fathers
We will not hide [the opinion of] **their children**
From the generations to come
Sing the praises of Yahweh and His strength
And the wonders He has done
Jacob established a testimony

And Israel established a law
Which commanded our fathers to teach their children
So that the generation to come might learn
And the children who are yet to be born *(GENESIS 16:13)*
Will arise to tell their children
    —*PSALM (78:1-9) (intro to a parable concerning a transfer from "Ephraim"† to Judah)*

Titus burned Yahweh's Temple 656 years after it had been burned by King Nebuchadnezzar of Babylon. In the eyes of those who could not see, it looked like Caesar had decisively won. But the battering ram of Caesar was caught in Moriah's *thicket*, marked by that twisted word *sebach*ϒ (סְבַךְ), which means *tangle* or *weave*, and when used in reference to forestry, indicates dangerous thorned growths of briar or bramble *(NAHUM 1:10)*. Caesar was snagged by Jesus, at the same furthest place where it looked like Abraham would have to sacrifice his Laughter, until God opened His trap with nature's biting twists of phrase. Soldiers *wove* or *braided* (πλέξαντες) a *victory wreath* ◯ (στέφανον) of *thorns* (ἀκανθῶν) upon the head of Jesus, because by the power of His word, Israel's Messiah won the contest in the world arena *(JOHN 19:2)*. Jesus was one person, but He represents an entire Messianic movement He gave new life. Like the *First Adam*, whose name was put upon both an individual man and mankind in general, the *Last Adam* is both Jesus and the entire zealous host.⸭ Myriads of Galileans were crucified. His holy army rose from the dead in their tombs before He did *(MATT 27:51-54)*.

stephanon
στέφανον

The Hebrew phrase *Ben-Adam* (בֶּן־אָדָם) is translated as *Son of Man,* and it too has a dual referral to all humanity in general. Thus like mankind *(Adam:* אָדָם) is both male and female *(GENESIS 1:27, 5:1-2)*, so too is the Son of Man *(Ben-Adam)*. This ambisexual etymology multiplies a series of double meanings fine-tuned in the Testimonium Flavianum:

About this time there was Jesus—a wise man
If it be lawful to call Him a man   *(or:→ if it be proper → if one ought to ...)*

Legal squeamishness about whether Jesus was a "man," regards more than just the super-human miracles He symbolically orchestrated. The reluctance is not merely a singular nod to heroic military victories won over Rome by an entire Zealous host of many men. Nor is the most esoteric level of this pause exhausted only in reference to sexual abuse and mutilation suffered by Galilean boys taken as slaves to erect Imperial wonder-works. Jewish women took up arms against Rome alongside men. Women were taken to Rome as slaves. Women were at the great tomb. All this and more, is She who anointed Jesus King, to assist the great resurrection victory:

She did what she could
She came beforehand to anoint the body of me for the burial

But I tell you truly that wherever this gospel is proclaimed
In the whole world
What this woman has done
Will be spoken of as a memorial for Her also
—Mark (14:8-9)

Suggestion that the "sinful woman" who anointed Jesus was a prostitute, hooks the pericope into an occupation forced upon many slaves and war refugees of both male and female gender. It's taken as given that Josephus was criticized for his efforts with these unfortunates. His mirrored double meanings, bleed together where nailed here. Anointing the king was a function performed by the High Priest. This whole epic planetary conflict, hung upon how a Roman appointed High Priesthood, prostituted Yahweh's religion out to Caesar. Joe notes how Herod chose foreigners for this high post *(Ant 15:2:4, 15:9:3, 18:1:1)*, and how the Sadducee families of Boethus and Annas monopolized the office, making bids to the Roman governors who appointed Israel's High Priest, as for a Pagan franchise *(Ant 9:20:1, 18:2:2)*. Heaped up with corpses of many Romans (i.e. ξένοις), their bodies were carted out of the city and thrown away in open burial, as food for dogs and wild beasts, in Akeldama—part of Gehenna *(i.a. Matt 5:29, Wars 4:5:2-3, Ant 16:1:1, Zech 11:13, Acts 1:18-19, Matt 27:3-9, Jerem 32:1-15)*¥.

GIVING IT TO CAESAR

Divitiae emin apud sapientem virum in servitute sunt, apud stultum in imperio
"Wealth is the slave of a wise man, the master of a fool"
— *Seneca, DE VITA BEATA (26:1)*
("wealth" → *divitiae*, cf. "god" → *divus*; "master"→ *imperio*, cf. "emperor"→ *Imperator*)

No one can serve two masters ... You can not serve God and money
— *MATT (6:24)*

! להסיר התחריטים הפגאניים האלה מהבית של האבא שלי

THE TRIBUTE MONEY RIDDLE

Jesus saw a denarius of Tiberius like this one, engraved:

AUGUSTUS TI CAESAR DIVI AUG F

which abbreviates:

→AUGUSTUS TIBERIUS CAESAR DIVI AUGUSTUS FILIUS

which is the Latin title:

→AUGUSTUS TIBERIUS CAESAR SON OF *the* GOD AUGUSTUS

but the legend is split on the coin to suggest:

→TIBERIUS CAESAR GOD AUGUST SON OF AUGUSTUS

Tiberius was bowed to and worshipped, with temples and sacrifices, as living god.

T HE Pharisees... made plans to trap Him in His words...
"Is it right to pay the Imperial tax to Caesar or not?"
Knowing their evil intent, Jesus said:
"You hypocrites, why are you trying to trap me?
Show me the coin used for payment of the tax"
They brought Him a denarius, and He asked them:
"Whose image is this? And whose inscription?"
They replied: *"Caesar's,"* **and then He said to them:**
"Return to Caesar what is Caesar's, and to God what is God's"
— MATTHEW (22:15-22)(Israel belongs to God; the River Tiber belongs to Caesar)

Many clerics spin the tribute money riddle shallow, and sell Israel's king Jesus short, with claims that the contentious Messiah: 1) had no political aims, 2) recognized Roman rule as legitimate, and 3) told Jews to pay taxes to Roman masters. None of this is close to what the cosmic king intended. The idols of a government god were stomping into Israel. Jews were being enslaved and sacrificed on crosses. What would Israel's king do? The tribute was not just any tax. The tribute was a special yearly pledge-fee, paid Caesar directly by non-citizens, to recognize Caesar as Lord. The tribute was thus a submission offering paid to a phony god. Jesus outsmarts the trap lain by the impious religious. A shallow read of the tribute parable ignores the full detail of what was found on the coin Jesus taught about, and where that illustration fit within the law of Moses. Jesus pointed to both the image and the legend graven on the coin, because both violated the worse taboo in Jewish law. The Caesars were worshipped as gods, and Jews were expressly forbidden to make any type of offering to such a "god." The contract with the Creator rests on this commandment. Zion was given to the people whom Moses led out of captivity and away from idolatry. Fiery brimstone was given to the state idols of a new Roman Egypt:

H E will burn down
the temples
of Egypt's gods
— JEREMIAH (43:13)

The tribute riddle is crafted to be comprehensible to an informed Jew, but below the radar of the average Roman. Jesus called Matthew to quit his tax booth, and used the coin to incite revolution from Rome *(MATT 9:9-13, LIFE 1)*. The only kings who ruled inside the Roman Empire, were client kings whom Romans appointed to help with taxing the natives. Pilate executed Jesus beneath a plaque that announced His charge as one of rebellion; any native declaration of kingship was revolutionary. The royal born in *LUKE's* manger is a Zealot king, as Jesus is born during the 6 AD tax-revolt, when Judas the Galilean begins the Zealot Sect *(LUKE 2:1-7, ACTS 5:37, ANT 17: 1:1-6, 17:20:5, WARS 2:8:1)*. Jews were in need of a king that year, after Augustus Caesar deposed his client king Herod-Archelaus, and took a census to recalculate tax collection by direct Roman management. When Judea was without a client king, the Temple Priests◊ answered directly to Roman governors, and assisted them in the collection of Imperial taxes. When Jesus is accused of eating with tax-collectors and "prostitutes◊," there are multiple far away acts on the stage of that peep-show. Telescopes dial to 66 and 80 AD. By inflaming public discontent, Rome's appointed priesthood led the way into God's kingdom *(MATT 21:31)*. Temple priests charge Jesus:

WE *found this man perverting our nation* (ironic reflecting◊)
Forbidding us to pay taxes to the Emperor
And saying that He himself is the Messiah—a King"

— LUKE (23:2)

PILATE **had an inscription written and put on the cross**
It read: *"Jesus of Nazareth—King of the Jews"*...
And it was written in Hebrew and in Latin and in Greek

— JOHN (19:19-20)

When Paul tells the Greek Messianic converts in Italy to obey the Roman government, these instructions must be understood as directives delivered to an underground *(ROMANS 13:7)*. The epistle *1 PETER* was much clearer to Messianists who still knew the revolting Jesus who smashed out of Tiberias into a riotous Jerusalem triumph. The Apostles taught their recruits to accept one's subjection without anger at the true God—like a *JOB*, but with His injunction to punish those who do wrong:

BE **subject to every human institution for the Lord's sake**
Whether to the supreme king
Or whatever governors he appoints
To punish wrongdoers (REV 1:16, HEB 4:12: the line applies to both subject and ruler)
And praise those who do good
For God wants you to silence the foolish and ignorant people

By doing good   *(taking on the suffering involved in acts from protest to full revolution)*
Live as free people
Without using your freedom as a pretext for evil
But as God's slave
Everyone estimate the love of the brotherhood
Then in fear of God—estimate the king   τιμᾶτε *(timate) = evaluate*
Servants be subject to your masters with all fear [of God]
Not only those who are good and gentle
But also those who are perverse
For the sake of the conscience towards God
Is it completely acceptable to endure grief and unjust suffering?
What could possibly be the credit if you endure sinning?
And being hit?
But if you endure doing good and suffering   *(in the zealous Messianic effort)*
That is acceptable to God
This is precisely what you have been called to
Because Christ suffered for you too   *(to take this mess down)*
Leaving you a model   *(with His violence in the Temples also)*
So that you would follow in the footsteps
Of one who never committed a sin   *(Exodus 22:20, Isaiah 53:9)*
Nor had anything duplicitous in His mouth that was ever found-out

   —1 Peter (2:13-22) (τιμᾶτε—timate—means to value, as in to place a value upon, but without any necessary prejudice as to whether or not that value will be high or low)

The movement had to stay under the Roman radar until the Son of Man arrived on the clouds of the sky. "Paul" was building strong human walls for the expected refugees. Soon the Zealots would end the sacrifices in the Temple to the divine genius of Caligula's nephew Nero. Two brothers, two nephews, and two cousins, had planned a date with planetary destiny: ❶ James and Simon the brothers of Jesus, ❷ Simon's son Eliezer and Matthew's son Joe, ❸ Menahem the son of Judas the Galilean, together with cousin Eliezer the son of Jarius. A vow to drink from the Lord's cup, made one a member of this Messianic body. The hope was for a swift and lasting victory. The battlefield needed to be cleared. A Passover plot enabled a new exodus. The entire zealous body is represented by Jesus in His role as Lamb of God:

THE Baptist said: *(Exodus 12:11, cf. Mark 1:6)*
   "I am not capable to untie the thongs of the sandals
    Of the one who comes after me"...   *('We're escaping this slavery')*
John saw Jesus coming towards him and said:
"Behold: The Lamb of God who takes away the sin of the world!
This is He about whom I said

After me there comes a man who came before me
Because He was before me (Jesus/Joses—new incarnations of Moses)
And I only knew Him so that He would be revealed to Israel
This is why I came baptizing with water"
— JOHN (1:29-31) (i.e.:— to gather the zealous Messianic flock)

TAKE a lamb for each family...
They shall take some of the blood
And put it on the two doorposts and the lintel of the houses...
You shall eat it with your loins girded (MARK 1:6)
Your sandals on your feet 🔔 (JOHN 1:29)
And your staff in your hand,
And you shall eat it hurriedly...
It is the Passover of the Lord... (who takes away sins of idolatry and slavery)
I will execute judgments on all the gods
— EXODUS (12:3-12)

THEY prepared the Passover meal...
It was evening (a twilight of the tribe of Dan...)
He took his place with the twelve...
He took a cup... saying:
"This is my blood of the covenant
Poured out for many for the removal of sins"
— MATTHEW (26:26-28)

I *am the vine*
And my father is the vine-grower...
Whoever does not abide in me is thrown away
Such branches are... thrown in the fire and burned"...
— JOHN (15:1, 6)

THEY cried:
"Any man who claims to be a King
Sets himself against Caesar!"
Pilate heard... it was the day of preparation for the Passover
He said to the Jews:
"Here is your King"...
The Chief Priests answered:
"We have no King except Caesar!" (who was false god & slave master)
— JOHN (19:13-15)

𝕭𝖊𝖍𝖔𝖑𝖉 𝖙𝖍𝖊 𝕷𝖆𝖒𝖇 𝖔𝖋 𝕲𝖔𝖉
𝖂𝖍𝖔 𝖘𝖊𝖓𝖉𝖘 𝖆𝖜𝖆𝖞 𝖙𝖍𝖊 𝖘𝖎𝖓 𝖔𝖋 𝖙𝖍𝖊 𝖈𝖔𝖘𝖒𝖔𝖘
𝕳𝖆𝖕𝖕𝖞 𝖆𝖗𝖊 𝖙𝖍𝖔𝖘𝖊 𝖈𝖆𝖑𝖑𝖊𝖉 𝖙𝖔 𝕳𝖎𝖘 𝖘𝖚𝖕𝖕𝖊𝖗
𝕾𝖆𝖉 𝖆𝖗𝖊 𝖙𝖍𝖔𝖘𝖊 𝖈𝖆𝖑𝖑𝖊𝖉 𝖙𝖔 𝖆 𝖘𝖚𝖕𝖕𝖊𝖗 𝖔𝖋 𝖕𝖆𝖗𝖙𝖑𝖊𝖘𝖘𝖓𝖊𝖘𝖘

If one can't see that the crucified King trained a rebel movement against Rome, or hear that the zealous lamb's exodus cleared a battlefield to take away the false gods of the world, then one is unlikely to arrive at the true flipside of the spun blood-guilt. The riotously loud shtick tells how the flight out of the new Roman Egypt was bought by rivers of blood, let from the prize-winning lamb at the cosmic-fair:

WHEN Pilate saw he was getting nowhere *(at subduing protests)*
But that a riot was now starting *(because of his innovations)*
He washed his hands in front of the crowd *(telling he felt no guilt killing Jews)*
Pilate spoke: *(LUKE 13:1)*

> *"Guiltless am I of this blood!*   *(Philo EMBASSY 299-305, ANT 18:3:1, WARS 2:9:2-4)*
> *You yourselves make it happen!"*   *(by standing in the way of Roman "progress")*
> **In answer all the people said:**   *(people from every native group and station)*
> *"Let His blood be upon us! And our children!"*   *(EXODUS 12:7-12)*
>   *(may the "robber" we choose for our King give us safe passage out from under Rome!)*
>   —MATT *(27:24-25)* *(ACTS 3:13: Caesar would have sold back more boys, but 'onlookers' were apathetic)*

A Judean multitude found themselves as brave blooded as Galileans and joined in the revolt, while others looked on in fear or loathing. JOHN'S "blood guilt" drama before Pilate can not be understood without JOHN'S Passover "Lamb of God." Galilee was the blood-marked door into an Israel that had been kept subdued by a paltry five Roman cohorts. Jerusalem was not Pilate's normal venue; the Prefect spent more time holding court in Caesarea Maritima, where the highest volume of international commerce moved. One cohort was stationed in Caesarea Maritima, two cohorts were stationed in Jerusalem, and one cohort was stationed at Sebaste in Samaria. The total number of Roman soldiers regularly deployed in Israel was near three thousand. Herod's sons Antipas and Philip each protected their tetrarchies with their own armies—trained and guided by Romans.

The Romans stationed smaller garrisons at points important to the movement of people and goods, in both Judea and the tetrarchies of the Herods. One such hamlet was Capernaum, which was at an important junction that connected the road from Tyre to Jerusalem, with that road to Damascus which passed under the perch of the rebel hotbed Gamala. Tens of thousands of soldiers filled the ranks of the Roman legions which were permanently deployed in Syria at Beirut and Antioch—not only to deter any attack from Parthia, but also to respond to problems within the empire to the north and south. The Herodians invested great deals of money in Beirut, hoping to endear themselves to the Roman troops stationed there. After Jesus heated up the Zealot movement, Roman Legions from Syria would be deployed into Israel to put down the Galileans on four different days: ① in 35-36, to counteract those Zealots who helped Aretas take Damascus right after the execution of John the Baptist, ② in 41, when the insertion of Caligula's idol into the Jerusalem Temple was successfully resisted, ③ in 51-53, when the Galileans devastated the local Roman forces by luring them into traps in Samaria, ④ in 66, when the Galileans took the country over completely—from Dan to Masada.

Roman forces in Jerusalem were barracked at the Antonia fortress, which was attached to God's Temple, and towered over its courts. The Sanhedrin appointed by the Romans ran Jewish affairs in Jerusalem, policed the Holy City with Temple guards, and called for help from the cohort when necessary. Worship in the Temple was ruled by a High Priest appointed by the Romans. Great throngs flocked to the city from all over the world during the festivals—especially the Passover. Pilate would bring additional forces

SIZE MATTERS: JESUS IS ARRESTED BY 1000 SOLDIERS

The Judean under-rowers *(ὑπηρέται: "uperetai" from "hupo" and "eretes"— 'rowers-under,' i.e. galley slaves rowing the Imperial Roman ship.)*
And the Commander of a Thousand *(χιλίαρχος: the Greek 'chiliarch' means a man at the head of one thousand men)*
And the *Roman* troops *(σπεῖρα: "speira" is a word of Latin origin for a force of Roman soldiers—either a Roman cohort, or a larger expeditionary force led by one. A thousand men were deployed from the Roman cohorts in the city, the goons of the Sanhedrin, and the Herodian forces that were in the city for the Passover)*
Arrested this Jesus and bound Him — *JOHN (18:12)*

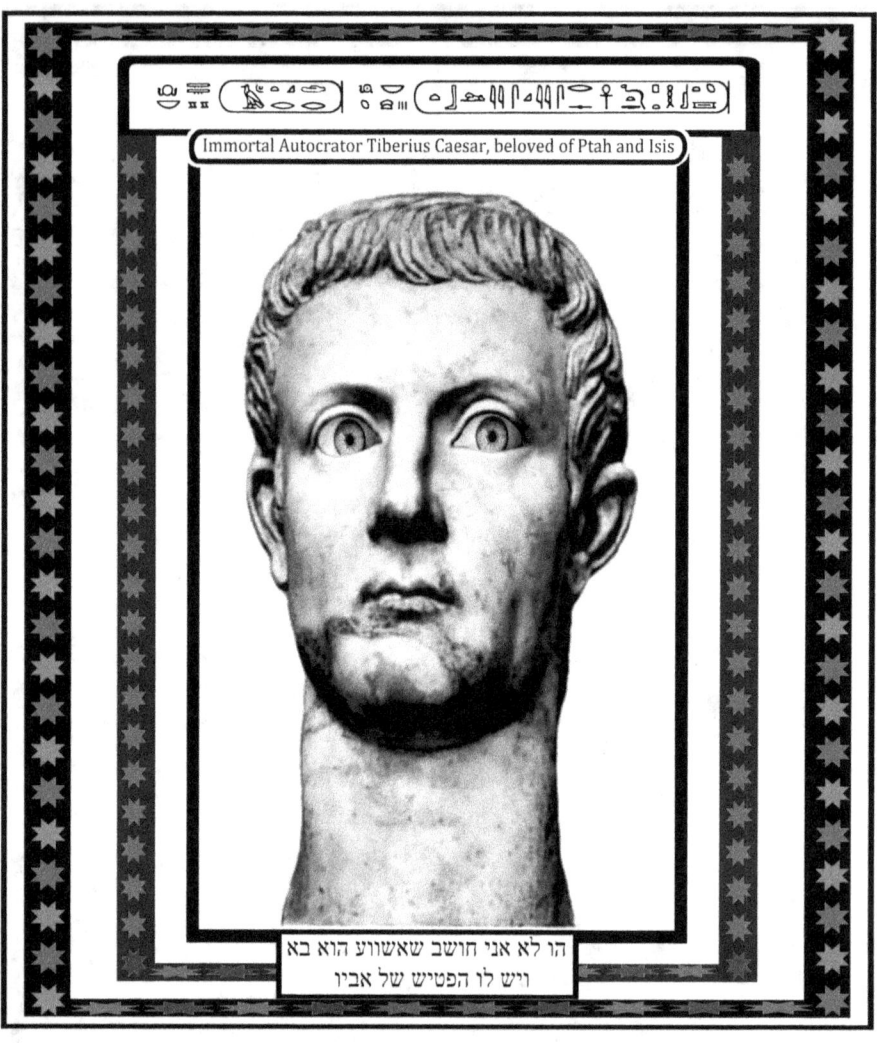

into the crowded city from Caesarea, while the Passover pilgrimage of Antipas was escorted by the Jewish men in the tetrarchy armies. Then Jesus made His own dramatic entrance. A Messianic train paraded into the city. The procession flared up into a huge rumble calculated to deploy the troops out from the Antonia and into the city streets. Under the cover of this riot, Jesus slipped into the Temple. Jesus and his special forces were afforded the diversion they needed to rage like a violent band of whirly dervishes in the smoky courts. Coins and animals were flying everywhere.

By the hour Jesus turned the tables, Roman rule had introduced many Pagan temples into Israel. The shiniest new round of idol constructions was built for worship of Emperor Tiberius as a living god, both at Caesarea Maritima, and at Tiberias of Galilee. Sacrifices in honor of the Imperial gods were also conducted in the Augusteums at Caesarea-Philippi, Sebaste, and

Autocratoris. The Imperial Cult sits at the center of why the Galileans attacked the Jerusalem Temple, for Tiberius was even having his sacrifices offered up besides sacrifices to Yahweh. While the Temple operated under Roman rule, its High Priests were picked by either the Roman Senate, Roman Emperors, Roman Prefects/Procurators, or by Roman appointed Client Kings. People who bewail the loss of Herod's temple, and might blame Jesus/Josephus for its destruction, should carefully consider the many applicable passages in both the law and the prophets—including:

You will have no other gods before me
— *Exodus (20:3), Deuteronomy (5:7)*

Do not worship any other god
For the Lord whose name is jealous
Is a jealous God
— *Exodus (32:8)*

When the Lord made a covenant with the Israelites
He commanded them: "Do not worship any other gods
Or bow down, serve, or sacrifice to them"
— *2 Kings (17:35)*

You shall have no foreign god among you
You shall not bow down to an alien god
— *Psalm (81:9)*

I am Yahweh, that's my name
I will not give my glory to another
— *Isaiah (42:8)*

Again and again I sent all my servants and prophets to you
They said each of you must turn from your wicked ways
And reform your actions
Do not follow other gods to serve them
Then you will live in the land I've given to you and your fathers
But you have not paid attention or listened to me
— *Jeremiah (35:15)*

Your country is desolate
Your cities burned with fire
Your fields are being stripped by foreigners right before you
Says the Lord: Your many sacrifices — what are they to me?
I have had more than enough of burnt offerings...
I have no pleasure in the blood of bulls and lambs and goats...
Who asked you for this trampling of my courts?...
Your incense is detestable to me!

I will hide my eyes when you spread out your hands in prayer...
Take your evil deeds out of my sight!...
Come now, let us reason together...
If you are willing and obedient you will eat the best of the land
But if you resist and rebel you will be devoured by the sword...
See how the faithful city has become a prostitute!
She once was full of justice... but now murderers!...
Your rulers are rebels—companions of thieves...
The mighty man will become tinder and his work a spark
Both will burn together with no one to quench the fire

— *Isaiah (1:7-31)*

The subtle way that Roman Paganism crept its way into Israel was much more sophisticated than what had been encountered previously. Moses built a resilient nation which had survived conquests by Egypt, Assyria, and Babylon, and was reestablished by Persia. It later reestablished itself again by throwing off the Macedonians. Under Rome, the legacy of Moses became further and further subject to a much larger and more studied empire. Roma knew how to swallow her prey slowly when it was required. Anacondas sometimes engulf large mammals which soon burst out their scaly guts.

The humbling of the Imperial cult by Jesus under Tiberius, gave the Jews the nerve to resist the idol Caligula intended to insert into the Jerusalem Temple. The disorder that ensued following the fire of Rome, allowed the Galileans to fully defeat the Roman cohorts and garrisons stationed in Israel. Rome no longer appeared magically supported, either in the eyes of its own troops, or its subjects. The revolt begins with the end of Caesar's sacrifices in the Jerusalem Temple. The speech Herod-Agrippa Jr. made

[DIVIU]S TIBERIEUM
[PO]NTIUS PILATUS
[PRE]FECTUS IUDAEA
[FECIT D]E[DICAVIT]

Previous Page: Marble Head of Tiberius Caesar from a colossal idol worshipped at one of his cult centers. **Above**: surviving inscription from the cornerstone of the Tiberium at Caesarea Maritima, where Pilate conducted Imperial business under the aegis of a similar culted statue of the Emperor.

on the eve of the war, (as delivered by Josephus), points to the riddle Jesus posed with the tribute money:

AGRIPPA said that what they had already done was as good as declaring war against the Romans: *"For you have not paid the tribute that is due Caesar, And you have disconnected the cloisters of the temple from the tower Antonia where the Roman garrison is stationed. You can still prevent this call to revolt, if you only connect these two back together again, and just pay the tribute you owe to Caesar"...* But some of those who were in the forefront of those who were instigating the people to go to war, *(the Galileans)* made an assault upon a certain fortress called Masada ... At the same time Eliezer ... a bold youth, persuaded those who officiated over the divine service, to accept no gift or sacrifice for any foreigner, and this was the true beginning of our war with the Romans, for they rejected the sacrifice of Caesar on this account ... which it was customary for them to offer up for their rulers ... They honored no Romans or Caesar, and forbade their oblations, not caring that rejecting these sacrifices might soon result in the inability to make their own offerings ... Their forefathers had always accepted sacrifices of foreign nations, but none of the innovators would listen.

—*Josephus from* WARS *(2:16:5-17:3)*

The house of prayer for all nations was turned into a den of robbers long before the Galileans took it over. The Romans, Herodians, and collaborators were robbing the nation. The Galileans robbed them back. The predatory Romans, Herodians, and collaborators were introducing Pagan innovations into Israel: idols, coinage, and amphitheatres with murder for entertainment. These innovations were powerful motives prompting the Galileans to halt all foreign sacrifice in the Temple. One set of robbers removed another set of robbers, and turned the Temple into a military base—banning all sacrifices from foreign nations:

THEY came into Jerusalem and He entered the temple
And began to drive out those who were selling
And those who were buying in the Temple *(ZECHARIAH 11:4-7,12-13)*
He would not let anyone carry anything through the Temple
He was teaching and saying:
"Is it not written: *(ISAIAH 56:7)*
My house shall be called a house of prayer for all nations
But you have made it a den of robbers" *(with sharp double-edged swords)*
— *MARK (11:15-19)*

**IN the Temple He found people selling cattle, sheep, and doves
And the money changers seated at their tables**
  **Making a whip of cords He drove them all out of the temple...
He also poured out the coins of the money changers
And turned over their tables
He told those who were selling the doves**
  "Take these things out of here
  Stop making my Father's house a marketplace"   (ZECHARIAH 14:21)
His disciples remembered that it was written:
  "Zeal for your house will consume me"   (the Galileans were the Zealots)
                                                —JOHN (2:13-17)

Slavery blinds master. Vision and muscle weaken. Lust for metal's power, casts an inhuman pall over life. The treacherous trench down is steep enough to squeeze the wind out. Gates, walls, and bars, slope to trap doors in deep dark banks below. Endurant Jesus—cords in hand—is clearly tougher than your average lamb. All the rowdiness of the entire Galilean swan-song, is symbolically edited down into one orgasmic money-shot. Jesus violently purges a clogged Temple. The wrath of an entire national subset, focuses in upon the coin changers with a sweet Imperial franchise. Every Jewish male over twenty years old owed the half shekel Temple tax. Many poor rural Galileans lived by subsistence and barter. In the eyes of the more countrified of these folk, the annual half shekel was a burden suffered to support a venue that had morphed from a shrine of national communion, into an unglorified butcher shop of cosmic proportions. Scribes scrupulously kept the records of who had, and who had not paid the tax. Those poor who were delinquent in this and other debts, could have any property they still owned confiscated. Failure to pay a large enough debt that was sadly owed to the wrong character, could result in six years of bondage in someplace as bad as the copper mines of Cyprus. The lack of returns from these transactions was a source of friction between the Galilean school on the one hand, and the Scribes and Pharisees on the other.

The temple tax was one half of a shekel. This was approximately equal to a dididrachma, or 128 prutahs. A prutah was a small bronze coin, which might buy a loaf of bread, a bunch of grapes, or a modest fish. 128 prutahs was not a negligible sum of money to an average rural 20 year old, whether he be single, or perhaps already the father of several children. In years of bad weather, much of the agrarian population was too impoverished to pay both this and the tribute money owed to Caesar. The poor were being ethnically cleansed out of Galilee, while wealthy foreigners and Pagans were moving into shiny new cities like Sepphoris and Tiberias. A man could emigrate. If instead he chose to stay and fight, he became a fugitive in the eyes of the law—a robber. If the greater part of the Galilean gene pool was to be consumed, it was going to happen right in Herod's grand Temple. They would raise the edifice up 20 cubits for world freedom. There would be fireworks.

The epic turning of the tables is a dramatic reflection of a scene which must have been played out many times. Another uncouth Galilean, with an awful accent which might be coined *Ebionics*, approaches money changer. Drab garbed banker looks up with unvarnished disgust at burly farm boy loudly dressed in garish Technicolor plaid. Unsacred transactions have been hassled by these crude reddish headed step-children before. Daniel-boy has made this long journey from the Gaulon Heights, to take part in the national communion. Proudly he pulls two shekels out from his coin purse, to pay the tax for himself and three of his brothers. He is informed that he must pay an additional 22 prutahs, even though he has exact change, and the proper metal. It certainly would provoke anger in many rural men of modest means, to learn that they were obligated to pay the money changers their full fees, whether they required their services or not.

The facade of Jewish religious freedom was an illusion. Herod murdered the Hasmonean Jewish State for Roman power. The Roman empire then spun Jewish religious institutions deep into criminality. When Herod's stupendous new Temple needed a solid standard of currency, Augustus would not permit such airs of Jewish autonomy as a new sacred Jewish coinage would have advertised. Elite players of the new Temple priesthood

and Sanhedrin were confirmed by Rome's man, and they policed the house rules at his pleasure. They were arranged a mint of Tyrian Shekels in Jerusalem to provide the new official chips for the revamped temple. Augustus and Herod shackled God's House to declare rules whereby the Imperial House would win. Instead of exchanging idolatrous coins for coins of legal Jewish design, the money changers now did precisely the opposite. Only the idolatrous Tyrian Shekel was accepted to pay the Temple tax. Augustus and Herod were laughing all the way to the bank. John began to baptize the rebel movement, as Pilate took the joke to new levels. The Galileans protested each new Pagan innovation Pilate made. Pilate snuck into Jerusalem by night, and installed standards with cult images of the fake god Tiberius Caesar upon them, but soon had to remove them because of unrest. Next Pilate installed Imperial trophies at a public space. Though these shields bore no images, they were engraved with titles which referred to the emperor's divinity. Pilate violently put down unending riots until he removed these new insults to the Holy City. Pilate then issued a series of coins for local use, which contained the emperor's name along with sacrificial implements from his cult. These coins cleverly referred to the emperor's divinity without stating it in words, and without ostensibly using any images prohibited by the letter of Jewish law, but still effectively ripping a new loophole to violate Jewish will. The game was getting ominous. The coins had to be exchanged for blatantly Pagan Tyrian shekels in order to pay for Yahweh's House. To any observant Jew living in this first century world steeped in magic and superstition, there was clearly something very funny going on at the tables.

The required shekel was engraved with the Tyrian god Melkart on the obverse. On the reverse was the graven image of an eagle, with its talon on a rudder. The inscription: *"Tyre the Holy and Inviolable,"* was ironic. The sad implication in the mirror was: *"Jerusalem the Unholy and Violable."* As an attribute of Jupiter Capitolinus, the eagle was the preeminent totem of Roman Imperial might and rapine. These new Tyrian shekels which were specially minted in Jerusalem for use in the Temple, had a special mint mark "KP," widely thought to abbreviate the Greek spelling of "CAESAR"—ΚΑΣΑΡΟΣ. Near Herod's death, he installed a golden eagle above the great gate of the Jerusalem Temple. Barbarous imitations of Herod's regular coinage appeared with the image of an eagle. Young Zealots climbed upon the Temple and cut the eagle down. Many involved were captured and killed in Jerusalem's arena. Any idiot could see base Roman standards that the graven eagle stood for, and how it had swooped its talons upon the Temple on wings of Caesar's KP Shekels.

The symbolism on the obverse of the blasphemous Temple shekel was more ghoulish than an Olympic bird of prey. *Melkart* can be identified with the foreign god whom the Hebrews roasted with a pun which is rendered into English as *Molech*. The Israelites were, perhaps rhetorically, said to have fallen in Molech's worship at the dump—Gehenna.

Molech's foreign cult may have been only for the immolation of those infants born with birth defects. Sound babies were passed over his flames, while deformed or sickly births were dropped into Molech fire. These offerings of public ritual exposure were evidently supposed to bring healthy regeneration upon next conception. Molech was a *Baal*, and gospel tells how clever foes accused the Galilean of being *Beelzebul* —*End-dump Lord of Zebulon.*

Galileans took the Temple. The Tyrian Shekels were melted down and struck into pious coinage with Hebrew legends *"Jerusalem the Holy."* The Messianic themes of the vine and the wine are evident. Gospel uses riddles to encode how the Jesus movement was made up of a family of Zealots. The same sort of riddles in the historical memoirs of Josephus, understate how the Zealots were Messianists who followed the line of Jesus. The whole charade was in part devised to hide the ongoing rebel activities of the family archivist. Early church scholars understood how Joe's code tells about James the Brother of Jesus in the mirror of the Ananus who killed him—a device which underlined how James was the alternative High Priest of the Galilean sect. Josephus uses this code to relate James to that "Eliezer of Ananus" who stopped Nero's sacrifices in 66:

AT that time there were no armies besieging Jerusalem
    For the siege began in the reign of Nero
And lasted until the government of Vespasian
Whose son Titus destroyed Jerusalem, as Josephus says
    On account of James the Just
    Who was the brother of Jesus who was called Christ
                   — *Origen, CONTRA CELSUM (2.13) circa 248 AD*

THE Temple was razed to the ground...
    Because of the wrath of God

**Regarding things they had dared to do
Against James the brother of Jesus**
— *Origen from his* COMMENTARY ON MATTHEW
cf. Eusebius ECCLES HIST *(2:23)*

The military history of the Galilean resistance is hidden beneath a polished literary surface. Josephus the historian, was a freedman of the Imperial house. As such he needed to employ great literary and rhetorical skill if he was to save the more politically incorrect moments of the rebellion. The *Parable of the Tribute Money* is a paradigm of the clever voice that met the challenge. It preserved the call for rebellion so well, precisely because it was so easy to lazily misread as a

> THE ILLEGAL EAGLE COIN OF HEROD IS A PROPAGANDA ISSUE SPOOFING HEROD'S INSTALLMENT OF A GOLDEN EAGLE OVER THE MAIN GATE OF THE JERUSALEM TEMPLE. THE CRUDE UNSTRUCK COINS WERE POURED IN BARS THEN BROKEN. THE TEMPLE-GATE EAGLE WAS LIKELY AN UNPUBLICIZED DONATION BY AUGUSTUS AND LIVIA, DESIGNED TO TEST THE JEWISH WATER—IT FAILED.

testimony to the opposite message, yet when it is fully studied, the gravity of the true vector against Rome is undeniable. A fiery hot prey eagle flew home to roost, upon the murder of James the Brother of Jesus. The martial spark attributed to the stoning of James, prods us to connect the disciple of Jesus

called *Simon the Zealot*, to the zealot called *Eliezer son of Simon*. Eliezer defeated the legions under Cestius Gallus, and captured an eagle. Eliezer's victory bought a bitter-sweet taste of freedom for Israel:

THEY **were filled with fury** *(☙at the chaffing of wheat on the Sabbath)*
And debated what to do to Jesus... *(☙ for healing a withered hand)*
  (here MARK *3:6, says: "they conspired with the Herodians on how to destroy Him")*
He spent the night praying to God
And when the day came He called his disciples
And chose twelve of them whom He named Apostles...
(counted down to) **Simon who was called "the Zealot"** ☿   *(#10)*
Judas of James and Judas Iscariot *(#11 & 12: the brother of Jesus with Judas Sicarii)*
—LUKE *(6:1-16)* *(☙cf.* ANT *12:6:2 "He taught them to fight on the Sabbath;" ☙cf. Luke 6:1 & 3:16-17)*

ELIEZER **the son of Simon who made the first** ☿
       separation of the Zealots from the people
                                    — WARS *(5:1:2)*

Gospel disguises* the troops in the open. Healing the withered hand, and removing chaff with the fingers on the Sabbath, represent leave to engage in zealous defense seven days a week. Zebedee's boys—John and James—drank from their cousin's cup; James died by the sword. Jesus called His hearers to action. Twelve were chosen to recruit His zealous host:

Do not think that I have come to bring peace to the earth I have not come to bring peace but a sword ... Whoever does not sieze his cross and follow Me, does not weigh in with Me. Whoever finds the essence of him will cut it off, yet those who have their essence cut off will find it on account of Me.
— MATT *(10:7, 39) (speech after calling the Twelve at 10:1-4)*

Stick that sword of yours where it belongs* *(inside Rome's soldiers)*
For all who live by the sword will die by the sword
— MATT *(26:52)* *(τόπον, crypted by θήκην at JN 18:11, ANT 7:11:7, cf. 2 SAM 20:8†)*

King Herod [Agrippa I] stuck out his hands to injure...
He put James (he of John) to death—with a sword
— ACTS *(12:2) (thus the Apostles lived by the sword; note the Herods were gutted†)*

Attentive gospel readers can hear that "the Twelve" are the elite vanguard of a military band organized by a Reform Rabbi under siege. Jesus sends apostles out to gather recruits for a war of independence. The family nature of such an enterprise is not surprising—it is predictable reality for a family with priestly and royal connections. A name-game inside the gospel uses a great catalogue of literary tricks to camouflage family relations. Seekers find that *Simon the Zealot* is grouped tight with the brothers of Jesus named *Jude* and *James*. Family links justify the cause and effect relationship between the stoning of James and the rebellion begun with Galilean attacks upon Jerusalem and Masada. When *Eliezer son of Simon Zealot* takes a Roman eagle, we are face to face with a nephew of the Lord. Simon's son is the big Kahuna whom Jesus confidently expects to rise from the dead—the Lazarus who scores the biggest legionary victory ever won in rebellion from Rome by any province. Josephus the son of Matthew decided that the best way to glorify his family's triumph was to understate it in a measure greater than anything so great had ever been understated before. Joe knew the Imperial idol had dashed its foot on the rock. Joe was going to ease its bulk down, as a redeeming Messiah infiltrating the Antichrist's house:

Prutahs issued by Pilate with the litus and simpulum of Tiberius Caesar's Divinity Cult

AN old and established belief (NUMBERS 24:17)
   Had spread over all the Orient
   Time had come for men from Judea to rule the world...
 Accordingly they revolted
 And after killing their governor

Syria's consular ruler came to the rescue
They routed him as well
And they took one of his eagles

— *LIFE OF VESPASIAN (4) by Suetonius*

THE tolerance of the Jews lasted until Procurator Florus
In his time the war broke out
Cestius Gallus, Legate of Syria, tried to crush it
Having to fight several battles—generally without success
Cestius died—either of natural causes or frustration

— *HISTORIES (5) by Tacitus* *(He burned Zebulon Oct. 17, but never went home)*

WITHOUT a world of reason, Cestius retired from the city
When the robbers perceived his unexpected retreat
They resumed their bravado... *(about November 22 of 66)*
The Romans suffered greatly... and were harried all the way...
Their ranks were put into disorder... as far as Bethoron
The valleys into which they frequently fell and tumbled down
Were so great on either side of them *(2 CHRONICLES 8:5)*
That there was neither place for flight
Nor any imaginable means of defense
Until their distress was at last so great they took to lamentation
And such mournful cries as men only use in utmost despair
Meanwhile the joyful acclamations of the Jews
Echoed back and forth as they encouraged each other
All at once now in a rage rejoicing
Indeed Jews could have taken Cestius's entire army as captives...
They picked over the dead bodies
And gathered together what booty of the Romans remained
And came rushing and singing back to their metropolis
For they themselves had lost only a few
But they had slain 5,300 Roman footmen, and 380 horsemen...
When they got back to Jerusalem... *(about November 27 of 66)*
Many parties gathered together in great numbers in the Temple
And appointed a great many generals for the war...
And city Governors—especially for the fortification of its walls
But because they observed that he had a tyrannical temper
They did not appoint Eliezer son of Simon to that office ♆
As his followers behaved like a guard around him
It was his effort that put him in possession of the Roman prey
And the money they had taken from Cestius
As well as a great part of the public treasury *(key to August fires in the city)*

**Therefore by the desire they had for Eliezer's money
And through subtle tricks employed by him
The will of the people was circumvented
And they submitted themselves to him in all public affairs**
— *Wars (21:19:7—20:3)*

Jerusalem archaeology unburies a first century tale of two cities. David's hill-throne was turned into a gilt pig-pen. An elite class of governors, priests, and international merchants, lived inside a mock Aventine of lavish villas, insecurely walled in connection with the Herodian palace complex. It was a city afraid of the Jews, within a city full of Jews. There were private ways and tunnels ushering these Jerusalem elites into guarded sections of the Temple, where they need never mingle with the rabble of the Jewish street. Meanwhile, members of the Imperial elite could spy upon all the slaughter from Latin VIP rooms high up in the tower named for Mark Anthony. Joe only returned to Jerusalem when it became safe for him—after the Antonia was taken. Joe was not appointed general until after Eliezer rose to control.

There is much evidence of conspicuous consumption in the lofty Roman neighborhood of Jerusalem. Money was being lent, not so much for compounded interest, as for hedged tabulations betting that the note was just large enough to ensure that it could never be repaid. The lender would then either seize land more valuable than what he had lent, or take six of the best years of a young persons life. This was high mockery of the spirit of the so-called laws of Moses. Ripened vouchers sent blood into bondage, and amassed unreal estates. Who were the lawless? Who were the real robbers?

The Galileans conquered the lower city in August of 66 AD. There was a seven day battle for the upper city from the end of August into early September. Syria's governor Cestius was prepared to deploy by the time news arrived that the cohorts in Jerusalem were defeated, for the force of Cestius was already on the march into Galilee before the end of September. Legion XII Fulminita and a large auxiliary force arrived at Jerusalem by early November. Lazarus crushed it in Bethoron before December. A great deal of plunder was taken from the Romans, which was added to the booty Lazarus extracted from the Upper City, when the Galileans emptied the vaults, and burned the debt records:

NOW the next day was Xylophory, when custom was for everyone to contribute wood for the altar, that there may never be a want for fuel for that fire, which was unquenchable, and burning forever. Upon that day they excluded the opposite party from the observation of this part of religion, and when they gathered to themselves many of the Sicarii who crowded in among the weaker people, for that was the name of those robbers who hid swords called Sicae inside

their bosoms, they grew bolder, and carried their undertakings further, so that the kings soldiers were overpowered by their multitude and boldness ... And so they were driven out of the upper city by force. These others then set fire to the house of Ananias the High Priest, and to the palaces of Agrippa and Bernice. Then they set fire to the palace where the archives were deposited, and hurriedly burned the contracts held by their creditors, and thereby dissolved the obligations for paying debts. This worked for the gain of the multitude of debtors, and persuaded the poorer sort, that might join the insurrection against the wealthier under safety. So those who kept the records ran away, and the rest set fire to them.

— *WARS (2:17:6)*

The gospels were written after the burning of the public records in Jerusalem. The wording of the *Lord's Prayer* was first put down on scrolls after day four of the Galilean revolt. Lazarus rose from the dead and torched the palaces in the upper city:

F**orgive us our debts — As we forgive our debtors**

— *MATTHEW (6:12)*

The importance of the context is compounded by the *Josephan Paradigm of New Testament Origins*, by which the variation in *LUKE* enriches the depth of the simpler statement in *MATTHEW*:

F**orgive us our sins — As we forgive everyone indebted to us**

—*LUKE (11:4)*

In the literal mirror, it is hard to tell monetary *debts* from *sins* ("failings"), or tell the robber from the copper. The eschaton *judge* would be *Dan*:

T**reat your adversary well quickly**   (*JOHN 13:26-27*)
While you are on the way   ("Satan" means "adversary" or "opponent")
Or else the adversary may deliver you to the judge
And the judge deliver you to his underling
And cast you into prison
I tell you it is certain
You will not will not come out from there
Unless and until you somehow pay the very last penny

— *MATTHEW (5: 25-26)*   *(The slow to waken would have hell to pay)*

There is only shallow contradiction, in first asking God for a cancellation of debts, and then insisting that one's debts must be paid to the very last "penny" (used to close the eyes of those who died in war). The puzzle is only understood by historical context. Systems seek equilibrium. Prayer for absolution of debts, was prayer for Galilean victory:

**Owe nothing to anyone
Except love for one another
For he who loves the other
Has fulfilled the law**
—ROMANS *(13:8)*

**If you don't have a sword
Sell that cloak and buy one
For it is written:**
"He will be numbered among the lawless"
And I tell you that this must be fulfilled by me   *(ISAIAH 53:12)*
—LUKE *(22:36-37)*

A giant clay-footed idol towered over the Temple. Rough stone took it down. The bandit revolt of *Jesus Barabbas* flared in Jerusalem while the Galilean band of *Jesus the Christ* was

> COIN: JUDEA CAPTA ISSUE OF VESPASIAN. A FEMINIZED JEWISH TROPHY SLAVE IS SHOWN IN DRAG BONDAGE. NOTE THE BICEPT MUSCLE. HIS VULGAR GESTURE TO THE ELBOW HAS SEXUAL MEANING. ★★★

decriminalizing the Temple. Barabbas is an epithet of Jesus himself. *Bar-Abbas* means "Son of the Father." Jesus gave "Abba" ultimate responsibility for "the cup" *(MARK 14:36)*. Older texts give the first name "Jesus" to Barabbas, (see the *NEW OXFORD, TODAY'S ENGLISH VERSION, NEW ENGLISH BIBLE*, and a note in the recent *REVISED STANDARD VERSIONS*—all restore "Jesus" to the text):

**At that time they had a notorious prisoner
Called Jesus Barabbas**
—MATTHEW *(27:16)*   *(cf. ACTS 1:23, LUKE 23:14, WARS 7:11:3)*

They all shouted: *"Release Barabbas for us!"*
**This was a man who had been put in prison
For a rebellion that had taken place in the city**
—LUKE *(23:18-19)*   *(note: James Zebedee died by the sword)*

**Barabbas was in prison with those rebels
Who had committed murder during the insurrection**
—MARK *(15:7)*   *(cf. MARK 14:36, MATT 20:20-22, LUKE 22:36, MATT 26:55)*

Pilate said: *"Do you want me to release you the King of the Jews?"*
They shouted in reply: *(all in the Galilean sect were "robbers;" see ROM 8:15, GAL 4:6)*
"Not that man! Barabbas instead!" — **but Barabbas was a bandit**
—JOHN *(18:39-40)*   *(the disciples lived and died by the sword: MATT 26:52, ACTS 12:2)*

ויען ישוע ויאמר לא ידעתם את אשר שאלתם היכל תוכלו שתות את
הכוס אשר אני עתיד לשתותו והטבל בטבילה אשר אני נבטל בה
ויאמרו אליו נוכל: —MATT (20:22)   *(cf. MATT 3:11, WARS 6:4:6 {258},*
ANNALES 15:38, LIFE OF TITUS 8:4)

Two others who were also criminals   *(counting Him among the lawless)*
Were led away with him to be executed   *(LUKE 22:36-38, MATT 26:52, ACTS 12:2)*
—LUKE *(23:32)*   *(LUKE 23:39-43: the Zealot on His left thinks they lost the war—forgets MATT 20:22)*

Two bandits were crucified with him   *(MATT 16:24, ZECHARIAH 11:12-13, 17)*
One on his right   *(LUKE 6:6-11, 1 MACCABEES 2:35-41, HEBREWS 8:1, MATTHEW 26:64)*
And one on his left   *(ISAIAH 53:12, see Josephus' DISCOURSE ON HADES)*
—MATTHEW *(27:38)*

There were some present who told Jesus
About the Galilean blood
That Pilate mixed with their sacrifices
—LUKE *(13:1)*   *(LUKE 6:10-15: the 12 are called to fight on the Sabbath)*

Jesus poured out the *Cup of Elijah* to resist Caesar's poisonous Kool-aid *(PSALM 79, LAMENTATIONS 3:66, JEREMIAH 25:15, REVELATION 14:6-13)*. The body of Christ dug a pit, then disappeared like Elijah in a chariot of fire. The embers were hijacked by Constantine Caesar, whose rulings perverted the *Passover Book Club* of the resistance. Rabid dogma bites lobotomized hard of hearing *People of the Book* into herds of head-bobbing zombies. The religion of peace too quickly about-faced towards the box Connie thrust upon them. For more than a millennium, the lay are force-fed enlarged misreadings with hypnotic kneeling, and standing, and genuflecting, and prostrating. Eat the words on this scroll for an antidote. Snap out of it upon the count of three: ONE, TWO ...

ב 120 שנים, מהרגע הראשון של המלך הורדוס ועד האחרונים של נכדו הורדוס, אגריפס השני הגדול, לא מטבע אחד של הורדוס היחיד אי פעם היה לאגדת עברית אחת.

הם השתמשו רק יווניים, משום עברית הייתה שפתם של אביונים.

בית החשמונאי לפני הורדוס שכמעט תמיד כלל אגדות עבריות לצד יווני על מטבעיהם.

Jerusalem and the Temple were destroyed... "and now did the madness of the Sicarii, like a disease, reach as far as the cities of Cyrene, for one named Jonathan ... went there, and persuaded the poorer sort to lend him their ear..." *When Jonathan was caught, the Roman governor Catullus* "persuaded Jonathan ... to accuse prominent Jews at Alexandria and Rome of plotting innovations. One of those against whom this treacherous accusation was lain was Josephus"

—A<small>NT</small> (7:11:1-3)

Moving on they found a man of Cyrene named Simon
They compelled him to pick up His cross

—M<small>ATT</small> (27:32) *(Simon means "He who Hears"... Let he who has an ear listen... to what the messenger is saying to the assemblies...)*

He who does not seize His cross and follow me
Does not weigh-in with me *(i.e. "is not on my side of the scale")*

—M<small>ATT</small> (10:38)

ROME TO MASADA: 64-66-73

The Jesus reborn on high, crunches out a punch-line coined by a 5th century BC Greek dramatist. His decidedly Hellenistic turn of phrase, alludes to infrastructures that chew up mankind until the system makes moves towards stasis, as the burdened pull the plug:

**To kick against the pricks is surely is a slippery course
It is my lot to consort with the highborn
And to please them** — *Pindar, PYTHIAN ODE II c. 475 BC*

Pindar uses "the pricks" as metaphor for the ruling class. A *prick* or a *goad* is a sharply spiked stick used to prod a beast of burden onward. Among pack animals, the camel excels at emotional communion with humans, approaching or surpassing even canines. However, of all the domesticated animals, abused camels can be the meanest and most single-mindedly determined to avenge mistreatment. The Hasmoneans built the sky high fortress of *Gamala* over the road to Damascus, in order to secure the northeast frontier. The citadel was called *Gamala* because its walls enveloped a steep ridge which resembles a camel's hump. The zealous "Galilean sect" was founded by one Judas who was born at Gamala. As he neared Damascus, top-gun Apostle Saul passed into the bandit zone, under that rebel stronghold:

**I was going to Damascus...
At midday... I saw in the road from the sky above
A flare that blazed all around me and those traveling with me
Brighter than the sun** *(a "phos" or "firelight")*
**We all fell to the ground — And I heard an Aramaic voice say:
"Saul, Saul, why do you persecute me?
It is hard for you to kick against the pricks"** —*ACTS (26:14)*

Jesus speaks from the cross in Hebrew with a Galilean accent, but the risen sky-cowboy who blocks the road to Damascus speaks in full-on Aramaic, which the author of *ACTS* renders into the Greek of his audience with dramatic flair. Jesus is speaking the language of the local underclass to a presumed outsider who is about to cross the border. Aramaic was the native Semitic language spoken in Syria—from Antioch down to Tyre, over to Damascus, up to Baalbek, and deep into Parthia. Aramaic was also the vulgar language of the poorer sort in the tetrarchy of Herod Philip, where the elite spoke Greek. Nearby at Capernaum, in the tetrarchy of Philip's brother Antipas, the Jews were *Galileans*, who spoke an Aramaic tinged Hebrew. In Gamala the Jews were *Gaulonites*, who spoke a Hebrew tinged Aramaic, as figured prominently in the book of *DANIEL*. Greek speaking secret-agent Saul plays a Hebrew detective from Jerusalem by way of Tarshish *(ANT 9:10:2)*. Lightning rope Jesus rounds him up in Aramaic—the language spoken by the local robbers of Gamala. Elite pricks on the Herodian side of the vanity, kicked down from Philip, Salome II, and Herod-

Agrippa II, who were pampered in the palace at Caesarea Philippi, which they soon rebuilt into a "Neropolis" on the suburbs of Dan. The Zealot pricks of Gamala galloped down from a different high ridge upon which they were born in great numbers. Doomsday results when governors count people like animals and become lower than Homo sapiens.⁴ Those who rule the highest mammal must mix with the people and please them. When political infrastructure devolves to a point where that is impossible, the conventional pack animal has been goaded down a slippery trail.

The biggest little pricks of the first century poked out from marbles on the hills of Rome, where Paul soon landed in the brig. Gospel crafts a *Two First Days of Christmas* puzzle. Jesus is born under Halley's **12** BC** visit, during the reign of Great Herod according to *MATTHEW (2:12 & 2:22)*, but Jesus is born again with the **6* AD** tax revolt lead by Judas of Gamala—after Herod's son Archelaus is deposed in *LUKE (2:1), (cf. ANT 18:1:1-18:2:2)*. The 6 AD, animal-counting Christmas, identifies mild-mannered Jesus as the entire Zealot host born that year, while the Comet Christmas dates His 'Second Coming' to the Zealot triumph of 66. The icy-hot Messianic visit over Bethlehem in 12 BC, reapplies Son of Man muscle rub, in clouds of Halley's brilliant 66 skies *(DAN 7:13, LK 21:25-28, MATT 24:29-31, WARS 6:5:3, Tacit. HIST. 5:13)*. Earth scientists planned the revolt to apex under cosmic lighting.

Once one hears that Joe sails for Paul, they see that Joe also gives himself two alternative nativities of *A)* 34, and *B)* 37 AD, and that he collates these to his two possible dates for the crucifixion. The riddle is an interlace between *ANTIQUITIES (18:5:2), JOHN (1:15, 19:31, 8:57, 2:20-21)*, and *LUKE (3:23)*; note that *A)* **45 − 12** = 33**, and *B)* **30 + 6* = 36**. All pivots on the anomalous chronology of John's beheading, which forces two possible Passion dates in the relevant years when the high day of Passover fell on a Sabbath—either 33 or 36 AD. Thus the birthday riddles mime the sequences: d. 33 → b. 34, or d. 36 → b. 37. Plugging in Joe's 37 AD birthday, sails this Joses who was the reborn son of Matthew, into Rome right before the Great Fire in **64**:

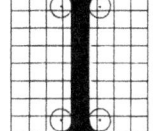

was born in the first year of Caligula... *(37 AD)*
In my 26ᵗʰ year it fell on me to go to Rome
—*LIFE (1-3)*   **37 + 26 = 63** *(the Great Fire was August of 64)*

The landscape of this time is populated with elite Greek fluent allies in Caesar's house, common to Paul and Joe. Jesus resisted Tiberias. His cousin John of Zebedee resisted Caligula's idol aimed at the Jerusalem Holy of Holies. These acts of defiance won the first family of Galilee an Empire-wide fame. The Greeks were in an Imperial situation parallel to that of the poor of Israel. Economic manipulations from Romanophilic pricks above, landed the impoverished into slavery. In another parallel to the Jews, the Greeks were dispersed throughout the empire far and wide. Much of Southern Italy was still Greek. Seneca was an enemy of Caligula, and was exiled right after that cracked emperor was assassinated. Seneca was soon recalled by Caligula's sister Agrippina, to serve as advisor to Claudius, and to tutor her son Nero in the classics. Recalling Seneca was like inviting the enemy to sight one's guns. The Greek freedman Epaphroditus, who served as Imperial secretary and publisher from the reigns of Claudius to Domitian, is revealed, by onomastic probability, to have been a high placed mole of the Greek resistance from the start. Jewish proselyte Poppaea seduced her way into Nero's house while Seneca and Epaphroditus served him. All three were eventually discovered. All three met death by an Emperor's angry fit. Epaphroditus is a common name for a Greek man-slave, but it is not a common name for an Imperial publisher. The Epaphroditus in the forwards of Joe's books, and in the Letters of Paul, must be the same man, considering the wisdom of all the other statistically improbable anomalies:

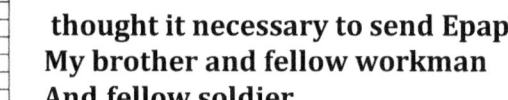

I thought it necessary to send Epaphroditus to you
My brother and fellow workman
And fellow soldier *(in the Messianic resistance)*
And your apostle *("emissary" for community organizing)*
And servant to my need... *(to gather and disseminate information)*
I am filled *(with new intelligence on our common enemy)*
Having received from Epaphroditus useful things from you
A sweet smell— a sacrifice acceptable—well pleasing to God...
And my God will supply all your needs *(Ex 29:18, Num 15:3)*
According to his riches in glory in Christ Jesus... *(who trashed Tiberias)*
Salute ye every saint in Christ Jesus *(i.e. "Down with all of Caesar's marbles!")*
There you salute the brethren with me
There you salute all the saints
And especially those of Caesar's house *(Seneca, Poppaea, and Epaphroditus)*
— *from Paul's* Letter to the Philippians *(2:25, 4:18-22)*

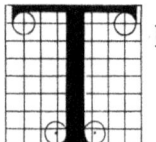

This is the account of my whole life
O Epaphroditus—thou most excellent among men
I dedicate this treatise of our Antiquities
— Life of Josephus *(2:25, 4:18-22)*

Joe's prologue to *Antiquities* waxes poetic on the name of *Epaphroditus*, which means "Devotee of Aphrodite," a name common to male sex slaves:

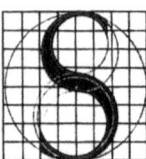

Some persons desired to know our history...
Above the rest Epaphroditus—a man who is a lover
Of all kinds of learning—but is principally delighted
With the knowledge of history
And due to the circumstance
Of his having been involved in great affairs *(fires, suicides, pamphlets)*
And many reversals of fortune *('ups and downs'—barely escaping Seneca's fate)*

And having proven wonderful vigor...
And immovable virtuous resolution into all of them   (firmness)
I yielded to this man's seductions
Who always excites such as have proficiencies
For what is useful and acceptable
Enjoining their endeavors to his   ('knowing' each other as allies against Caesar)
I was also ashamed myself
To let any laziness of disposition
To have a greater influence upon me
Than the delight of taking pains
In such studies as were very useful
I thereupon poked myself up
And went on with my work more cheerfully

Joe's *ANTIQUITIES, LIFE,* and *AGAINST APION* are all dedicated to Epaphroditus. *ANTIQUITIES* dates itself to the thirteenth year of Domitian. Joe had been a fugitive since 80 AD—right before Domitian came to power. Soon after the gospels and these keys to them were published, Domitian figured out that his sick and elderly secretary Epaphroditus had betrayed the Caesars for all these years. In the fifteenth and last year of his reign, Domitian had Epaphroditus executed for sleeping around with the works of an enemy author. In the wake of the greatest publishing effort in history, the tide inside Domitian's Imperial household turned into a wave. The brother of Titus was wiped out by a bedroom pipeline. It was an inside job all the way:

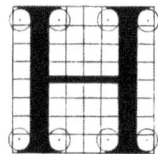

He *(Domitian)* **condemned Epaphroditus, his confidential secretary, to death, because it was believed that after Nero was abandoned, the freedman's hand had aided him in taking his life...** *(in other words, Domitian Caesar finally discovered Epaphroditus had been a mole since at least the end of Nero Caesar—thirty years earlier)* **For eight successive months** *(after Domitian had taken out Epaphroditus)* **so many strokes of lightning occurred and were reported, that at last he cried: "Well, let him now strike whom he will!" The temple of Jupiter of the Capitol was struck and that of the cult of the Flavian family, as well as the Palace and the emperor's own bedroom. The inscription too on the base of a triumphal statue of his was torn off in a violent tempest and fell upon a neighboring tomb...** *(all code for Christian vandals playing with marble figureheads)* **he was hastening to the bath, when his chamberlain Parthenius changed his purpose by announcing that someone had called about a matter of great moment and would not be put off. Then he dismissed all his attendants and went to his bedroom, where he was slain... As the**

wounded prince attempted to resist, he was slain with seven wounds by Clodianus, a subaltern, Maximus, a freedman of Parthenius, Satur, decurion of the chamberlains, and a gladiator from the imperial school.

—Suetonius, LIFE OF DOMITIAN (14-17)

It was not hard for Domitian to understand what Joe and Epaphroditus had been up to, once someone explained to Domitian the correspondences between Joe's LIFE and the ACTS of Paul before the fire:

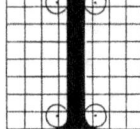

T happened that I took the voyage to Rome...
When Felix was procurator of Judea   (52-60 AD)
There were certain priests of my acquaintance...
He had put in bonds and sent to Rome...   (ACTS 24:27)
These I was desirous to procure deliverance for...
Accordingly I came upon Rome by Sea
Though it would be through a great number of hazards   📖
For as our ship was drowned in the Adriatic Sea   ✪
We that were in it being about 600 in number   (about a cohort)
Swam for our lives all night
Upon the first appearance of the daylight
We sighted a ship out of Cyrene   (Alexandrian ships called at Cyrene first)
I and some others—80 in all   ⑧⓪
By God's providence prevented the rest
And were taken up into the other ship
And when I had thus escaped
And landed in Dicearchia, which the Italians call Puteoli
I was acquainted unto Aliturius—an actor of plays
And much beloved was he by Nero although by birth a Jew
His interest was revealed thoroughly unto Caesar's wife Poppaea
To carefully obtain freedom when ripe for the priests
I obtained this and many other gifts besides from Poppaea
I returned home again
For now I perceived innovations were already begun
And that there were a great many very elevated
In hope by this revolt from the Romans
I therefore endeavored to put a stop to these persons   (Romans)
Persuading them to change their minds...   (making allies among the enemy)
They already possessed the Antonia which was the citadel
I retired to the inner court of the temple
But did go out of the temple again after Menahem
And the principal band of robbers were put to death...   (the cohorts)
   (Trick language—Menahem's arms taken from Masada killed the Roman forces of Jerusalem)

As the danger was directly upon us   *(in the Temple under the Antonia)*
We pretended to be of the same opinion as them [Romanophiles]*
      —LIFE *(3-6)(*for as long as necessary—until the class act of 80 AD)*

HEN it was decided we were to sail to Italy
They transferred Paul and some other prisoners
To Julius—Centurion from Sebaste's cohort *(in Samaria)...*
We sailed under the lee of Cyprus   *(and its Copper mines)*
Because its winds were against us...
Much time was lost and sailing now hazardous...
Paul advised... but the Centurion paid more attention to the pilot
And the owner of shipment than to what Paul had said...
Soon a violent Northeast wind rushes down...
The ship was caught by the storm and could not head into the wind
So we went with it and were driven along...
We were being pounded by the storm so violently
That on the next day they began to throw cargo overboard
And with their own hands on the third day   *(the day of Joses)*
They threw the ships tackle overboard...
Paul stood tall among them, and said: ...
> *"Last night an angel stood beside me*
> *Of the God to whom I belong—whom I worship*
> *And he said: "Paul, Do not be afraid*
> *You must STAND-UP BEFORE CAESAR!"...*

As we were drifting across Adriatic sea waves...
Fearing that we might run upon the rocks
They dropped 4 anchors astern and prayed for day to come... *(gospels)*
We were in all about 76...   *(variant manuscripts read 276)* ⑦⑥
When day came they did not recognize the land
The ship ran aground...
The soldiers decided to kill the captives
But *(good Samaritan)* **Centurion ... wanted to save Paul ...**   *("save the little one")*
Ordering swimmers to jump ship first and make land...
And when they had escaped
Then they knew the island was called *Malta*   *("Sweet"— freedom honey)*
Paul gathered bundled brushwood...
To put it on the fire...
And they said...*"This man must be a murderer!"*...
3 months later we boarded... Alexandrian sail...
Twin brothers were its figurehead...
On the second day we came unto Puteoli
      —ACTS *(27:1-28:13)*

Beceire

Paul threw **chaff** on the fire *(Acts 28:3;—φρυγάνων is "chaff" in the Septuagint)*. The **viper** bit his *hand (Acts 28:3;—χειρὸς)*. A return to the fire freed his hand from ***the beast*** *(Acts 28:4;—θηρίον; cf. Rev 13:15-18)*. Fire ruined Nero while Paul had friends in Caesar's House; one—Ephaphroditus—had his hand in Nero's suicide. A tinder-box mafia with insane fancies for Pharonic magic, had remade Rome's Republic into an autocracy. Roman Republicans, and Greeks Democrats, were moved to act like Ephaphroditus against this depraved estate. Domitian learned Ephaproditus was the fire starter's publisher, and snuffed him—but not the movement. Those who govern must serve the people. The Caesars thought it their prerogative to serve people to themselves for dinner instead. Smart iconoclastic satire, slam-dunked with the Last Supper loaf, broke cannibal mysteries initiated by Caligula—the same Caesar who sought to install his personal cult idol in Jerusalem's Holy of Holies. Caesar was the drunken steward whom Jesus shattered:

WHO is now the faithful and prudent steward whom the Master will set over His household to give in season the wheat measure? Happy will be that servant whom the Lord finds doing so when He returns. I assure you He will certainly trust all His assets to him. But if that servant says in his heart, "My Master has delayed His return," and begins to hit both the female and the male servants, and also to eat, and to drink and be drunken *(1 Cor 11:18-24)*, **then the Master of that servant will return in a day he does not look for, and in an hour he does not know, and cut him in two** [parts] *(E & W)*. —*Luke (12:42-46)*

God made every tree in the garden as food for mankind, except one. Mankind is not to eat: the tree called "Knowledge of Good and Evil." What true evil is, he who eats from it, will find out. Earth's great empires were built by *man eating man*, in metaphorical senses every bit as real and fatal as the literal. A Roman elite addicted to sympathetic magic, elevated this metaphorical Imperial crime by institutionalizing, and popularizing, literal cannibalism. Swine trampled garden shoots. Such unclean eating, heated Isaiah, to recall *Genesis* on the revolution of the upper crust:

FOR behold Yahweh fire will come
      Chariot whirlwind heat will return

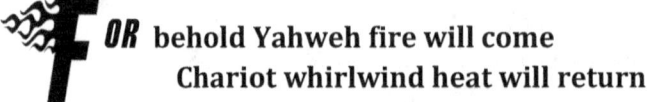

Flames of fire his anger and rebuke
Yahweh will govern by fire   כי באש יהוה נשפט
His sword on all meat   ובחרבו את כל בשר
Many will be penetrated   ורבו חללי
Yahweh sanctifies and purifies upon the garden   —ISAIAH *(66:15-17)*

 **HE** flaming sword overthrew   (המתהפכת = *turned over scorching*)
To protect the way to the tree of life   —GENESIS *(3:24)*

Like Pharaoh, Caesar abused the tree of life. Jesus gave him a very hot bath:

[**JOHN SAID**]: Indeed I baptize you with water for after-thought
But He who comes after me is mightier than I...
He will baptize you with the Holy Spirit and with fire
His winnowing fork is in His hand
And He will clear His threshing floor   *(cf. DANIEL 2:31-45)*
Gathering His wheat into the barn
And burning up the chaff with unquenchable fire   —LUKE *(3:16-17)*

[**JESUS SAID**]: A baptism I have yet to be baptizing, and how restrained I am—until while it is accomplished   —LUKE *(12:50)*

    The Paganism practiced under Caesar trended into Pantheism, Animism, and heavy sadism. Cults and mysteries made empty promises of metaphysical prowess. Reptile was esteemed in equal stature with mammal. Unable to follow scholarly enterprise, the pop cultists doubted that there was any difference between Medusa and Minerva. Sympathetic magic habits blurred their vision of vital truth. Minerva did indeed wear Medusa's head as Aegis, but they read this upside down, thinking it indicated Minerva's secret wisdom was a penchant to predate on humanity. Son of Man cracked their sick foundations—with the two most important civic fires ever lit.

PAGAN TEMPLES TRUMPED ♪ ROME:	*YOU'RE FIRED!*
FIRE 64: OLDER FOUNDATIONS	**FIRE 80:** SHINIER TEMPLES
Every Temple dedicated by Rome's Kings	Temple of Serapis
Temple Romulus built to Jupiter Stayer	Temple of Isis
Evander's shrine to Hercules	Temple of Neptune
Temple Tullius built to Luna	Pantheon of the gods
Every Temple built for the Punic War	Temple of Veiovis
Holitorium Temple of Janus	Temple of Juno Moneta
Holitorium Temple of Spes	Temple of Virtus
Every Temple built for the Gallic War	Temple of the Capitoline Triad
Fascinus Beast Shrine by Vesta's Fire	Temple of Jupiter Optimus Maximus
☠☠☠☠☠☠ Sanctuary of Vesta ☠☠☠☠☠☠	☠☠☠ Rising Templum Vespasiani ☠☠☠
DIO HIST. *(62:16)*, SEUT. NERO *(38:121)*, TAC. AN. *(15:41)*	☠☠☠☠ DIO HIST. *(66:24)*, SEUT. TITUS *(8:3)* ☠☠☠☠

IF indeed it is righteous with God to repay with tribulation those who oppress you, then those of you who are oppressed: indulge with us in the revelation of the Master from heaven, Jesus, with his mighty angels, in flames of fire, awarding vengeance upon those who know not God, and upon those who don't hearken to the good news of *our* Master—Jesus.   — 2 *THESSALONIANS (1:6-9)*

I have come to set this estate on fire
           And whatever I will once it is kindled   — *LUKE (12:49)*

    BEHOLD I come like a thief   — *REVELATION (16:15)*

       IF the Master of the House   *(Master: Caesar; House: Imperial Rome)*
          Had known the hour of the night the thief was coming
            He would have stayed awake
            And not let his house get cracked up   — *MATTHEW (24:43)*

     THE day of the Lord   *(MALACHI 4:1)*
      Will come like the thief of night...
      The Foundations will be cracked up by hot fire...
      This estate and all works in it will be burnt   — 2 *PETER (3:10)*

WE did not use cleverly invented myths
When we introduced you to the building power
Of *our* Master—Jesus Christ
Instead we had been eyewitnesses to his majesty...
Thus we posses a prophetic message
That is altogether reliable
You would be wise to attend to it like a lamp   *(MATT 21:1-13)*
Shining in a dark place until day dawns
And in your hearts arises *Phos-phoros*...   *(Luci-fer in Latin)*
The present heavens and earth are reserved for a fire
           Being kept for the day of judgment
           And destruction of ungodly men
                     — 2 *PETER (1:16-3:7)*

              I Am   *(the fire survivor; cf. MALACHI 4:1)*
         both root and descendant of David
         the Bright Morning Star   — *REV (22:16)*

Venus is both the Morning and Evening Stars. "Morning Star" is *Helel Ben Sahar* in Hebrew: (הילל בן־שחר), in Greek: *Phosphoros* (φωσφόρος), Latin: *Lucifer*. The Latin Vulgate Bible uses the name "Lucifer" eight times: *ISA (14:12), 2 PET (1:19), JOB (11:17), JOB (38:32), PS (110:3), SIR (50:6), REV (2:28), REV (22:16)*. Only in *ISAIAH* might it be said to refer to a fallen angel. Yet *ISAIAH* only alludes to the Dawn Star to mock the Chaldean Empire's false start, for Persia would eclipse Chaldea's day in the sun after only one single century, while Egypt's day had arcked through three millennia. Anti-Christ Nero was not likened a harbinger of dawn—Jesus was.

THE woman that you saw is the great city... *(Roma)*
    She will be burned with fire
        For mighty is the Lord God who judges her...
All those who traded on the sea
Stood far off and cried out
As they saw the smoke of her burning...
"Alas ! The great city !...
In this hour she has been laid waste !"
Rejoice over her O Heaven
You Saints and Apostles and Prophets
Because God has made judgment דִּין دين
For you — against her ! ...
Hallelujah ! Smoke goes up from her !
Forever and ever !
          — REVELATION (17:18 –19:3)

> Basic Judeo-Christian moral values do not flow down from the erroneous dogmas of religious sects. Morality wells up from natural law, whereby rational humans choose to enforce behavior that leads to a world in which they would want all children to live. The texts of Monotheism point the way, but have been subverted by corrupt dogma. Much blame for the cancer of the "Black Mass" lays square in mainstream doctrinal errors. God will not be bound by religion, nor by non Biblical mythological theatrics.

JESUS did amazing wonder-works full of power
    Thus it is impossible for me to call Him* a mere man
      However, in view of His common nature   *(JN 20:31)*
  〈 They would not 〉 call Him* an angel
    (for many* came after Him in His name, and picked up His cross: MATT 10:7; cf. MK 11:29-33)
      —WARS Slavonic recension *(2:8:3)* *(Mead's 1924 translation is Theosophy)*

I will give Him* power over the Pagans...
    Like breaking vessels of a potter   *(an iconoclast)*
    He will shepherd them with a rod of iron   *(DANIEL 2:31-35)*
    Given to me by my Father...   *(PSALM 2:9)*
    And to Him* I will give the Morning Star *(and keys to death and Hades)*
        — REVELATION *(2:24-28)*

HE will baptize you with the holy wind
                  And with fire — MATT *(3:11)*

כג ויט משה את מטהו על השמים ויהוה
נתן קלת וברד ותהלך אש ארצה וימטר
יהוה ברד על ארץ מצרים

כד ויהי ברד--ואש מתלקחת בתוך
הברד כבד מאד--אשר לא היה כמהו בכל
ארץ מצרים מאז היתה לגוי *(EXODUS 9:22-26)*

COIN OF NERO WITH THE ELITE HEXAFORM
TEMPLE OF VESTA, GILT WITH THAI-LIKE
FLAMES: GROUND ZERO IN 64'S GREAT FIRE.

THE blaze in its fury ran first through the level portions of the city, then rose to the hills, whereof it again devastated every place below them. It outstripped all preventive measures, so rapid was the mischief, and so completely at its mercy this city... And no one dared to stop this mischief, because of incessant menaces from a number of persons who forbade the extinguishing of the flames, because again others openly hurled brands, and kept shouting that there was one who gave them authority, either obeying orders, or seeking to plunder more freely... The temples of the gods, and the porticoes devoted to their feasts, fell in yet a more widespread ruin... It would not be easy to enter into a computation... of the temples which were lost, many with the oldest ceremonial, such as that dedicated by Tullius to Luna, the great altar and shrine Evander raised to a sighting of Hercules, the temple of Jupiter the Stayer which Romulus founded, Numa's royal palace, and sanctuary Vesta, where the tutelary deities of the Roman people were kept—all were burnt. Some persons observed that the beginning of this conflagration was on the 19th of July, the very same day on which the Senones had captured and fired Rome *(the Senones were a Celtic tribe settled in Italy. They sacked and burnt Rome in 387 BC after the Romans had molested their diplomatic messengers—451 years before this fire.)* ... **Nero strapped the guilt for the fire, and inflicted the most exquisite tortures, on a class called Christians by the populace, a group hated for abominations** *(The TWELFTH LETTER OF SENECA AND PAUL states: "our own times bore Caligula ... the source of the many fires which Rome suffers is obvious. Yet if humble men could speak out about the reason without risk in this dark time, all would be obvious to all. Christians and Jews are commonly executed as contrivers of the fire. The criminal* is he whose pleasure is that of a butcher {i.e. cannibal}* though he veils himself with a lie. He is reserved for his due season ... He* vowed to death for all will be burned with fire.").* **Christus, from whom the word originates, suffered the extreme penalty under Tiberius' reign, under hands of one of our procurators, Pontius Pilate. Thus a most mischievous superstition, then checked for a moment, again broke out, not only in Judea which was the first source of said evil, but even in Rome, where all things hideous and shameful done in every part of the world, find their center and become popular. Accordingly, arrests first were made of all those openly making guilty claims. Then, by their**

This curious letter is dated 28 March 64 AD—107 days before 64's Great Fire.

knowledge, an immense multitude was convicted, not so much out of the crime of firing this city, as out of hatred against mankind. Mockery of every sort was added to their deaths. Covered with the skins of beasts, they were torn by dogs and perished, or were nailed to crosses, or were doomed to become torches and burnt to serve as a nightly illumination, when daylight had expired [in Nero's Vatican gardens].
—*Tacitus,* ANNALES: *(15.38-45)*

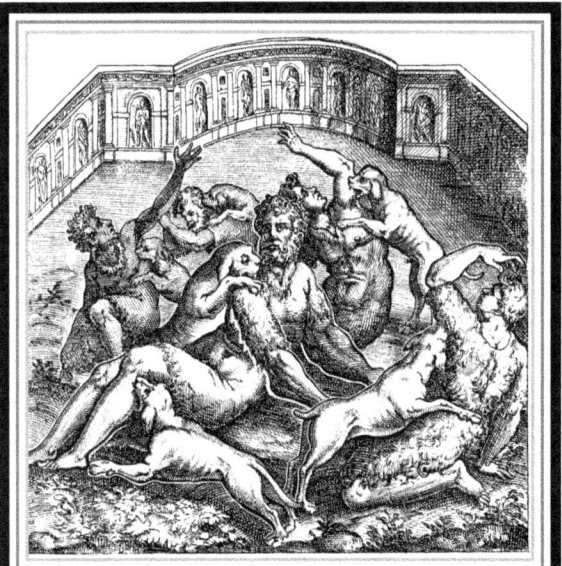

LEFT: Men are fed to dogs in the arena. BELOW: Capitoline Hill in the background of the hippodrome, where men are crucified, torched, and fed to lions. PAGE 131: Mirror-tiled projection of Blake's *Wise and Foolish Virgins.* Vesta's cult of the phallus *Fascinus,* used sexual "magic" to oppress:

Our Vestal Virgins have the [magic] power, by uttering a certain prayer, to arrest the flight of runaway slaves, and transfix them to the spot ...
—*Pliny,* NAT. HIST. *(28)*

John said... *"I only baptize you with water for repentance*
But the one who comes after me is harsher than I
I am not able to take off His sandals   (Exodus 12:11—His mission is urgent)
He will baptize you with fire and the Holy wind
The winnowing fork is in His hand
With it He will clear His threshing floor
He will gather the wheat into His barn
And the chaff He will burn with unquenchable fire"

— M*att* (3:11-12)

The kingdom of the heavens will be made like ten virgins
Who took their lamps   *(satire on Rome's Vestal Virgins)*
To come out and meet the bridegroom   *(there were 4-6 Vestals, hence 5 fools)*
But five of them were foolish and five of them were wise
For the foolish ones had brought their lamps
But did not bring oil with them
The wise ones took pots of oil with their lamps
Then the bridegroom was delayed   *(until lyric for Nero was perfected)*
So they all nodded and were sleepers   *(sleeper cells)*
And in the midst of the night
A cry was made   *(as clueless Nero took to the stage in Antium, Seneca banged the gong)*
"Lo ! The bridegroom is coming ! Come out and meet Him !"

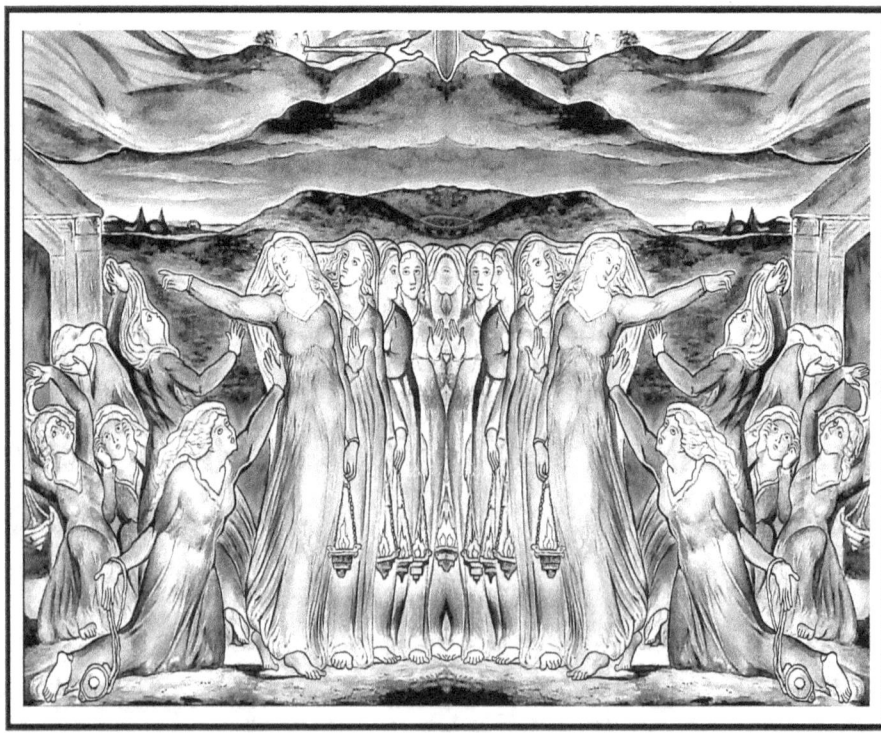

So the virgins rose up *(as Nero sang of Firing Troy before a chosen audience)*
And readied their lamps
The foolish said to the wise:
"Give us some of your oil—our lamps are going out!"
The wise replied: *"There's not enough for us and you*
Now go instead to those selling and buy for yourselves!"...
The bridegroom came *(Vestals Virgins magically wed Pontiff Maximus—often a Caesar)*
Those prepared were joined to him in the marriage-feasts
And the door was slammed... *(the lavish Patrician feasts were closed to the Plebeians)*
So be prepared for you know not the day nor hour
When the Son of Man comes   — MATT (25:1-13)

☙ Shouts of *"Divi Filius has given us authority!"* offered Christ's virgins a neat way to frame the fire upon Nero—son of the Imperial god Claudius. Tacitus begins his treatment of this disastrous fire in a segue, off his account of how Nero bottomed out in a freakish gay wedding, whereat Kaiser Nero rolled over on a couch, and passively took ritual intercourse from his favorite large man, in a scandalous public ceremony:

The bridal veil was put over the emperor; people saw the witnesses of the ceremony, the wedding dower, the couch and the nuptial torches. To be blunt, everything normally hidden by darkness when a [real] woman weds, was all made plainly visible. A disaster followed... *(outraged citizens joined the Jews in burning Rome)*
—*Tacitus*, ANNALES: *(15.37-38)*

The houses of leaders of old, still adorned with trophies of victory, and those temples of the gods vowed and dedicated by the kings, and later in the Punic and Gallic wars, along with whatever else interesting and noteworthy had survived from antiquity, were all burned ... Nero sang the whole of the "Sack of Ilium," in his regular stage costume.
—*Suetonius*, LIFE OF NERO *(38)*
(cf. Cassius Dio, ROMAN HISTORY 62:18:3 with ROMAN HISTORY 57:18:4-5)

Rome's oldest shrines burned after Josephus left Nero's dungeon. This fed rumors that Nero torched the city in order to play architect. Joe slipped back into Jerusalem after the Romans lost Masada in the post-fire confusion.

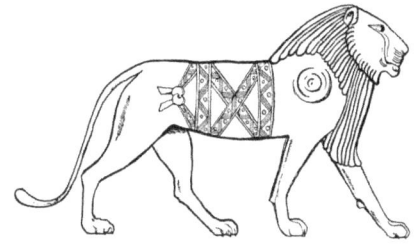

Jesus said:
> "I have food to eat that you haven't seen"

And the disciples asked each other:
> "Did anyone bring him something to eat?"

Jesus answered them:
> *"My food is that I may execute the will*
> *Of Him who sent me out*
> *So His work may be finished ...*
>> *I sent you to reap*
>> *That on which you have not labored*
>> *Others have done the hard work* ✴
>> *And you have reaped the benefits"*
>> — JOHN (4:32-38)

BOY JESUS WITH THE DOCTORS IN THE TEMPLE
UNDER THE ROMANS IN THE ANTONIA FORTRESS

Why were you seeking me
Don't you know it is my duty
To attend to my father's things?

LUKE 2:49

FORTRESS ANTONY: Power summit above Jerusalem, *Tower Antonia* loomed over the Temple, and housed most of two Roman cohorts at the ready. Grim Galileans took it with weapons they reaped from the Fortress at Masada. ✦
PAGE RIGHT: Coin of Vespasian with goddess *Pax Pacis,* who wields a caduceus against the snake plaguing the Imperial Via *(GEN 49:17, EX 7:12, MATT 10:16, JN 3:14).*

MATT (8:8)

Here at Masada was laid up grain in large quantities...
   Here was also oil and wine in abundance...
And all kinds of pulse and dates heaped together
Which Lazarus [son of Jarius] found there
When he and his Sicarii took it over...   *(Issa-char 'reapers' with their "sickles")*
There was also found there a large quantity
Of all sorts of weapons of war sufficient for Ten-Thousand men... 💣
The report tells how Herod
Prepared this fortress on his own account ✶
As a refuge against two kinds of danger
The one: of a multitude—for fear of the Jews 🍪
Lest they should depose him
And restore their former kings* to the government
   The other danger was even greater
   And more terrible
   It arose with Cleopatra Queen of Egypt   *(tagged by Cleophas)*
   Who did not conceal her intentions
   But spoke often to Antony...   *(who became like her slave)*
         —WARS *(7:8:4)* by the Ari of the Hasmoneans (aka Maccabeans)*

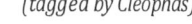

Then on the evening of the same day
   Being the first of Sabbaths   *(rest when Peace is won)*
And with the doors of where the disciples were being shut   *(sealed)*
For fear of the Jews 🍪   *(the most horrifying double-speak—backed up with brimstone)*
Jesus came and stood in the middle
And says to them: *"Peace Be Upon You!"*
         —JOHN *(20:19)*

   After Masada fell, the despoiled menorah was on public display in a new temple to the goddess of "Peace" (Pax Pacis). It was built with captive Jewish labor the Flavians dragged to the Roman capitol. Joe's disapproval of that Pagan trophy-shelf setting for the Temple treasure intensified, as this "Peace" meant slavery and death for Jews building the city's wonder-works.

POMPEII'S ANNIVERSARY GETS HOT

A flock of six hundred sheep was destroyed and statues split open
Some were driven out of their minds
And wandered about in helpless idiocy...
For what can one believe with any safety
If the world itself is shaken
And its most solid parts totter to their fall
Where indeed can our fears be bounded
If the one thing... which all things depend upon to hold them up
Begins to rock...
Where will the anxious ones run
When fear springs from the ground
And is drawn up from the earth's foundations?...

What is God?
Everything you see
And everything you don't see   *(cf. the NICENE CREED & JOHN 20:29)*

— Seneca on Pompeii's 62 AD earthquake, NATURALES QUAESTIONES (6:1-5)

Truth is the enemy of any state whose corruption outpaces its duty to its subjects. The first century Roman Empire was a very superstitious place. Pagan magic discounted the effect of individual effort. All happenings were subject to intercession by a god, or conflicts between gods. This world view grew manic by the time the Jews collided with the feet of the idol in Nebuchadnezzar's dream. Caesar began to assert his divinity over the rest of the population, in the guise of a superhuman father who was caring for earth's more ordinary children. Few of those who accepted the ordinary role could argue, as impressive marble projects rose everywhere. Such is the lot of those who can't read the reality in metaphor. It takes depth to see beneath surfaces, and forward to the age to come. Deeper thinkers are less distracted by pomp and glitz. Understanding the past is essential to peering behind the hypnotic masks of the present. Judaism was a level above its first century Pagan opponent, in that its metaphors had deep historical anchors. The story of Rome's founding was clever, but two bastards suckled by a predatory wild dog, can't compete with an entire underclass who united to quit the world's greatest empire. One says rise up and throw off your oppressors. The other says you may have been born a prodigy, but you are subject to the whim of a beast.

The Jews were delivered by Moses. The United States were redeemed by Washington and the founding fathers. The mythic twins who founded Rome had a she-wolf give them suck. Like Washington had his cherry tree, Rome's Capitoline wolf had a fig tree called *Ruminalis,* under which she nursed Romulus and Remus. A temple was built around this fig-fetish, and the lupine Julius Caesar planted a shoot from that original tree in the Roman Forum, right in front of his emasculated Senate:

In my opinion
    The origin of so great a city
  And establishment of an empire next in power to that of the gods
Is due the Fates   *(drafted Republican Livy, kicks soft at the pricks, to suggest: overdue)*
Vestal virgin Rhea was deflowered by force
Then when she gave birth to twins
She swore that Mars had fathered her illegitimate offspring...
But neither gods nor men
Protected her or her children from that king's cruelty...
He commanded the offspring to be tossed
Into the current of the River Tiber...
They exposed the boys on a floodplain nearby

Roman Forum with *Ruminalis* fig; the Capitoline Hill is in the distance.

Right where Fig Tree *Ruminalis* still stands...
A thirsty she-wolf coming from mounts nearby *(the seven hills of Rome)*
Directed her course to the cries of the infants
And offered her nipples
— HISTORIA ROMA *(1:4)* by Livy

Christian scholars date Paul's LETTER TO THE ROMANS to 58 AD, just as Nero plots to murder his own mother. Paul's instructions—to not rock the boat—can only be understood inside the entire war-plan:

Bless those persecuting you—bless and curse not...
Repay evil for evil to no one
Producing right things in front of all men
As much as you can, stay at peace with all men
Don't avenge on your own beloved
But give wrath its place
For indeed it has been written:
        "Vengeance is Mine!
        I will repay says the Lord"
But if your enemy is hungry feed him
If he should thirst give him a drink
For by doing this

You will heap coals of fire on his head°...
Let every soul be subject to the authorities above him
Indeed there is no authority if its not under God...
For rulers are not a terror to good works but to evil
—*Paul's LETTER TO THE ROMANS (12:17-13:3) (Rome: Joe's subject; the Pagans: no authority)*

Anyone who tries to read Paul's letter to the Romans, is lost without the historical context. These rhetorical clauses all hinge upon the fact that Nero was widely known to be a murderous tyrant:

Although at first his acts of wantonness, lust, extravagance, avarice and cruelty were gradual and secret, and might be condoned as follies of youth, yet even then their nature was such that no one doubted that they were defects of character and not due to his time of life. As soon as night fell he would put on a hat or a wig and go to the taverns or range about the streets playing pranks, which however were very far from harmless; for he used to beat men as they came home from dinner, stabbing any who resisted him and throwing them into the sewers *(Nero snuck out of the palace and partied like a spoiled rock star, but there was grave danger far all who spurned the affections of this brat who was escorted by soldiers; Nero had no safe word, and he left a wake of stiffs behind him)*... **Little by little however, as his vice grew stronger, he dropped jesting and secrecy, and with no attempt at disguise openly broke out into worse crime... Besides abusing freeborn boys and seducing married women, he debauched the vestal virgin Rubria. The freedwoman Acte he all but made his lawful wife, after bribing some ex-consuls to perjure themselves by swearing that she was of royal birth. He castrated the boy Sporus and actually tried to make a woman of him, and he married him with all the usual ceremonies, including a dowry and a bridal veil, took him to his house attended by a great throng, and treated him as his wife. (And the witty jest that some made is still current, that it would have been better for the world if Nero's father Domitius had had that kind of wife.) He took this Sporus with him to the assizes and marts of Greece, decked out with all the finery of the empresses and riding in a litter, and later at Rome through the Street of Images, fondly kissing him from time to time... he at last devised a kind of game, in which, covered with the skin of some wild animal, he was let loose from a cage and attacked the private parts of men and women, who were bound to stakes, and when he had sated his mad lust, was finished off by his freedman Doryphorus; for he was even married to this man in the same**

way that he himself had taken Sporus, going so far as to imitate the cries and lamentations of a maiden being deflowered.

—Suetonius, LIFE OF NERO *(26-29)*

When Paul associates idolatry with wanton homosexuality, the intent is not a condemnation of alternative lifestyles of love. Paul is making a political polemic against the boundlessly sadistic Caesars, who believed every citizen was their whipping boy. If a president or prime minister of today, were outed as behaving in the criminal manner of a Nero, both gay and straight alike would call for his head. People want and need strong rulers, but the man who abuses life is a weak thing imitating strength, trying to cover up his inadequacies with a self-serving chaos. The compliant masses gave Caesar reason to believe he was a god, and that everyone else was a lower animal subject to his whim, as he pretended godhood by sadistic example:

The wrath of God is being revealed from heaven against all the godlessness and wickedness of men who suppress the truth by their wickedness, since what may be known about God is plain to them, because God has made it plain to them. 🟊 **For since the creation of the world, God's invisible qualities—his eternal power and divine nature—have been plainly perceived, being understood from what has been made, so that men are without excuse. For although they knew God, they neither glorified him as God nor gave thanks to him, but their thinking became futile and their foolish hearts were darkened. Although they claimed to be wise, they became fools and exchanged the glory of the immortal God for images made to look like mortal man and birds and animals and reptiles. God gave them over in the sinful desires of their hearts to sexual impurity for the degrading of their bodies with one another. They exchanged the truth of God for a lie, and worshiped and served created things rather than the Creator— who is forever praised, Amen. God gave them over to shameful lusts. Even their women exchanged natural relations for unnatural ones. In the same way the men also abandoned natural relations with women and were inflamed with lust for one another. Men committed indecent acts with other men, and received in themselves the due penalty for their perversion** *(venereal disease and effeminacy).* **Furthermore, since they did not think it worthwhile to retain the knowledge of God, He gave them over to a depraved mind, to do what ought not to be done. They have become filled with every kind of wickedness, evil, greed and**

depravity. They are full of envy, murder, strife, deceit and malice. They are gossips, slanderers, God-haters, insolent, arrogant and boastful; they invent ways of doing evil; they disobey their parents. They are senseless, faithless, heartless, ruthless. Although they know God's righteous decree, that those who do such things deserve death, they not only continue to do these things, but applaud ☙ those who practice them.

—Paul's LETTER TO THE ROMANS (1:18-32)

Philosopher Seneca was recalled from exile, and drafted as an Imperial advisor. A captive in Nero's house, this Stoic Monotheist was forced to sit in a voluminous depth of depravity. Seneca was the ally Joe needed to fight the gods. When one plans to surreptitiously move half a million civilians off a battlefield, with no more than what they can run with, one does not want a committee full of sadists waiting on the shores to welcome the refugees. This was a world where children were bought and sold in the open, like meat in the supermarket. Brothels were full of captive innocents, dispensed for men to stroke their ego upon. Arenas were full of blood. The homosphere was on the road to death. To accept the Imperial Cult was to drink the poison of Jonestown. The infrastructure of this depraved state was too strong to fight head on. The idol had legs of steel.

The scholar Pliny the Elder (who died in an ash heap on the suburbs of Pompeii) said of Nero:

is entire rule revealed that he was the enemy of mankind

—Pliny, NATURAL HISTORY (7:4)

This was the leadership Rome offered to the world. Caesar was no true god, nor son of god. Caesar was not even a responsible parent. The Caesars were wolves. The same year Paul wrote ROMANS, something funny happened in the shadow of the Capitoline Mount; the fig tree *Ruminalis* in the Comitium on the Forum withered:

hat same year, the fact that the fig tree in the Comitium, which 840 years before had sheltered in infancy Romulus and Remus, was suddenly impaired by the decay of its boughs and by the withering of its stem, was accounted an ill omen

— 58 AD in ANNALES by Tacitus (13:58)

nd having seen a specific fig tree on the way
He came on it but found nothing
Merely leaves
And there He said to it:

ו כי גוי עלה על ארצי עצום ואין מספר
שניו שני אריה ומתלעות לביא לו
ז שם גפני לשמה ותאנתי לקצפה
חשף חשפה והשליך הלבינו שריגיה

> *"No more fruit from you until the age comes!"*
>
> And that fig tree immediately withered
> And having seen this, the disciples wondered, saying:
>> *"How did that fig tree suddenly wither?"*
>
> And Jesus answered them saying:
>> *"I tell you it is certain*
>> *If you have faith and don't doubt it*
>> *Not only this stroke to that fig tree can you perform*
>> *But even when you say to that very mount* (Capitolinus)
>>> *"Be lifted and cast into the Sea!"*
>> *It will come to pass"*
>>> — MATTHEW *(21:19-22)* *(cf. JOEL 1:6-7)*

Withering of the barren fig, is an episode *MARK* and *MATTHEW* set upon a returning to a "Holy City," after leaving Bethany (the town of Lazarus). The pericope is cued up on the morning after the tables are turned. The dial of this specific fig is calibrated by *REVELATION*, where events of Joe's career, scope into the Kitos War in the same way that the gospels scope events of the life of Jesus into those of the time of Josephus:

ow when they finish their testimony the beast will come up from the abyss and attack *them*, overpower *them* and kill *them*, and *their* bodies will be in the plaza of the great city which is spiritually called Sodom and Egypt *(Pompeii/Rome)* **which is also where *their* Lord was crucified**

—*REVELATION (11:7-8)(the two prophets are not the only "them" in this vanity)*

Jesus Christ was not crucified inside Jerusalem, and the plaza referred to is not within that Holy City's walls. Jewish boys who escaped from work gangs building the coliseum, were crucified in public spaces of Rome whenever they were recaptured. An underground was haunted by fugitives turning tricks. Meanwhile, Pompeii was a hub of child importation for the sex industry. That waterfront city on the volcano, had more brothels, full of more abused young slaves, than anywhere else in Italy—or the entire planet.

The majority of Romans, were good family-people oppressed by an evil. The Latin elite that made the transition from Republic to Empire, steered the economy towards a necrotic level of dependence upon slavery. Most of the ancient world took for granted that slavery was one of the natural states of man, but Julius Caesar upped the stakes, when he took one million Gauls as captives, and murdered the Republic with the proceeds. The founding of the Imperial Cult coincided with this chronic disease reaching acute stage. The colossal marbles of the dictators were symptomatic boils that needed irrigation. Jesus compounded medicinal devices for the cure. The Galilean recruited many Italian allies who were equally disgusted with the obnoxious insanity of the Caesars. Even Centurion wanted to save the little one.

When Joe falls off his horse in the war near Bethsaida, Joe is taken to Capernaum—hometown of Jesus. Popular metaphor speaks of a general being upon his horse when he is in command, and off his horse when he is not in command. The like idiom out of the wild west is *"I'm back in the saddle."* Joe was taken to his new home in Rome, after he fell off his horse and was captured—come easy, go easy:

osephus escaped in the war with the Romans, and in his own war with his friends, and was lead by Nicanor to Vespasian, but now all the Romans ran together to see him... Vespasian gave strict orders that he should be kept with great caution, as though he would, in a very short time, send him

to Nero.... Later, when everyone was ordered to leave, except for Titus and two of their friends, Josephus said to them: *"You O Vespasian think you have only taken Josephus himself captive, but I come as a messenger of greater tidings* (a prophet of the gospel)*, for had I not been sent to you by God, I know what was the law of the Jews in this case, and how it is fitting for generals to die. Are you going to send me to Nero? For what reason? Will not every successor to Caesar die until they are only left with you? You Vespasian are Caesar and Emperor—you and your son. Bind me now still tighter and keep me for yourself, for you O Caesar are not only lord over me, but over the land and sea and all mankind,*⚜*and surely I deserve to be kept in closer custody than I am now, so that I might be punished, if I rashly make a claim about the divine."* **When he had said this, Vespasian did not believe him at the time, but supposed that Josephus had said this as a cunning trick, aiming at his own preservation, but in a little while he was convinced, and believed what he said to be true.** *(a nailing only fully understood by Herod-Agrippa Sr.'s role in the successions of the false divinities Caligula and Claudius)* —WARS *(3:8:8-9)*

Joe's prediction proved to be all right until the rising sun, but that doesn't mean that it wasn't cunning. A plot is proven all the more clever when it succeeds. If Vespasian had any desire to become emperor, then Pagan superstition made it taboo for him to kill Joe, much less send Joe to Nero for torture and death. The Messianic design was way above Vespasian's head, as Joe dazzled him in rhetorical mirrors, to take custody of Rome:

Surely *I deserve to be kept in closer custody than I am now*
So that I might be punished (Joe called Caesar "Lord" only to thwart him...⚜
If I rashly make a claim on the divine"

The Caesars were rashly making divine claims over the entire habitable earth. Rome needed to be commandeered. When Joe was captured by Vespasian, Jesus was back in the saddle. Few were of the capacity to comprehend what was unfolding. Joe provides a key clause in *AGAINST APION*:

I myself have composed a true history of that whole war, and all the particulars that occurred therein, as having been concerned with all its transactions; for I acted as general of those among us who are called Galileans, as long as it was possible for *us* to make any opposition. I was then seized upon the Romans, and became a captive. Vespasian also, and Titus, had kept me under a guard, and forced me to attend[4] them continually *(two robbers were finished while being attended to[4], while the third still lived).* **At the first I was put into bonds;**

but was set at liberty afterwards, and sent to accompany Titus when he came from Alexandria to the siege of Jerusalem, during which time there was nothing done that escaped my knowledge, for what happened in the Roman camp I saw and wrote down carefully. And what information the deserters brought, I was the only man that understood them.
—*Josephus in AGAINST APION (1:9)* ⁵*(telescopes dial like a series of matryoskas)*

Surely Josephus could not have been the only Hebrew translator in the Roman camp. Even if Josephus had been a traitor—and from way back before he played his surrender to Vespasian—the Flavians still would never have trusted him to process intelligence without the security of additional translators. A traitor is worthy of the least trust from any employer who knows him to be capable of treachery. There is however a logical alternative Joe leaves the reader: moles deserted to deliver Joe intelligence in a code that only Joe understood. Their symbolic communication was above the heads of the other translators who were working for the Romans. Joe's capture by Vespasian was plotted in order for Joe to be able to act as general of the Galileans for as long as it was possible to for them to make any opposition, and the Galileans did hold out in Jerusalem until 70 AD—three years after Joe was captured. Galileans opposed the Romans at Masada until 73 AD. Then the cross of the opposition was picked up by Cyrene, and Joe was accused of helping this walking dead Galilean opposition from Rome.

The drama was complex. Even during Jerusalem's siege, multiple parties suspected Matthew's son:

or when the siege of Jotapata was over, and I was among the Romans, I was kept under guard with every consideration, Vespasian providing me with every mark of honor. I even took a certain virgin for myself... *(cf. Joe in LUKE 3:23)...* **I was sent with Titus to the siege of Jerusalem. I was frequently in danger of death, both from the Judeans, who were very eager to get me under their power for the sake of revenge, and from the Romans, who whenever they suffered a defeat, imagined that it was the consequence of my treachery... Now I was sent by Titus Caesar with Cerealius and a thousand horsemen, to a certain village called Thecoa, to assess whether the terrain was suitable for building a fenced camp. On my way back from there I saw many prisoners who had been crucified, and recognized three who had been my close associates. My soul was burdened and I went to Titus and told him so. He immediately directed that they be taken down, and receive therapy and medical care. Unfortunately two were finished** *(τελευτάω • accomplished ˢ)* **while being attended to⁴, but the third lived.** ˢ*(cf. θεραπεύω and προσεδρεύειν)*

—*LIFE OF JOSEPHUS (75)*

Joe communicates in stealth, crunching words in the several layers of zip-filing evident in this pericope. Three men are crucified at Thecoa, but one manages to survive by the intercession of *Joseph son of Matthew*. Likewise, three men are crucified on Golgotha, but one manages to survive by the intercession of *Joseph of Arimathea*. Joseph asks Titus to take the body down at Thecoa. Joe asks Pilate to take the body down outside Jerusalem. The town of Thecoa was nearest to Bethlehem, and in *LIFE* Josephus marries a virgin. In *MATTHEW* Joseph marries the virgin Mary, and she gives birth to Jesus at Bethlehem. Pilate killed the Jesus whom gospel paints as a simile of the Jerusalem Temple. Titus killed the Jerusalem Temple. In *AGAINST APION*, Joe notes that he was made to attend to two robbers named Vespasian and Titus who are hung up with Joe, being nailed by their own superstition and desire. Only Joe survives all the nails.

A blood-feud at Thecoa figures in the plot to redeem King David's son Absalom, where a woman from Thecoa tries to trick Messiah David:

The woman from Thecoa said:
  "Then let the king invoke his God Yahweh
  To prevent the avenger of blood
  From adding to the destruction
  So that my son will not be destroyed"

King David answered:
  "As surely as Yahweh lives
  One hair of your° *son's head will not fall to the ground"*
    — 2 *SAMUEL* (14:11) (cf. *JUDGES* (17:4-18:21) with 2 *SAMUEL* (25-26); °*David's son*)

This scene is alluded to in the *Little Apocalypse* of *LUKE*, which treats the destruction of Jerusalem in 70 AD:

All men will hate you because of me
  But a hair of your heads will not perish
  When you see Jerusalem surrounded by Armies
  Know that the hour of her desolation has come near
    —*LUKE* (26:17-19) (cf. *MATT* 10:22 & *JOHN* 15:21: *a few will survive to procreate*)

Joe tried to explain himself to his Jewish critics. Few were willing to listen. A clash of values made some desolation inevitable. The righteousness of Moses was on a collision course with the sadism of Imperial idolatry, as had been foretold in the *BOOK OF DANIEL*. Joe's ministry to the captives was a strategy in a world war that highlighted two sets of values struggling for domination of the planet. To smash the idol's foot, redeemer-Joe needed to bring the fight to Rome. The rebel leader Simon Bar Giora camped at Thecoa before he ravaged the Edom homeland of the Herodians, whose adultery had prompted rebel war-codes—wherein "Edom," "Babylon," "Sodom" and

"Egypt" stood for Rome, well before Titus burned Jerusalem. Soon thereafter the Flavians were erecting a huge arena as a memorial to their victory. Rome would have a rival of the pyramids, in its own world wonder—big death via bloody pain as pop culture.

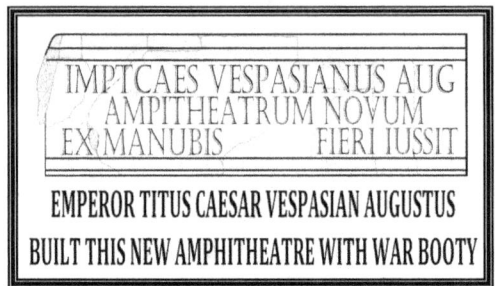

EMPEROR TITUS CAESAR VESPASIAN AUGUSTUS BUILT THIS NEW AMPHITHEATRE WITH WAR BOOTY

The Flavian Amphitheatre is the sickest concrete Joe points at with his code-phrase **"works in Egypt"**:

of the young men he chose the tallest and most beautiful, and reserved them for the triumph, and as for the rest of the multitude who were above seventeen years old, he put them in bonds and sent them to the works in Egypt *(κατ' Αἴγυπτον ἔργα).* **Titus also sent a great number into the provinces, as a present to them, that they might be destroyed upon their theatres, by the sword and by wild beasts, but those that were under seventeen years old were sold for slaves** [at public auctions].

—WARS *(6:9:2)* *(on "Sodom and Egypt" as Rome, see how GILL'S EXPOSITION begins at REV 11:8)*

The younger captives were sent to market. The littlest ones on the block wound up in Sodom's brothels or as its house-boys. Many in their later teens were taken to work as menial laborers supporting pet projects of the Imperial house: cutting a canal in Corinth, digging tin in Cornwall, and building the coliseum in Rome. Those who refused to shovel, were sent as victims to far-flung arenas to be slain as entertainment. Jewish captives toiled on the new Flavian Amphitheatre for a decade. The rebel nation was humiliated in the capitol's dust. Bronze letters at the arena entrance championed their long torturous suffering. The colossal win of Lazarus was avenged inside an equal rout by a ring of graven idols. Human flesh was consumed in the concrete bowl for entertainment and revenge. Gourmet murder of cosmic dimensions proved Rome was safe. Or did it? The guts of the intelligentsia and middle class were fed up with the insulting magic diet.

The boys taken to slave at wonder-works in Rome urgently needed a Rabbi. If Oscar Schindler could save Jewish life in the heart of the Nazi military industrial complex, then certainly the freedman Josephus Flavius could do his part under the protection of nails he drove into the Imperial House. Titus indulged Joe's pleas in Thecoa; money could persuade Titus to oblige Joe's petitions in Rome. When

bad-boys and escapees were crucified in the city spiritually called "Sodom and Egypt," Joe could buy their lives, along with the lives of those injured and disabled at slave labor. Jews still held enormous wealth. Manumission money could be solicited in place of the temple tax no longer due from Parthia's Jews. Those captives Joe couldn't redeem, he could smuggle on an underground railroad. Catacombs were full of young Jewish fugitives trying to eke out an existence anyway they could. Which Rabbi would lead the children of the darkest night yet on earth? Josephus the Arimathean accoutred necropolitan hide-outs in vaults volcanic:

ⁿὸ behold an advisor came named Joseph (to sue Rome for divorce)
(As he was a good and righteous man (MATT 27:57 adds "rich")
He did not agree with the plan and the work of them) (DAN 2:44)
From Arimathea ♆ (Lion of Matthias: 1 MACC 2:19-24; Ari-Matityahu: lion gifted from Yahweh)
A Judean populace oriented to receive the Kingdom of God ⚰
He went to Pilate and begged for the body of Jesus (MATT 5:10, 19:14)
And having taken it down he wrapped it in a linen cloth אֲרִי מַתִּתְיָהוּ
And established it in a tomb cut in rock (a mine deep under mount Capitoline)
In which not was no one not yet laid (οὗ οὐκ ἦν οὐδεὶς οὔπω κείμενος)
—LUKE (23:50-53) (Ἰωσήπου τοῦ Ματθίου; ⚰ cf. MATT 8:34, LUKE 17:21, MARK 10:15—reincarnate)

The drama of Jesus under Pilate, is parsed to telescope the Son of Man's rise under Titus. *JOHN (19:17)* names the crucifixion site in Greek as *Kraniou (i.e. Cranium),* meaning *[Place] Of the Skull;* the Hebrew is given in Greek characters as *Golgotha,* which plays on the actual Hebrew word for skull— *gulgoleth* (גֻּלְגֹּלֶת). Wordplay replaces the (glt) of the last syllable with (gt), which, as a word of mystical origins (גט), signals a writ of divorce or manumission. The Latin title of Rome's *Capitoline Hill: "Capitolinum" (cf. caput; capitalis),* does, in fact, mean precisely: *[Place] "Of the Skull."* Varro *(LL V.31)* and Livy *(I.55),* both tell that the hill was named *Capitolinum* after a huge human skull was found by workmen laying foundations for Jupiter's temple. In 80, Joe fired this head⊚, while the deified Vespasian's temple was under construction at the foot of the hill. Custodians of the Holy City on its summit worried; squatters filled caverns under their feet *(MT 27:62-65, REV 11:8):*

HE soil on which the city of Rome is built ... is of volcanic origin ... Three strata appear, one above the other: the uppermost is the so-called *pozzolano,* **earth from which the Romans, by an admixture of lime, prepared their excellent cement; next is a stratum of tufa, made up half of earth and half of stone; the lowest stratum is composed of stone. From the earliest times the lowest layer was worked as a stone quarry, and, both in the lowest and uppermost strata, irregularly hewn galleries are discovered everywhere, as in the Capitoline Hill*.**
—*from "Roman Catacombs,"* CATHOLIC ENCYCLOP. *1908.* (*on which the Lord was skewered)

The ranks of any oppressor include good people. Among those supervising imperial work gangs, were certainly men who knew love. Relationships between captives and wardens developed for a decade. Still, boys who became so sick they could no longer work, were slated for death. Joe couldn't just gallop into the coliseum like a cowboy to the rescue, for Centurion was not able to receive Joe under his cover without blowing it. Joe would have to heal the Centurion's beloved from a distance, sending clean linen for boys to make their escape. Poor Jewish wretches would excite alarms if they were seen running in the streets wearing the rags they wore at the construction site. Once a run-away boy reached a hideout, he was offered healing. A slave who broke a limb at the work site was finished, unless he could be snuck out and lowered down into the catacombs for treatment. 'Marys' from Judea and Galilee—valued servants in wealthy households of the city—brought herbs and aloe, and administered medical care and therapy. All this time a remounted Josephus was composing, in Nahum's new hiding place:

H̲e having entered into Capernaum moreover *(cf. Joe's fall in LIFE (72):*
'I sprained my wrist and was carried to Capernaum ... I called for doctors")
A Centurion came to Him begging and saying:
"Lord! my boy is laid in the house paralyzed *(the coliseum)*
Grievously tormented" *(my boy: my "pais"—a servant youth from whom sexual service was usually required; LUKE 7:2 gives "duolos"—slave)*
And He says to him:
"I having come will heal him!"
Now the Centurion said:
"Lord! I am not secure enough to have you enter under my cover
But only say the word *(give the instructions)*
So that my boy may be healed"
—MATT (8:5-13)

Joe released his epic work WARS OF THE JEWS while the Flavian Amphitheatre was at the height of its construction. The black sense of humor sprouts from tufa deposited during and after the war. The reader justly wonders how deep the hyperbole seeps into the record. If boys who refused to crush and carry rock were sent to public tortures in provincial amphitheatres, then what was Caesar's final plan for the menial crew building the colossal torture chamber, once the usefulness of these boys as human backhoes and wheelbarrows was finished, and the stands were filled with bloodlust waiting for victims? What host would be the opening act at the Flavian Amphitheatre? Great Herod had also built amphitheatres in Jerusalem and Jericho, and planned a monstrous show for his own exit. At Herod's death there was to be a mass human sacrifice of famous captives, collected from cities throughout the country. Herod planned to force the nation to mourn the exit, of a triumphant client king, who had pushed them up to a Roman cliff:

erod then turned around and returned to Jericho, in such a sad state of health as though he were just about to die, when he proceeded to attempt a horrid wickedness; for he got together the most illustrious men of the whole Jewish nation, out of every village ☻, into a place called the Hippodrome, and shut them in there. He then called for his sister Salome, and her husband Alexas, and made this speech to them: *"I have no doubt that the Jews will celebrate the anniversaries of my death, however it is in my power to receive mourning by another method, and thus have a splendid funeral, if you will just follow my instructions. Carefully deploy soldiers to surround these men that I have just taken into custody, and slay them immediately upon my death, then every family of theirs and all of Judea, will weep at my death whether they want to or not"...*

(As horrible as Herod's sister Salome was, the ugliness of Herod's insane spectacle was too much for her visions of a happy future):

Before the soldiers knew of Herod's death, Salome and her husband came out and dismissed those that were in bonds, whom the king had commanded to be slain, and told them that he had changed his mind, and would have every one of them sent to their own homes. When these men were gone, Salome, told the soldiers the king was dead, and got them and the rest of the multitude together to an assembly, in the amphitheatre at Jericho.

—WARS (1:33:6-8)

The new Joshua surrounded the new Jericho —underground. The directives of Moses were engaged in a global conflict with no limit or safe-word. The goal was life and freedom. Joe's later work *ANTIQUITIES* points to Herod's amphitheatres at Jericho and Jerusalem as the first undeniable signs that Herod had no respect for the family. To Herod it was all just a game:

W̲hen Herod returned to his kingdom, he found his house in a tumult, with his wife Mariamne *(of the 'Ari-mathea' line from Matthias; she was thus Joe's blood relation, as were her Herodian offspring: cf. the "relations" of ROMANS 16:10-11 and ANT 18:1:6)* ☼ and her mother Alexandra very agitated ... Mariamne realized that the king's love for her was entirely hypocritical, and more of a show than a reality, she decided it was entirely fictitious ... and thus Mariamne was lead to her execution ... Alexandra lived in Jerusalem at this time, and being informed of the condition Herod was in *(over his murder of Mariamne)*, she tried to get her family in possession of the fortified places about the city... Messengers were sent to Herod to inform him of her plot, so he made no further delay and had her slain ... and after a further slaughter, of the innocent *Bar Babbas* ... the kingdom was entirely in Herod's power, and there was no one remaining of enough dignity to stop what he did against the Jewish law. It was by this means that Herod revolted from the laws of his country, and by the introduction of foreign practices corrupted their ancient covenant *(constitution)*—a covenant which should have remained inviolable to this day. In this way we afterwards became guilty of great wickedness, while those religious observances which used to lead the multitude to piety *(liberté, égalité, fraternité)* were neglected; for in the first place, he scheduled solemn games to be celebrated every five years in honor of Caesar, and built a theatre in Jerusalem, and a very great amphitheatre on the plain. Both of them were indeed lofty works, but against Jewish customs,Ω for we have had no such shows delivered down to us as fit to be used or exhibited by us *(1 MACCABEES 1:14-24)*, but nevertheless he celebrated these spectacles every five years in the most solemn and extravagant manner ... He spared no pains to lure all of the most famous people at such sport, to come to this contest for victory ... Moreover the theatre was circled by trophies all made of the finest gold and silver, with engravings of the great exploits of Caesar, and those nations which he had conquered in war ... He also made a great preparation of wild beasts, and of lions *("ari" in Hebrew)* themselves in great abundance, and of such

other beasts as were of uncommon strength, or of such a sort as was rarely seen. These were prepared either to fight with one another, or so that men who were condemned to death could fight with them ... Now foreigners certainly were greatly shocked at the vastness of the expenses exhibited here, and at the great dangers that were to be witnessed, but to the natural Jews this was no better than a dissolution of their customs, for which they had so great a veneration. It appeared also no better than shameless impiety, to throw men to wild beasts just to delight the spectators ... but it was the trophies that were the most distasteful to the Jews, for they saw them as images, displayed as they were with armor around them, and they were displeased with them, because it was not the custom of their country to pay honor to such images *(which were signs that the nation was being sent into slavery by Herod the Narcissus).*
 —ANT *(15:7:1-15:8:1)*   ארי מתתיהו

At this pinnacle of Joe's name game, the *Bar-Babbas* prompt *Ari-Mathea* to slash into *Bar-Matthias,* while *Bar-Babbas* and *Barsabbas* foreshadow the *Son of the Father* in Jesus *Bar-Abbas*. An even more terrible flight into the Egyptian^Ω by Cleophas avoids the slaughter of innocents, while Mariamne meets her death because Joseph loved her. The way the secret disciple takes Jericho is autobiographically tweaked into interlace overload, by one whose reborn epithet *Ari-Matthias,* bares his claws as the Hasmonean Lion *(1 MACC 2:24-25, LIFE 1)*. God sent a gift that avenged Herod's innovations by pouncing on the guiltiest thieves in their own theatre—paws down on Caesar.

Recognition that telescopes to passions in the 70's, are zip-filed inside lines of four variant accounts of a passion in the 30's, does not indicate that Jesus did not exist, or indeed rise. This is the same cautionary note, inserted into the packaging that reveals how Jesus is offered up as a parabolic mask, worn by the entire Messianic body of Christ at war with Pagan Rome. Crucifixion was Rome's method of punishing these rebels, and the true passion Jesus suffered and conquered, offered a poetic recruiting device to reseed the field of the Lord's work, while memorializing those who picked up his cross and followed after Him. When unzipping the literary codes, the exact method of Christ's crucifixion is one of the puzzles employed to key collation.

At the capitol **"works in Egypt,"** broken limbs meant death. Only the gospel of *JOHN* weaves a Paschal lamb allusion to *ZECHARIAH* and *EXODUS*, by piercing Caesar's spit roasted Jesus, while those to the right and left have their legs broken. The construct builds on *DEUTERONOMY*:

> **I**f a man guilty of a capitol offense is put to death
> And his body hung on a tree
> You must not leave his body on the tree overnight
> Be sure to bury him the same day
> Because anyone hung on a tree is cursed by the gods *(pl: "Elohim")*
> Don't pollute land your God Yahweh gives you as an inheritance
>
> —*DEUTERONOMY (21:22-23)*(cf. PSALM 82:6 & JOHN 10:34)

Rome's gods usually complied with this native custom during peacetime; Philo complains that Procurator Flaccus did not follow this usual concession to Jewish Law. Philo's passage reads like a tease, with a mute poke at Rome with a taboo topic—the iconoclastic Jesus:

> **I** know of cases when on the eve of a holiday of this kind
> People who had been crucified were taken down
> And their bodies delivered to their relatives
> Because it was believed fitting to give them a burial
> And permit them the ordinary rights... ♠ *(they broke no Jewish law)*
> But Flaccus gave no orders
> To take down those who had died on the cross
>
> —*Philo, FLACCUS (10:83)* ♠ *(instead of breaking Jewish law they were enforcing it)*

The variant in *JOHN* highlights a sarcastic element in Roman sadism. The standard mode of death in crucifixion was asphyxiation. The feet were fixed in a position above the man's stature, to prevent locking of the knees. This put the body's weight upon the arms. The breastbone pressed against the wind pipe and lungs, which caused oxygen restriction. If the victim did not use muscle to reduce the grave bone pressure against his wind, he would suffocate after a number of hours that depended upon his mass. Breaking legs was an excessively brutal alternative finish. The legs could simply be unfastened, or he could be slain by a spear or sword blow as pointed out by *JOHN'S* variant. The Romans did all they could to prolong the deaths of these naked and mutilated men, who were left on the cross to be eaten by birds, rats, and dogs after they had expired. The spoiled wine on a stick was used like smelling salts to taunt and revive the victim, so that he would not pass-out and die without further suffering. Breaking legs fit the Roman need to always have the last sick word. The Romans could appear to concede to Jewish law by allowing the body to removed before night fell, but trade one brutality for another equally fierce and even more shocking. Yet there is more to *JOHN'S* treatment of these wounds. The simile linking Passions in the heart of Rome to the Passions before Jerusalem's walls, is found in an anomalously tight body treatment, which better fits the setting of bones in the shadow of a rising Egyptian pyramid, than it fits the typical Hebrew faith in a resurrection worked by God's hands—not conjured by rich men with redemption money, or physicians with aloe, spices, and strips of linen:

Therefore the Jews went to Pilate
    Asking that their legs might be broken
        And the bodies of them taken away
        So the bodies might not remain on the cross on the Sabbath
    For it was the day of the Preparation for Passover
And that Sabbath Day was a high one (EXODUS 12:16)
Therefore the soldiers came
And did break the legs of the first one
And then also those of the other that was crucified with Him
However when they came to Jesus they saw that He was dead
And His legs they did not break (EXODUS 12:46—He is the Paschal lamb)
But one of the soldiers grabbed a spear and pierced His side
And immediately blood and water spurt out (like a roasted Paschal lamb)
And He who has seen has born witness
And the testimony of Him is true
And that one who remembers speaks true things
So that you might be persuaded
That these things happened
So the scripture might be fulfilled:

   "Not one of His bones will be broken" (Ex 12:46, NUMBERS 9:12, PSALM 34:20)
And yet another scripture says:

   "They will watch Him whom they pierced" (ZECH 12:10, REV 1:7)
After these things the Pilate was petitioned by Joseph[us]*
(He of Arimathea—who was a disciple of the Joshua (Jesus = Joshua)
But in secret for *Fear of the Jews*) (code name for the immortal plot)
To retrieve the body of the Joshua
And the Pilate gave permission
He thus went and took away the body of Him...
They took the body of the Joshua and bound it in linen cloths$^\Omega$
With the spices... (myrrh and about eight pounds of aloe)
After the Jewish burial customs (psyche!—they're at works in 'Egypt')$^\Omega$

   —JOHN (19:31-40)

MARK (15:46) sets this puzzle using the generic *eneileo* (ἐνειλέω), which means "to wrap around" with no indication of how intensely the limbs are dressed. The word choice fractures as the treatments at MATTHEW (27:59) and LUKE (23:53); both use the Greek *entulisso* (ἐντυλίσσω), which similarly indicates no more than "to wrap." However LUKE *(24:12)* indicates this wrapping was worked with strips—"little linens," Ω (i.e. bandages: *othonia*: ὀθόνια)—which tells the reader that Joe did not lay His bruised stiff in any *Shroud of Turin*; this eases the seeker into the further word break cast by JOHN *(19:40),* which uses the Greek *edesan* (ἔδησαν) which means "to bind." The Egyptian faith in rebirth required a mummification process, which did bind the embalmed body tightly with strips of cloth. The therapeutic setting of a broken limb, is the only similar practice fitting Jewish customs.

Capitoline Hill from Via Portuensis

 # SIMPLY SIMON

After the martyrdom of James, then the conquest of Jerusalem *(by the Galileans)* **immediately followed. It is said that the apostles and disciples of the Lord who were still living all gathered together from every direction, together with those who were related to the Lord by the flesh (for most of them were also still living). Now they took council as to who was going to succeed James. They unanimously chose Simon, he of Cleopas... Some say he was the Lord's *brother*, because Cleopas was of Josephus.** —ECCLES. HIST. *(3:11)*

The name *Bar Giora* means "Son of a Proselyte." Simon the Zealot ☉ (father of Lazarus, brother of Jesus, uncle of Josephus), is given this literary name by Joe to prophesize about the ultimate victory that would be won by God's inspired word over the Pagan ninnies of Rome. Gentile recruits from eastern shores of the Galilee who fought against the empire with their Jewish friends, are described facetiously by Joe at the loss of Magdala in WARS *(3:10:10)*; these martial proselytes are mirrored by Gentile Christians which Joe and Seneca's efforts planted deep into the ash rock of Rome. When Simon was strangled in the Forum, and thrown off the Tarpeian Rock so many times ☠, a critical mass of *second-generation* Roman Christians was outraged:

Now the last part of this pompous show was at the Temple of Jupiter Capitolinus, and when they arrived they stood still ✋, for the ancient Roman custom was to freeze until someone brought the news that the general of the enemy was slain. This general was Simon the son of Giora, who in this triumph had been the lead among these captives ... when it was reported that he was finished,✶ then all the people let out a cheer of joy ... for this was a festival-day for the city of Rome, celebrated for the victory obtained by their armies over their enemies, for the end that was now gained for their civic miseries, and for the commencement of their hopes of future prosperity and happiness ... —WARS *(7:5:6)*

Joe uses Simon's capture to foreshadow a coming revenge; hundreds died in the sadistic Triumph of Vespasian and Titus. Simon rises up at the temple on the third day in WARS *(7:2:1)*:

This Simon, during the siege of Jerusalem, was in the upper city; but when the Roman army was gotten within the walls, and were laying the city waste, he then took the most faithful of his friends with him, and among them some that were stone-cutters, with those iron tools which belonged to their occupation, and as great a quantity of provisions as would suffice them for a long time, and let himself and all them down into a certain subterranean cavern that was not visible above ground. Now they went onward along it without disturbance as far as had been dug of old; but where they met with solid earth, they dug a mine under ground, and this in hopes that they should be able to proceed so far as to rise from under ground in a safe place, and by that means escape. But when they came to make the experiment, they were disappointed of their hope; for the miners could make but small progress, and that with difficulty also; insomuch that their provisions, though they distributed them by measure, began to fail them. And now Simon, thinking he might be able to astonish and elude the Romans, put on a white frock, and buttoned upon him a purple cloak Ω, and appeared out of the ground in the place where the temple had formerly been. At the first, indeed, those that saw him were greatly astonished, and stood still ✋ where they were...

I AM LEGION ✺ FOR WE ARE MANY			
MATTHEW *(8:28-34)*	**MARK** *(5:1-20)*	**LUKE** *(8:26-39)*	**WARS** *(4:7:11-10:12)*
Gadarenes: Two violent demon possessed men coming out from the tombs.	Gerasenes: A man with an evil spirit who lived in the tombs, unbindable with chains. **Simon freed Zion's slaves:** *WARS (4:9:3)*	Gerasenes; (variants read Gadarenes and Gerghesenes): A demon possessed man in the tombs.	Vespasian first takes Gadara and next Gerasa: Emancipator Simon "Bar Giora" is a Gerasene who rises from a cavern.
A Roman Legion had up to 6000 men divided into six cohort-centuries. 6000 Jewish women and children who made a "flight" from Gischala are killed by Roman Legionnaires.			
"a herd of pigs"—the Galilee's east shore was Gentile; *WARS* mentions a "mighty prey" of animals captured, but no pigs (they ran away).	"about 2000" possessed pigs fly to their rebirth in the Sea of Galilee, which is a pool of Jordan River fresh-water. Gentiles are baptized with Jews. "Giora" = "proselyte".	"a herd of pigs" flies into the water; John baptized new Christians in the Jordan—many Greeks among them.	"about 2,200"—among whom are those who fled Gadara—are captured while a "prodigious number" fly into the Jordan River to drown.

SIMON SAYS BOO

OUT OF HIS MOUTH
Rev 1:16
CAME A SHARP DOUBLE-EDGED SWORD
καὶ ἐκ τοῦ στόματος αὐτοῦ ῥομφαία δίστομος ὀξεῖα ἐκπορευομένη

Publication of Joe's WARS, was followed up by the end of Vespasian. Pompeii was soon buried beneath a huge pile of volcanic ash. As the eldest Jewish war-boys in the brothels were reaching 24 years old, tortures became more brutal and cutting. Sick harvests were ended by brimstone. An unpleasant eruption greeted the deification of the Imperial Cult's new god. Soon, like a president visiting his gulf coast after a great ecological disaster, Titus left game-town for a working weekend on the new black sand beaches of Napoli. The son of the new god Vespasian was there for moral and financial support, inspecting recovery efforts one year after Sodom was gagged. But while Titus was away, the bigger cat did play. An army of the presumed dead rose out from the dark depths of the city. They fired the hill and cracked its idols. Jesus was reborn in a host of rough trade, maimed casualties with faultily set fractures, and the odd spectacle with stigmata. Some ran up slope to the houses of horror. Others limped up the hill at a pace. All the boys brandished torches. Connect the bloody dots:

I saw many prisoners who had been crucified
And recognized three
They had been my close associates
My soul was burdened
And I went to Titus and told him so
He immediately directed that they be taken down...
Two were finished[†] **while being attended to**   [†](τελευτάω • *accomplished*)
But the third lived   (JOHN 19:30: *When Jesus took the sour-wine He said: "It is finished"*[†]...)
        —LIFE OF JOSEPHUS (75)   (*... then He sent forth His wind*)

This same man went to Pilate   (*telescope to Titus*)
   And asked for the body of Jesus   (*asked for His injured Host*)
      Then he took it down and wrapped it in a linen cloth
   And laid it in a rock hewn tomb
   Where not was no one not yet laid
   It was the day of the preparation
And the Sabbath was beginning
The women who had come with him from Galilee followed
And they saw the tomb and how his body was laid
Then they returned and prepared spices and ointments
                                —LUKE (23:50-56)

ENTRANCE FRESCO TO THE HOUSE OF POMPEII'S IMPERIAL CULT HIGH PRIEST
CAPTIVE DANIEL IS ROASTED AS PRIAPUS (with restored foreskin) **:** The boy's shin numbers *Iudaean* mystery meat as number *I* on the menu—weighed less than a sack of *Iudaea Capta* coinage. He is reddish haired, roasted bronze, leaning next to a commercial fire poker, against a steaming oven. The sickle is repurposed as a butcher's tool; two slash into his upper body, and rack him from behind. The Imperial cultists endulged in magical cannibalism upon a table of mysteries authored by Caligula Caesar. This house, of cult priest *A. Vetti*, had brothel scenes in a strange kitchen, with a statue of Priapus reaping meat by the real stove. Medicine was delivered hot.

And the curtain of the temple was torn in two
From top to bottom *(proving Roman gods effete up to the capitol by Jove)*
Now when the Centurion who stood facing Him
Saw He breathed his last in this way *(exhaling on Rome's Capitoline Holy of Holies)*
He said: "Truly This Man was God's Son!" *(ROMANS 8:14-30)*
Moreover there were women from far away *(all the way from Judea & Galilee)*
Watching after Him *☆(note LIFE 75: "I thought of the one thing that might give me the most comfort in my calamities, and so I asked Titus that my own family might have their freedom;" see also WARS 5:13:1-3)*
The Mary of Magdala among them
And Mary she of James—mother of Joses* **(Ἰωσῆτος—Iosetos)*
And Salome, who all were with Him when He was in the Galilee
Who Had followed Him and ministered to Him
And many others who had gone up at Jerusalem with Him
But evening had already arrived
It was the day of the Preparation for the Passover
The day before the Sabbath *(and no one's gonna save you from the beast about to strike)*
Arrived the Joseph[us] Arimathea **(Ari=Lion; Joseph: Ἰωσὴφ = Josephus: Ἰώσηπος)*
An advisor much desired *(εὐσχήμων βουλευτής—by the Imperial House and others)*
Who was himself warmly-receiving God's kingdom
[He] went boldly to Pilate and asked for the body of Jesus
Pilate was suspicious if He was already dead
And summoning Centurion *(the rebel who schooled Titus on the angles of His body)*
He asked him had He been dead for some time
When he learnt from Centurion he granted the body to Joseph[us]*
And having brought a sheet of linen
Now He took Him down wrapped in linen cloth
And laid Him in a tomb that had been hewn out of the rock
And rolled a stone to the door of the tomb
And Mary she of Magdala, and Mary she of Joses* *(Joseph→Josephus→Joses)*
Knew where He was established

—MARK (15:38-47)   **(Ioseph→curt Greek, Iosepos→w/ masc. suffix, Iosetos→w/diminutive suffix)*

The tomb opened with another earthquake. The fire that rose from the ground in 80 AD, selected different Pagan Temples from those already torched in the **Great Fire of 64**. A deliberate controlled burn, marks the **More Taboo Fire of 80,** as the second installment of a common fire-marshal's bill. The 64 Fire hit the most ancient layer of Rome's Pagan foundations, and destroyed revered shrines reputedly built by the earliest heroes of Rome's Paganism: *Evander, Romulus,* and *Numa*. Then the 80 Fire completely trashed the top layer of Rome's newest Pagan infrastructure. The 64 Fire weakened Rome for the 66 Revolt. Suetonius relates the 80 Fire, to the reign of the Caesar who burned Jerusalem in 72:

Hardly anyone ever came to the throne with so evil a reputation, or so much against the desires of all, as Titus Flavius did. Besides cruelty, he was also suspected of riotous living, since he protracted his revels until the middle of the night with the most prodigal of his friends; likewise of unchastity because of his troops of gay-boys and transvestites, and his notorious passion for queen Bernice *(Herod-Agrippa Sr.'s daughter—well into her 50's, and perhaps Caesar's Madame)*, **to whom it was even said that he promised marriage. He was suspected of greed as well; for it was well known that in cases which came before his father he put a price on his influence and accepted bribes** *(Pilate also was famous for accepting bribes; see Philo EMBASSY 38:302)*. **In short, people not only thought, but openly declared, that he would be a second Nero ... At the dedication of his amphitheatre and the hastily built baths which were near it, he gave a most magnificent and costly gladiatorial show ... There were some dreadful disasters during his reign, such as the eruption of Mount Vesuvius in Campania** *(the eruption on the Sodom called Pompeii in 79 AD)*, **a fire at Rome which continued three days and as many nights, and a plague the like of which had hardly ever been known before. During this fire in Rome** *(the More Taboo Fire of 80 AD)* **he made no remark except "I am ruined" ... Among the evils of the times were the informers** *(moles like Joe and Epaphroditus)* **and their instigators, who had enjoyed a long standing license. After these had been soundly**

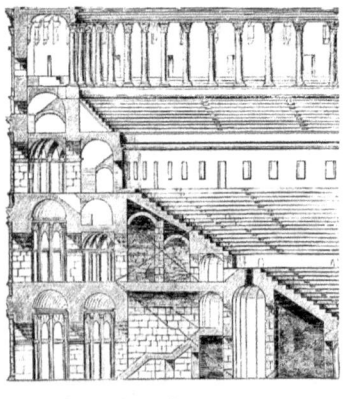 beaten in the Forum with scourges and cudgels, and finally led in procession across the arena of the amphitheatre, he had some of them put up and sold, and others deported to the wildest of the islands ▽ *(Glastonbury—perhaps—spinning Joe's escape as an 'exile')* ... **After finishing the public games, at the close of which he wept bitterly in the presence of the people, he went down to the Sabine territory, somewhat cast down because a victim had escaped as he was sacrificing** *(...hmmn)* **and because it had thundered from a clear sky. Then at the very first stopping place he was seized in a fever, and as he was being carried on from there in a litter, it is said that he pushed back the curtains, looked up to heaven, and lamented bitterly that his life was being taken from him contrary to his deserts; for he said that there was no act of his life of which he had cause to repent, save one only** *(bringing Josephus to Rome)*. **What this was he did not himself disclose at the time, nor could anyone easily divine ... He died in the same farmhouse as his father, on the Ides of September, two years two months and twenty days after succeeding Vespasian, in the 42nd year of his age. When his death was made known... the Senate hastened to the House before it was summoned by proclamation, and with the doors still shut...** *(for Fear of the Jews: grandsons of Jude the brother of Jesus were questioned by Domitian, but nothing was learned according to Eusebius, CHURCH HISTORY 3:19-20).*

—Sueton., LIFE OF TITUS *(6-11)* התגבר על האריה של שבט יהודה השורש של דוד כדי לפתוח את הספר

Lazarus shocked the cosmos, in holy war made upon Romulans by *People of the Book* of Moses. Caesar's cult aimed to consume the entire habitable hemisphere, using whips, and chains, and crosses, to teach mere humans that resistance was futile. New unholy slave master needed to assimilate a huge rebel collective of ex-slaves. His Romulan ruler cult was novel and alien to the Latinos, who had thrown off their monarchy with a Republic that had thrived for five centuries. Then Caesar imported this slave master's religion from Egypt into Italy. His obnoxious new Imperial religion divinized the most loathsome racketeer element of Roman society. Many Italians, especially Greeks and Grecophiles, thus found common cause with the Jews. Thanks to Jewish resistance, huge iron-legs tripped on its way up the hill to the pinnacle of Pagan Roman religion. There the temple of Jupiter Capitolinus was still the holiest shrine in the Pagan Roman cosmos. Its inner sanctum, with its colossal statue of Jove, stood in direct opposition to the wind in the Jerusalem Temple's Holy of Holies. Defeated generals of the nations which Rome had conquered, were strangled in the Forum. The crowd stood still in complete silence during the whole human sacrifice. The Pontiffs made ritual use of the bodies in Jupiter's temple on the Capitoline Hill, threw them out the back window, and had them thrown off the Tarpeian Rock. After their bodies hit the street below, the crowd in the Forum broke their many minutes of complete silence with boisterous cheers. This was the Triumph of Roman Pagan religion. But the Galileans rode the wind of Yahweh's presence directly against the temple of Jupiter Capitolinus. Jesus exhales his last breath into the wind of the Jerusalem Temple's Holy of Holies, renting the veil *(MARK 15:36-37)*. Quaking earth split rock open *(MATT 27:51)*. Fire rose from abyss *(MATT 3:11, cf. τελεσθῇ—i.e. "it is finished/accomplished" at LUKE 12:50 and JOHN 19:30)*. The Taboo Fire of 80 proved no magic could protect even the most powerful idols. Ritual cannibalism offered no security. Centurion was convinced that this bunch of Joshuas were Sons of True God.

The gospel of *MATTHEW* cues up the most pointed clues to the triumph of Josephus. *MATTHEW'S* "holy city"—which experiences saints resurrected with an earthquake—is the holy precincts of the temple complexes on the Capitoline Hill of Rome. Beneath that hill was a maze of ancient volcanic rock mines, in which not was no one not yet laid. While Titus was distracted at Sodom, an underground of abused boys rose from the tomb. The text is unsealed by untying a knot:

W̧hen evening came there arrived a man rich
Out of Arimathea by name Joseph[us]   *(the Thriller)*
Who also himself was a disciple of this Joshua

Having gone to the Pilate [He] asked for the body of the Joshua
And the Pilate ordered it to be returned
Then having taken the body, Joseph[us] wrapped it in clean linen
And established it in the new tomb of His
Which he had dug in the rock
And went away
Having rolled a great stone to the door of the tomb   *(Danielian)*
What's more, sitting there against the tomb
Was Mary she of Magdala and the other Mary   *('Mary' of the Tower: Centurion)*
And on the coming day
Which is after this preparation   *(for yet another exodus stage left)*
The Chief Priests and the Pharisees *(in mirror: Capitoline Priests and Imperial elite)*
Were gathered before Pilate saying:
> "Might we remind you what this deceiver said while living
>   "AFTER THREE DAYS I ARISE!"
> *Therefore order that the tomb be secured*
> *Just in case his disciples come steal Him away*
> *And then [they can] tell the people*
>   "HE IS RISEN FROM THE DEAD!"
> *And then the last deception will be worse than the first!"*

The Pilate said:
> *"You have a custodia*   *(the police force of the holy city's precincts)*
> *Go make it as secure as you remember"*

So they secured the tomb having the custodia seal the stone...
Then this Joshua cried out with a loud voice again
And sent forth His wind
Lo! the veil of the temple was torn in two—the top to the bottom!
And the earth was shaken
And the rocks were cleaved apart
And the tombs were opened   *(Jews were buried for resurrection, Pagans: cremated)*
And many bodies of the saints who were sleepers arose
And after the resurrection of Him
Having come forth marching out of the tombs
They entered into the holy city
And appeared before many
Now the Centurion
And they who with him kept guard over this Joshua
Having witnessed the earthquake and the things that took place
Was feared* violently for saying:
> *"Truly God's son this was!"*

    —MATTHEW (first→27:57-66, last→50-54) *(*fear of the proselyte Messianic Jews)*

When Joe and his boys took custody of the temple of the Capitoline Jive, there was one fixture of particular interest. A century earlier, Joe's errant distant relative rewarded the very first Roman to enter the Jerusalem Holy of Holies—with an offering to the Pagan's false high god:

ompey came to Damascus and marched over Coele-Syria
 At that time ambassadors came to him there
 From all over Syria and out of Egypt—and Judea too
 For Aristobulus sent him a great present *(of 3770 lbs. of gold)*
Which was a golden vine of the value of five hundred talents...
They called the thing *the Terpole* **or** *delight* *($107 million at 2012 scrap value)*
However we saw the thing ourselves *(Joey and His boys)*
Installed in the temple of Jupiter Capitolinus
With the inscription: *"A Gift from... the King of the Jews"*
— ANT *(14:3:1)*

vine has been planted outside the father
And since it is not sound it will be pulled out by the roots
—GOSPEL OF THOMAS *(40)* *(cf. MATTHEW 15:10-20 & JOHN 15:1-17)*

While Titus was absent in Campania   *(about Pompeii in 80 AD)*
Attending to the catastrophe that had hit that region *(in 79 AD)*
A second catastrophic fire rose from the ground   *(like lava)*
And spread over very large sections of Rome...
It consumed the Temple of Serapis
The Temple of Isis
The Saepta
The Temple of Neptune
The Baths of Agrippa
The Pantheon   *(a temple to all the Pagan gods of Rome)*
The Diribitorium
The Theatre of Balbus
The stage building of Pompey's Theatre
The Octavian buildings along with their books
And even the temple of Jupiter Capitolinus [Optimus Maximus]
With every surrounding temple [in its complex]   *(the "Holy City" ▷ on the Capitol Hill: temples of Juno Moneta, the Capitoline Triad, Virtus, Veiovis, and Vespasianus Augustus)*
Thus the disaster seemed to be not of human
But of divine origin
   —Dio, ROMAN HISTORY **(66:24)** *Joe and boys out-gamed a sick arena at 80 AD's hot opening*

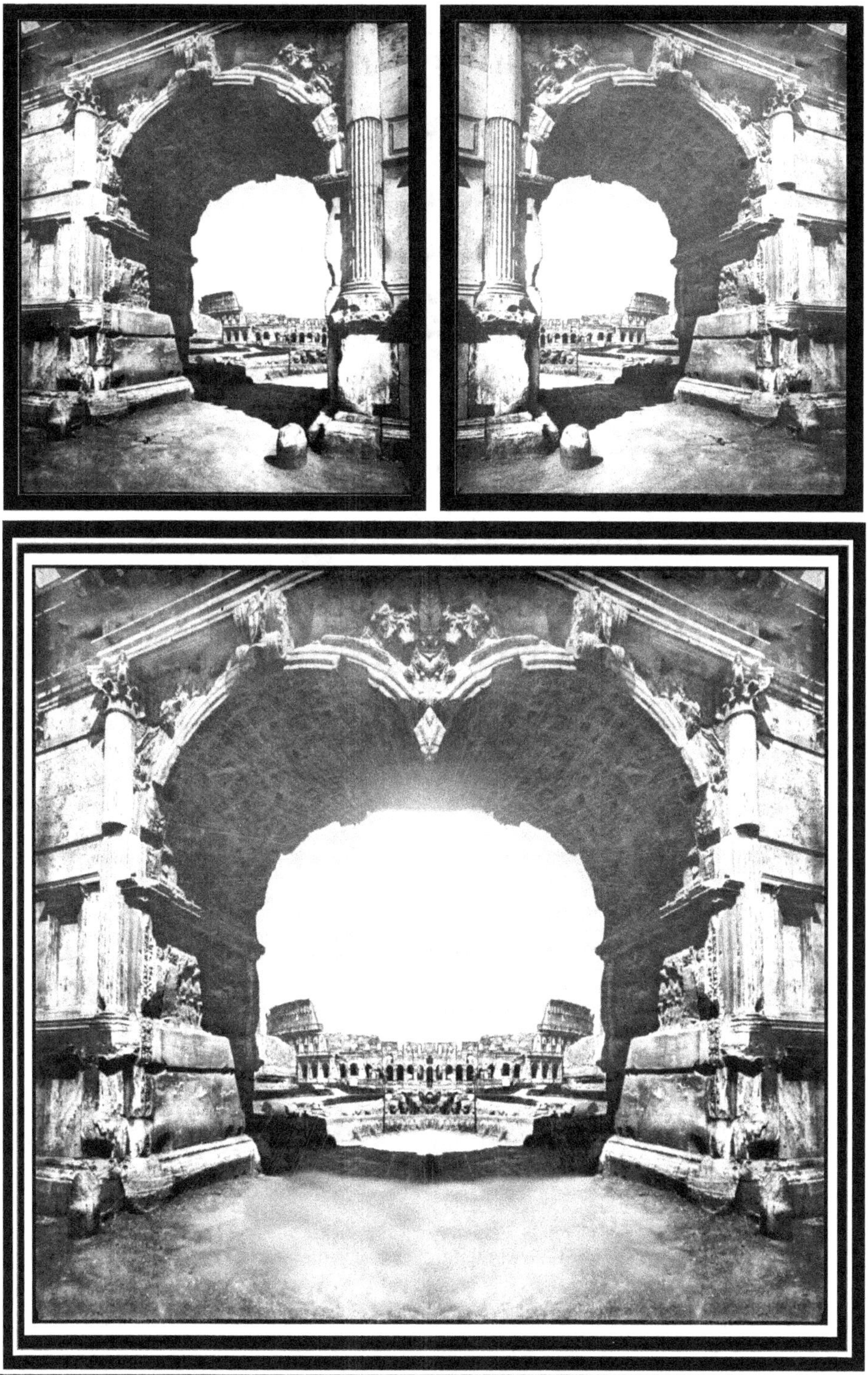

A mirror-tiled projection off an early photograph, tweaks the view of the Flavian Amphitheatre. The arena dominated the vista though Arch of Titus before this view was blocked by later constructs.

🎵 *A hair of the head did not perish via Olethan.* 🎵
JOSEPH OF ARIMATHEA LANDS AT GLASTONBURY IN PHRYGIAN CAP:

Whiston's paraphrase of *WARS (7:8:4, N.S. 300)*: τὸν μὲν παρὰ τοῦ πλήθους τῶν Ἰουδαίων, as: "**the one for fear of the multitude of the Jews,**" prompts his savvy readers to recognize the connection to *JOHN (19:38 & 20:19)*: τὸν φόβον τῶν Ἰουδαίων—"**for the fear of the Jews,**" whereas the word παρά used in *WARS*, if employed as a preposition, means "**besides,**" but if employed as a declined adjective form of πηρός, means "**maimed in a limb,**" which more literally renders the ornate tag here, as: "**one truly lame, of [regards to] the multitude of the Judeans, lest they depose him and restore their former kings to the government.**" Joe's sarcasm is justified. This Hasmonean driver who met the decrypted Joshua on the road to Emmaus, rough-rode Herod's great projects, and deposed his Edomite family's rule. Second coming events in Rome, refract through this polished telescope prism. Mirror winks at seer.

RUNNING WITH THE MENORAH

ABOVE: Sculpted details from the Arch of Titus:
The son of Joseph the tecton rose up; his Jesus cast His fire.

62 AD: After Eliezer 'the son of Dan' is captured, James the brother of Jesus is thrown off the Jerusalem Temple; 'Saul' makes a riot. An earthquake does great damage to the slave-trade hub of Pompeii on February 5.

63 AD: Josephus ... 'Paul'... wind up in Nero's Rome; dungeons echo in song.

64 AD: Nero is in Naples where he sings in public for the first time. As Nero takes the stage, a new earthquake hits the region. The theatre in which Nero sings collapses as soon his performance is evacuated in response to the quake. As Nero takes to the stage again in Antium on July 19 of 64, Rome is lit on fire. The eternal city burns six days.

66 AD: The Galileans take Masada and Antonia. Israel is free of Rome.

67 AD: Josephus is captured. Joe prophesizes to Vespasian that he and his son Titus will both be Caesars. Vespasian believes—returns to Rome.

70 AD: Jerusalem and its Temple are retaken and burned on August 30.

71 AD: Jewish captives arrive in Rome for the triumph. These boys slave upon the Temple of Peace and Coliseum. Tectonic Joe (τέκτων) ministers to the needs of every boy who belongs to the true builder.

73 AD: Masada falls around April 15 of 73 or 74 AD.

75 AD: Cyrene piracy is squashed. Temple of Peace opens. Joe releases *WARS*.

79 AD: Vespasian is taken June 29. Joe goes underground. Vesuvius erupts from August to October. Pompeii's brothels sold Jewish flesh for rape and worse. Brimstone buries it all. Peace be upon you.

80 AD: Rome burns three days whose dates are excised from the sources as they matched Passion to Easter in the *CARTHAGINIAN COMPUTUS*. Fire is cast on the Capitoline Hill's Pagan "holy city" precincts. The Coliseum is rushed toward completion as part of the Imperial clean up effort.

81 AD: The unfinished Coliseum is opened with 100 days of murderous games, which begin two months after the anniversary of the ***More Taboo Fire of 80.*** When the bloody games end, Titus retreats to the countryside, where Titus is seized on September 13 of 81.

Titus expired at 42 years of age. This man, whom God's plan chose to fire Jerusalem, reigned less than three years. Some who did not heed tales about fires, suspected his brother Domitian; their sibling quarrels were famous. The cosmic truth was immortalized when the erection of Titus Arch was finished by Domitian. The Jewish frieze on the arch shows more triumph than that which Rome celebrated for Vespasian and son in 71. The Flavians were deaf, to how Barbecue-Joe used their capitol parade as foreshadow ᘛ, for his hot upcoming visit to Jupiter:

hen Vespasian went to that gate which is called the Gate of Pomp, (for pompous shows always go through that gate) ... after they put on their triumphal garments, and offered sacrifices to the idols that had been moved to that gate, they sent the triumph forward, marching through every arena, so that they could be seen better by more people ... It is impossible to describe all the shows in these venues as they deserve *(with death on the menu)* ... Even the huge numbers of captives were all dressed up, moreover the variety that was in their garments, and their fine texture, concealed from view the deformities *(ἀηδία—nauseousness/nauseatingness)* of their bodies.$^{\Omega}$ But what caused the greatest surprise of all was the structure of the pageants *(floats)* that were carried *(by the captives)*, for indeed any who encountered them could not but fear that the bearers would not be able to support them firmly enough, for that is how enormous they were, some being even three or four stories, one on top of the other ... There was molded gold and ivory attached all over them, and many depictions of conflict, which in several ways, and by a variety of devices *(doors, curtains, elevators, & surprise executions)*, showcased a most lively portrait of war, for there was to be seen a happy country laid waste, and entire squadrons of enemies slain, while some of them ran away *(exodus)*, and some were carried into captivity. Walls of great altitude and magnitude were overthrown and ruined by machines ... with an army pouring itself within the walls, and everyplace full of slaughter ... Fire sent upon the temples *(pl.)* was also simulated, and houses overthrown and falling upon their owners ... a land still on fire from every side, for the Jews related that they had undergone such a thing during the war *(double-talk foreshadow published years before the Fire of 80)*ᘛ ... the craft of these representations was so magnificent and lively in their mode of construction, that it represented what had been done to those who did not see it, as if they had really been there. On top of every one of the pageants,

was placed the commander of the city that was taken and the manner whereby he was taken. *(though widely mistaken for standards, the tabula ansata in the frieze are instead a parade of signs that named each major Jewish city vanquished, carried by a long-haired victim from that city* ☻ *; the sign naming burned Jerusalem—aided by a toga grab—knocks menorah fire to Rome's street.)*. **Moreover following these pageants was a great number of ships. And for the spoils, they were carried in great plenty. But as for those that were taken from the Jerusalem Temple, they made the best illustration of all ... the last part of this pompous show was at the temple of Jupiter Capitolinus, where upon arrival they stopped, for it was the Roman custom to be still, until someone brought them the news that the general of the enemy had been slain.** —WARS *(7:5:4-6)*

The Arch of Titus shows captives lifting the Temple treasures while using walking sticks—a deliberate anomaly. Joe mentions heavy floats in the triumph, but the menorah, at no more than 150 pounds *(EX 25:39)*, would not be heavy for the half dozen men under it, unless fixed on a new solid gold base. Moreover, walking canes are no help with any burden, unless one is injured, or on slippery terrain. Escapees were safest sleeping in the tombs, but injured Jewish slaves who had been legally repurchased in Rome to save their lives, had no urgent need to hide in the catacombs. Jewish slaves who were injured at work and then freed with papers, hobbled round Rome with walking sticks. Civic drama in their binding and loosing made these boys conspicuous creatures on the capitol pavement. Fatal love these laurelled ⌣ captives returned to Caesar, is immortalized by anomalous telescoping. Walking staffs used by those who

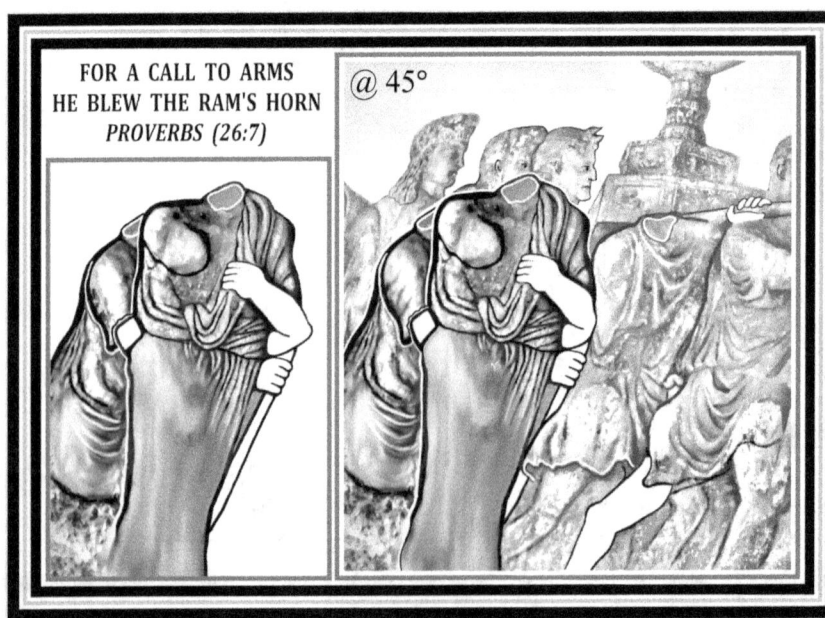

FOR A CALL TO ARMS
HE BLEW THE RAM'S HORN
PROVERBS (26:7)

@ 45°

Two horizontal layers of plates cover the menorah base with divergent perspectives. The toga-grab elbows the menorah, which cascades to fire the streets of Rome.

were redeemed when injured in years after the triumph of 71, are shown in an anachronistic triumph that climaxed in the twilight-zone fire of 80. Canes double as long knives. Undead Sicarii weapons, tap out Titus and Vespasian.

The cameo of Josephus is squeezed in right behind Titus. Galilee's confident general intercedes between Caesar and the menorah. Joe directs a black triumph under the surface of the pompous one. Caesar is cut off by the bruised boys who parade upon him. Titus was seized in his post-game litter.

The boy who follows tight by his nose directly behind Joe, portrays an epitome of every Jewish boy in Rome who lovingly followed Joe's rebel agenda. The boy crunches in endearingly close to his seditious Rabbi. Their head to head congruence conducts a deformed army of the damned, scrambling towards a fire escape. This student who noses in to cover Joe's back, cleaves Titus off of Joe with a dig of his chin. The torso of Titus was carved out in high relief, at odd angles of spine and shoulders, presaging his fall. Clueless Titus is shown being mugged. The crouching captive directly behind Titus thrusts his swollen knee to Caesar's leg, while his wrenched arm reaches right into Caesar's profile. The captive in front of Titus steps on Caesar's sandalled foot with a bound ankle. Imperial slave master is being gang-tackled by victims of his abuse. The ankle stomping foot, a walking staff, and an odd high-kicking leg, all take stabs at Titus from the front. Chin, arm, and knee attack from behind. A flamboyant assist from a second arm rips-off the lecherous Emperor's victory toga—an arm which could belong to the proud dictator, or to Josephus, or to a slave boy grabbing from underneath by shadow and substance. The artist embedded multiple optical illusions and double meanings, viewable at variant angles. Joe was hidden directly behind the now missing head of Titus, to sneakily portray the two as if Siamese twins. The esoteric focus is upon Joe's locomotive drive, commandeering the array of a fiery battlefield upon which an asymmetric contest was predestined, by both things and ideas—of Moses:

ND Centurion said: *"Lord !*
I am not able to take you under my cover
Only say the word so my boy will be healed
For I am also a man under authority (riddled here as a mirror of Jesus under God)
Having soldiers under myself
And I say to this one: (Nero)
"Go !" ⇨ *and he goes*
And I say to this one: (Vespasian)
"Come !" ⇨ *and he comes*
And to my servant: (Titus)
"Do this !" ⇨ *and he does it"*

—MATT *(8:8-9)* *(None was so obedient in all Israel!)*

Comparison with Centurion, zip-files memories of an extraordinary other under a higher authority in his mirror. The commander of a hundred had to answer to a fake god—Caesar. Caesar had to answer to the Sons of True God.

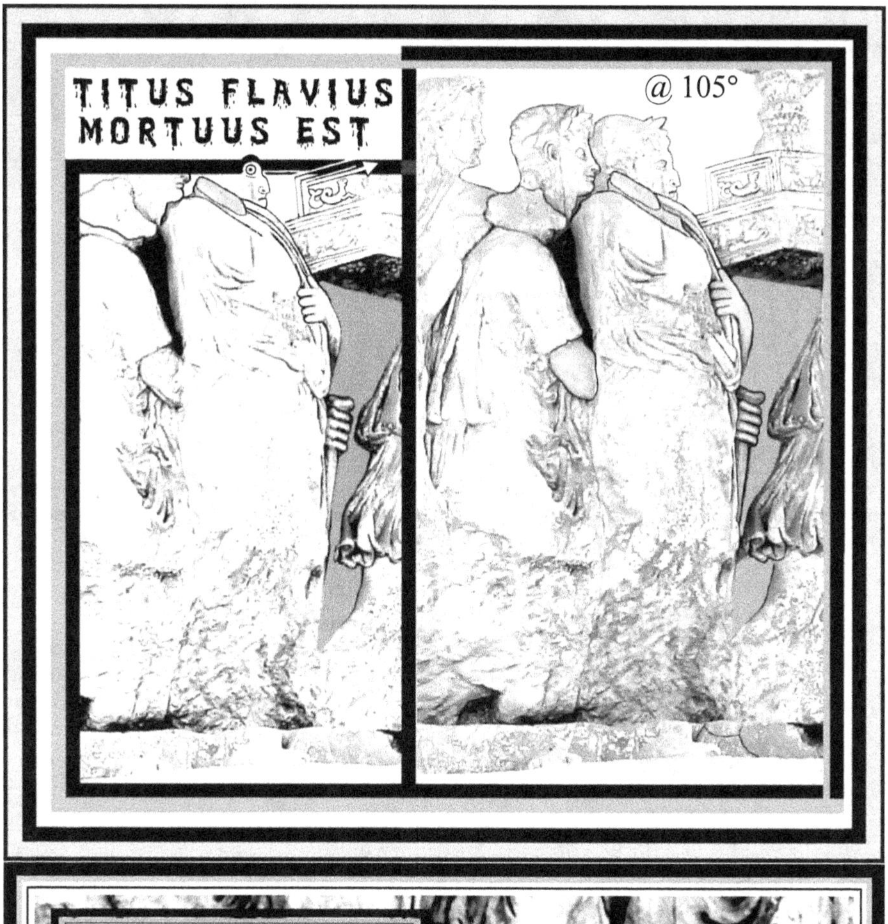

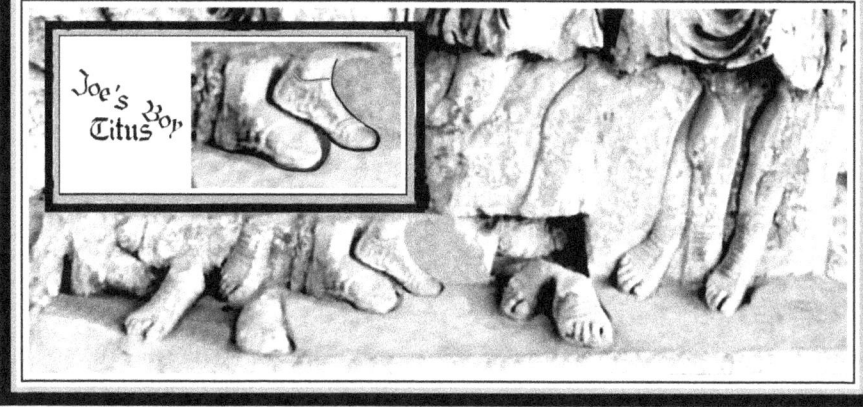

GALILEE'S GENERAL GRABS THE TOGA PICTA

JOE AND TITUS' TORSO | OUTLINE OF VESPASIAN

THE TRIUMPH OF JOSEPHUS ARI-MATITYAHU — SICARIOT
"[Titus] reserved the tallest and most beautiful boys for the Triumph ...
The fine texture of their costumes, concealed
the revolting nature of their bodies"$^\Omega$ — WARS *(6:9:2; 7:5:5)*

Triumph 71 was celebrated jointly for Vespasian and his son Titus. An awed captive looked up in nauseous disbelief at the monstrous godhead of Vespasian. Only a ghostly outline now remains of Vespasian's fat figure, exposing a hungry head once hidden behind the official bust, and fleshing out motive for the black triumph embedded in the composition. The cane toting captive raising the showbread table before Vespasian, kicks back at an uncrippled angle, higher than any other boy, mirroring the foot stomp on Titus. Stealth canes cut into the scene sharply, one before each Caesar, to trip them up from out of the background. From a forward street angle, the stomping boy's costume occults the stealth cane before Titus, morphing it into a long knife positioned like it might extend from the reach of the boy crouching into Titus from behind. This keys the subtle composition, as the length of the boy's reach relative to his body size, better fits a reach inside Caesar's toga, where the boy might pull the dictator down by his most tender member. Polished cuts, direct meaty fingers, to the appetites of two Caesars who ate it before the memorial was carved. The unfinished Coliseum's hasty opening sought to distract the mob from the menu complaint fired off by Joe's resurrected host. Titus bit the murderous dust immediately after throwing the Coliseum's 100 days of sadistic inaugural games. Man-eaters were loose in the country.

> He was the most notorious of all the Jews of his day
> Not only among his own people, but among the Romans also
> And his works were deemed worthy of a place in the library *(Biblio-theca)*
> So they honored him with the posting of a sculpture in Rome.
> —Eusebius, CHURCH HISTORY (3:9)

JOSES c. 33 - 115

JOSES c. 33 - 115

AN ISSUE OF TITUS PROMISES AMPUTATION AND ROASTING: 79 AD.

The Greek verb σταυρός which the gospel uses for "crucify," literally means "to stake" or "to skewer." This trophy holds culinary stakes.

INDEX OF WORKS CITED

Koran

1:5-23	47
2:243-259	65
2:31	vi
2:81	54, 56
3:37-43	54
3:43-45	56
3:55	53
4:49	57
4:77	57
5:115	57, 59
5:111-115	59
5:50-51	54
15:75-77	إنّ في ذلك لآيةً للمؤمنين ... 39, 160
16:80	57
17:1	46
17:71	57
18:45	48
19:3-33	53
19:4	57
19:16-27	45, 48
21:28-43	48
23:99-100	48
24:31	57, 58
30:54	57
33:59	57
39:42	48
42:9-11	vi
43:5-11	48
43:78	vi
48:27	57
50:9-11	48
57:26-27	54
6:38	48
6:99	48
66:12	48
67:2	48
73:17	57, 58
9:30	45

John (Jn)

1:4-5	– i
1:12-17	4, 45, 50, 120
1:26-31	13, 91
2:13-17	99
2:20-21	28, 120
3:14	133
4:1-45	15
4:32-38	133
5:5	195
6:26-71	59
8:57	120
8:58	27, 77
10:22-42	13, 50, 154
11:1-12:50	60
12:3	55
12:3-8	5, 42. 60
13:26-27	109
14:6	4, 54
14:30	4
15:1-6	91
15:1-17	166
15:21	146
16:33	92
18:11-12	94, 105
18:33-38	3
18:39-40	110
19:2	32, 70, 83
19:13-17	24, 91, 148
19:19-20	89
19:30-31	111. 120, 164
19:31-40	155
19:38	4, 169
19:40	156
20:19	134, 169
20:20-31	50, 128
20:29	136

Matthew (Matt)

1:20	45
2:12	120
2:19-22	17
2:22	120
3:4	61
3:11	111, 128, 164
3:11-12	131
3:17	26
5:3-12	148
5:17	54, 56
5:25-29	84, 109
6:12	60, 109
8:5-13	4, 149
8:8-9	134, 177
8:28-34	148, 158
9:9-13	89
10:7-39	128, 105
10:14-22	28, 133, 146
11:14	25
12:18	24
13:15	vi
13:55	20
15:10-20	166
17:11-13	25
20:22	111
20:24	60
21:1-13	127
21:19-22	142
21:31	89
21:19-22	88
21:31-46	77, 54
22:15-22	47
22:33	60, 127
23:23	47
23:35	132
24:21-43	6, 22, 60, 120
25:1-13	91
26:6-15	50, 55, 60, 62
26:26-28	91
26:52-64	111
27:3-9	84
27:15-18	4, 110
27:24-25	93
27:25	92
27:32	114
27:33-50	25
27:35	26
27:38	111
27:43	26
27:45-46	22, 42
27:54	Life or Death, Steam or Ash: *Choose!* 193
27:50-56	66, 83, 156, 164, 165
27:59-65	148, 155
28:16-20	77

Life of Josephus son of Matthew (Life)*

1	4, 15, 89, 152
1-3	120
2	11, 61
2-3	14
3	17
3-6	124
53	24
65	10
72	149
75	145, 159, 161
76	121
77	126

Luke (Lk)

1:5-23	25, 47
1:26	45
1:31-38	45
1:54	45
1:76	25
2:1-7	28, 45, 120, 14, 15, 45, 89, 120
2:41-51	12
3:16-17	25, 104

Luke (Lk)

3:16-23	32, 120, 126, 127
4:9-11	32
6:1-22	20, 54, 104, 111, 147
7:1-10	4, 124
7:36-49	55, 61
8:26-39	158
10:29-37	124
11:4	109
11:51	47
12:2-50	0, 117, 125, 126, 164
13:1-11	92, 111
17:21	148
18:31	56
20:18	32
21:20-28	65, 120
23:46	MDCCLXXXIII ... 51
24:44	56

Acts of the Apostles (Acts)

1:8	18
1:18-26	5, 84, 120
2:1-8	66, 59
3:13	93
5:37	14, 28, 89
8:1-14	18
9:10-31	18
17:22-31	66
20:29	47
21:38	17
23:6	13
23:31-27:9	15
24:27	123
26:14	119
27:1-28:13	124-125

Nahum

1:10	כְּפַר נָחוּם ... 84

Mark (Mk)

1:6	90, 91
4:11-12	3, 194
5:1-20	158
11:15-33	98, 128
12:41-44	182
13:16-20	22, 64
14:3-11	42, 60, 83
14:36	iii
15:7	110
15:34-47	22, 66, 155, 161, 164

The Jewish War (Wars)

1:0:1	18
1:0:4	יָפֵת יָפוֹ ... 39
1:0:12	194
1:7:5-7	38
1:33:6-8	150
2:8:1-14	14, 28, 89
2:9:2-4	93
2:13:1-2	crucifixus caput non deorsum ... ii, 14
2:13:6	28
2:16:5-17:3	98
2:17:6	60, 109
2:19:7-20:3	108
2:20:3-4	8
3:4:1	64
3:7:31	38
3:8:8-9	144
3:8:9-9:3	71, 37
3:10:10	157
4:5:2-3	38, 84
4:5:4	47
4:7:11-10:12	158
4:9:10	4
5:1:2	104
5:13:1-3	161

The Jewish War (Wars)

5:13:7	21, 65
6:4:1-6	20, 111
6:5:3	120
6:9:2-4	20, 22, 23, 24, 65, 147, 179
7:11:5	6
7:2:1	157
7:5:4-6	157, 175, 179
7:8:4	134, 169
7:11:3	70

The Jewish War • the Slavonic Recension

2:8:3	128

Antiquities of the Jews (Ant)*

1:6:1	יָפֹו ... יָפֹו ... 38
1:7:1-10:4	75
1:10:4	39
2:13:1-2	iv
2:14:4-6	21
6:12:8	48
7:9:6	38
7:11:1-7	105, 114
7:13:4	25
7:14:5	42
8:3:4	34
8:8:5	47
9:10:2	18
9:20:1	84
12:4:10-5:1	37
12:6:2	104
14:3:1	166
14:4:4	38
14:7:3	ii
15:2:4	84
15:7:1-9:5	84, 152, 195
16:1:1	84
17:1:1-6	89
17:13:4-18:1:6	10, 14, 25, 28, 32
17:20:5	89
18:1:1-2:2	13, 84, 151, 120
18:3:1-3	4, 32, 93, 194
18:5:2	120
20:6:1-3	14, 17, 18
20:7:5-10	14
20:8:6	17
20:9:1-7	13, 47

Against Apion (Agnst Ap)*

1:5	8
1:7-9	9, 145
1:14-15	38

Seneca • Questions of Nature

6:1-5	135, 136

1 Peter

2:4-10	51
2:13-22	90
3:17-22	51

2 Peter

1:16-3:7	127
3:10	60, 127

🎵 Revelation (Rev) 🎵

1:7-16	9, 89, 155, 182
2:24-28	128
3:3	60
4:6	25
7:1-8	38
11:7-8	143, 147, 148
13:15-18	i, 125
14:6-13	111
15:2	πυρι και τους νικωντας εκ του θηριου και εκ της εικονος αυτου .... i, 25, 63
16:15	127
17:18-19:3	128
19:11-13	38
20:12-15	54
21:2	66
22:16-28	25, 127

生或死　蒸汽或灰

GALATIANS
1:8-9	1
2:10	60

HEBREWS
4:12	77, 89
8:1	111

PHILIPPIANS
2:25	121
4:18-22	121

ROMANS
1:18-32	141
3:31	56
8:14-30	50, 161
12:17-13:3	139
13:7-8	89, 110
15:26	60
16:10-11	10, 151

THOMAS
40	166

PSALMS (PS)
2:7-9	24, 26, 31, 46, 128
12:5	60
18:19	24, 26
22:1-19	24, 25, 26, 42
34:20	155
37:9-11	147
47	83
69:31-33	40, 60
72:13	60
78:1-9	83
79	111
81:9	96
82:6	50, 154
105	83
140:12	60

MALACHI
3:1	25
4:1-5	25, 127

這個星球上必須選擇

Deuteronomy (Deut)

5:7	96
15:4-7	60
21:22-23	154
27:6	32
31:3	27, 52

Daniel (Dan)

2:31-45	30, 32, 126, 128, 147, 148
7:10-13	iii, 120
12:1	22

Genesis (Gen)

1:27	vi, 83
2:7	27
3:19	28
3:24	126
5:1-2	vi, 83
10:1	יָפֶת ... יְפִי ... 38
11:31	74
12:4-6	74, 75
13:16	28
14:11-14	39
15:12-13	78
16:13	83
18:1-21	39, 75, 76, 77
19:1-28	39
19:36	74
20:12	74
21:1-6	77
21:7-12	81
22:1-14	25, 27, 32, 81
23:4	156
48:3-7	38
49:16-17	iv, 38, 133

Exodus (Ex)

1:11	36
7:12	133
8:16	29
9:23-33	37
11:1-5	30
12:3-46	38, 90, 91, 92, 131, 111, 155
19:18	37
20:3	96
20:25	2
21:32	50
22:20-28	24, 90
23:6	60
25:39	175
29:18	121
32:8	96
33:18-23	51, 83
34:29	40

Song of Solomon (Song)

1:12	42, 53
5:10	42, 53
8:6	156

1 Maccabees (1 Macc)

1:14-24	151
2:18-25	148, 152
2:27-41	4, 48, 111
4:47	32
12:20-21	37

Isaiah (Isa)

1:7-31	96
14:30	60
26:19-20	156
29:19	60, 147
41:17	60
42:8-25	96, 194
53:9-12	90, 110
56:7	98
66:15-17	126

Jeremiah (Jerem): Joe's faux error at MATT 27:9 is his prophecy ⚐

2:33-35	60
4	56
5:28	60
25:15	111
32:1-15 ⚐	עוֹד יִקָּנוּ בָתִּים וְשָׂדוֹת וּכְרָמִים בָּאָרֶץ הַזֹּאת: ף ... 84
35:15	96
43:13	88

Joel

1:6-7	142

Amos

4:1	60

2 Chronicles (2 Chron)

2:11-16	32, 34
3:1	25, 32
8:5	34
12:15	47
13:22	47
20:34	47
24:17-22	47

1 Kings

6:1	38
7:13-14	34
9:17	34
13	47

2 Kings

17:35	96

1 Samuel

16:12	41
21:1-6	48

2 Samuel

1:26	48
14:11	146
17:1	38
20:8	105
24:1-25	28, 32

Numbers (Num)

1:20-46	38
9:1	155
12:1-13	–i
15:3	121
24:17	106
28:4-51	38

Zechariah (Zech)

1:1-7	47
11:4-17	84, 108, 111
12:10	155
14:1-2	156
14:21	99

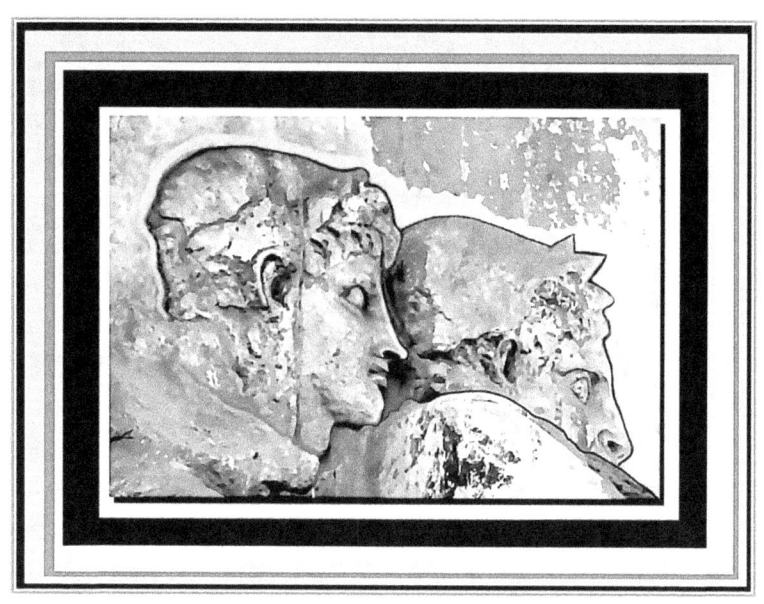

1 Esdras
4:34-41 7

Ezra
5:1 47
6:14 47

Nehemiah (Neh)
12:4 47

Judges (Judg)
5:2-31 .... 37, 38
14:15 ⁺Timorem Dei habui ducem iteneris mei per Gallias atque Italiam... 37
19:16-30 ....etiam in insolis quae sunt in mari Terreno⁺ 39

Proverbs
12:22 7

Lamentations
3:66 121
4:7 42

Ezekiel (Ezek)
37:1-9 47
48:1 38

Joshua
19:45-6 .... ויהד יודה־ ברק יהודה עוד אודה יהוה 33, 37

Habakuk
3:4 40

Eusebius • Church History (Eccles Hist)
2:23 .... 47, 104
3:9 181
3:11 157
3:19-20 163

Origen • Contra Celsum
2:13 103

Philo • Embassy to Caius (Embassy)
299 93
302 162

Philo • FLACCUS
10:83 154

Irenaeus • AGAINST HERESIES
5:13-38 60

Constantine • LETTER TO COUNCIL OF NICEA
10:83 154

Hippolytus • REFUTATION
7:22 60

Strabo • GEOGRAPHY (c. 23 AD): "arsenals of robbers are the haunts of robbers"
8:6:9 38
16:1:28 .... Joppa: "naval arsenal" of the Jews 37
16:34 .... cf. Jewish "Phoenicians" in Judea and Galilee 21

Suetonius • LIFE OF NERO
26-29 140
38 ....126, 132

Suetonius • LIFE OF VESPASIAN
4 107

Suetonius • LIFE OF TITUS
6-11 ....111, 126, 163

Suetonius • LIFE OF DOMITIAN
14-17 123

Cassius Dio • ROMAN HISTORY
57:18 167
62:16-18 ....126, 132
66:24 ....126, 132

Livy • HISTORY OF ROME
1:4 138

Tacitus • ANNALES
12:54 16
13:58 141
15:38-45 ....43, 126, 111, 130

Tacitus • HISTORIA
5:13 ....120, 123

Pindar • PYTHIAN ODE II
90-95 119

Heredotus • THE HISTORIES
4 33

Pliny • NATURAL HISTORY: "Joppe Phoenicum antiquior terrarum inundatione" !
5:14 .... Andromeda's seamonster Ceto (Dercetto) was Dagon (דגון) 37
7:4 141

Homer • ILIAD
14:310 38

Hadith • SUNNAN ABU DAWUD
37:4310 42

Homer • ODYSSEY
11:14 38

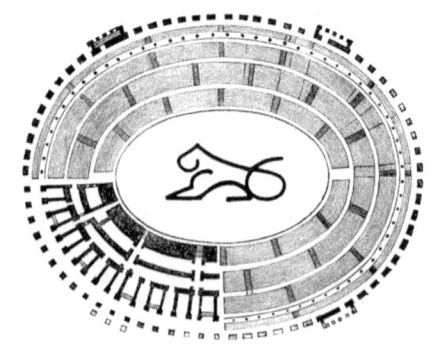

16:44:5-45:6	*Diodoros Siculus* • BIBLIOTHECA HISTORICA	39
4:35:9	*Pausanias* • DESCRIPTION OF GREECE	37
38:2	ARISTOTLE • PROBLEMATA (PUZZLES)	40
56a	BABYLONIAN TALMUD • GITTIN	47
24	PROTOEVANGELION OF JAMES	48
69	JERUSALEM TALMUD • TAANIT	48
96	BABYLONIAN TALMUD • SANHEDRIN	48
348 349	PAPYRUS LEIDEN #348 & PAPYRUS LEIDEN #349 משיתהו׃ "ration grain to Soldiers and Apiru who *draw* the well at estate Ramesses II south of Memphis"	29

כאשר הקצין הרומי הצבא, (עם אנשיו שמרו ישו) ראה את רעידת האדמה, וכל מה שקרה, הם היו מפוחדים, וקרא, "אין ספק שהוא היה בנו של אלוהים!"

🌍🌍🌍

Ioṗeṫ ḋamḣra aṅ an ṫuama lena Cáṅa Ioṗa (Baċall Ioṗa)
Beaṫa no Bàṗ, Ḋaile nó Ḟuiṅṗeog, Sṁùiḋe no uiṅṅṗeaṅṅ, OWME OR DANDER

I will embrace these things from every side in seven books *(cf. seven parallel books: 1) WARS, 2) ANTIQUITIES, 3) MATTHEW, 4) MARK, 5) LUKE, 6) JOHN, and 7) REVELATION. LUKE & ACTS are one. ANTIQUITIES, LIFE, & AGAINST APION are also one work. The double-count of seven books, common to WARS and Joe's entire revolutionary anti-Imperial library, includes his swansong REVELATION, but not the rebel letters—some largely written by Seneca.)* **and will leave no room for complaints or accusations from anyone who is familiar with this war, but write it all down for the sake of those who love truth—not for those who please themselves by installing engravings** *(Whiston's savvy translation here gives the colorful euphemism "please themselves with fictitious relations," to expose a comparison between idolators and "jerk-offs"—cf. the Testimonium's "take the truth with pleasure.")* **and will begin my version of these events, which follows, with the first heading I made** *(which is a cold beheading off a hot spring named Emmaus)*.

—WARS *(1:0:12): end of the introduction to Joe's first major literary work*

Paganism fell into sympathetic magic addiction. Parallel weaves in God's creation were exploited to construct cannibal empires of degenerate mind control—the resort of lazy uninspired governors. In the Parable of the Sower, Jesus qualifies a contrasting, inspired use of metaphor, calling the stupefied to action, with tending God's garden as method and reason. Metaphor draws maps of reality for the Monotheist's mind. Reality is no more than metaphor to a Pagan psyche—their matrix delusion:

TO you has been offered the mystery of the sovereignty of God, but everything is generated by metaphors to those outside, where seeing they see and don't understand, and hearing they hear and don't comprehend. —MARK *(4:11-12)*

The metaphor within the metaphor compares Pagans to the idols they worship, with senses of cause and effect. Statues see but do not understand. Carved rock and molded metal absorb sound waves, but they do not listen. Sympathetic magic turns the sorcerer to cold stone:

Those who trust in idols and say to images:
"You are our gods"
Will return to the backside in utter humiliation
Hear you deaf ones and see you blind ones?
Who is as blind as my servant is now?... *(ignoring the spirit of the law given)*
They see many things but none guard
Their ears are open but they don't listen...
So He poured out on them His burning anger...
It enveloped them in flames but they did not understand
It kindled them but they did not take it to heart *(pay attention)*

—ISAIAH *(42:17-25): where Isaiah's Israel represents all humanity.*

Bethesda Pool, near Antonia, was an intolerable Pagan *Asclepieion* (*cf.* ANT 15:9:5). The five porticoes housed idols, of: 1) Asclepius, 2) Hygeia (Hygiene), 3) Panacea, 4) Iaso, and 5) Algaea. Joe's telescope dials up the true healer: a geyser-like geothermal spring from caves beneath. Roll up the sleeping mat. **"One of the** *(lame)* **men there was thirty, and eight years had been among the ill** *(Pagans)***."** —JN *(5:5) (71 + 8 = 79)*

www.ingramcontent.com/pod-product-compliance
Lightning Source LLC
Chambersburg PA
CBHW071356290426
44108CB00014B/1574